Holy Terror

Holy Terror

Understanding Religion and Violence in Popular Culture

Edited by

Eric Christianson and Christopher Partridge

LONDON   OAKVILLE

Published by Equinox Publishing Ltd

UK: 1 Chelsea Manor Studios, Flood Street, London SW3 55R
USA: DBBC, 28 Main Street, Oakville, CT 06779

www.equinoxpub.com

First published 2010

British Library Cataloguing-in-Publication Data

A catalogue record for this book is available from the British Library.

ISBN   978 1 84553 359 5   (hardback)
ISBN   978 1 84553 360 1   (paperback)

Library of Congress Cataloging-in-Publication Data

Holy terror: understanding religion and violence in popular culture /
edited by Eric Christianson and Christopher Partridge.
     p. cm.
Includes bibliographical references and index.
  ISBN-13: 978-1-84553-359-5 (hb)
  ISBN-13: 978-1-84553-360-1 (pbk.)
1. Popular culture—Religious aspects. 2. Violence in mass media.
3. Violence—Religious aspects. I. Christianson, Eric S. II. Partridge,
Christopher H. (Christopher Hugh), 1961–
  BL65.C8H65 2010
  303.6—dc22
                              2009031002

Typeset by S.J.I. Services, New Delhi
Printed and bound in Great Britain by Lightning Source UK Ltd, Milton Keynes

Contents

Part Three: A Case Study: The Violence of *The Passion of the Christ*

Part Four: In Sport

Introduction

Eric Christianson
Christopher Partridge

The second annual meeting for the Centre for Religion and Popular Culture held at St Deiniol's Library, Hawarden, drew an impressive range of papers across different disciplines, including theology, sociology of religion, biblical studies and media and film studies. Perhaps unsurprisingly, the main focus of the papers was on the depiction of violence as it relates to religion in visual media. In comparison, the previous year's conference on the lure of demonology in popular culture drew more broadly on literature and music with a relatively small sampling of visual media. This may indicate our culture's tendency to think of violence in visual terms, to make use of the constant stream of visual stimuli in order to inform our thinking, consciously or not, on violence and the sacred.

"Religion and violence" together are simultaneously sensible and incongruent. Their coupling is an everyday reality of cultural discourses, yet as Nadia Delicata states, "violence within religion, or violence in the name of religion, causes the greatest scandal to human sensibilities... It highlights ever more sharply how in our personal, social, cultural existence, we are fundamentally torn apart—within ourselves, from each other, from our infinite hope" (2009: 13). While such a bold statement begs definition of terms, in this collection of essays one will not find contestation over definitions of violence (the implicit definition of physical and/or psychological force to inflict injury underwrites these essays), and religion is defined throughout with contextual specificity. The authors of these essays are, however, interested in dissecting the multitude of contexts in popular culture in which religion and violence confront, or combine with, one another. That process cogently lays bare a range of themes and questions: on the way in which violence is used to recover religious identity or human dignity; on how violence can be seen to pave a way towards experience of the sacred; on the roles of censorship, audience response and spectacle in shaping the degree to which we are willing to accommodate violence in religious contexts; on the growing multiple forms of media that perpetuate ideas about violence and religion, including television news and the internet; on how we respond to religious violence which may have the appearance of the heroic. These questions are all in some way about negotiation and contestation: over the multiple meanings of "religion and violence"; over reflection on, and even protest against, their unholy alliance; over the public and private spaces where that reflection takes place.

Since 9/11, terrorism's relationship to religion has taken on new dimensions in public discourse. In Jolyon Mitchell's essay, "Seeing Beyond Fear of Terrorism on the Web," Mitchell takes as his case study public responses to the July 2005 bombings in London as mediated on the internet. Mitchell does not limit himself to explicitly religious responses and as such identifies more subtle forms of religious influence, as well as the internet's role in the formation of community identity. Mitchell focuses in particular on the posting of digital imagery online and offers a taxonomy to understand its variety. The images are defined by defiance, solidarity and, in the case of Islamic image archives especially, the reconstruction of a more positive religious identity. Mitchell deftly demonstrates that sites such as the hugely popular We're Not Afraid archive are successful models of semi-religious discourse as peaceful protest against terrorism. The scenario Mitchell maps out reveals a new and creative site for reflection on the meaning of religiously motivated violence.
    Emma England examines a more specific example of terrorism-related violence, this time in connection to the biblical Judith. England begins by aligning the figures of Judith and Wonder Woman as superheroes. Both figures share archetypal superheroic traits: absent parents, god-like nobility, salvific abilities and even costume changes! Both defeat tyrannical dictators and save their respective communities. The details of Judith's narrative also enhance the comparison; for example, Holofernes whom Judith defeats is not unlike a comic supervillain, with an unquenchable appetite for chaos and destruction. Both female protagonists resort to excessive violence (both murder a man; in Wonder Woman's case, villain Maxwell Lord). Wonder Woman is punished in her narratives for transgressing the superhero code of murdering only non-humans. Although Judith is celebrated for her violence, in the end she returns to her domesticated widow status. The final part of the essay introduces the controversial figure of Lynndie England, the American soldier indicted in the 2004 Abu Ghraib prisoner abuse scandal, seen by millions in photos where she is shown sexually humiliating inmates. Uncomfortably, Lynndie liminally shares some superheroic traits, but even more so is shown to be villainous in her use of vengeful violence. Through this seemingly unholy comparative triad, England successfully raises questions about cultural responses to "heroic" violence, in religious (Judith), semi-religious (Wonder Woman) and non-religious (Lynndie) discourses.

Opening an analysis of film, Jo Carruthers examines the place of Raoul Walsh's 1960 biblical epic *Esther and the King* within a tradition of reading that seeks to rationalize and sanctify violence against the traitor. As a product of the Cold War era, the film embodies tension between loyalty to the State and individual religious freedom. The film, in line with Esther's reception history, renders the biblical Haman as traitor, but further as an embodiment of "unmanly vanity," an affront to modern America's self-identity. The film makes explicit what is at best implicit in the biblical text. Haman is made the unforgivable traitor, building on a long-standing religious discourse on the theological legitimacy of violence against enemies of the State. The violence that Haman is seen to inflict on the Jews in Walsh's film is, as Carruthers shows, aligned to the recent memory of the Shoah, helping further to legitimate Haman's eventual punishment by the State. Carruthers aligns the film's structure of violence to the theoretical triad of Victim (the Jews, esp. Esther), Victimizer (Haman) and Rescuer (the State, in the figure esp. of King Mordecai). Carruthers sees in the film's response to Haman's terrorism a parallel to modern approaches to counter-terror, namely the misguided elimination of a "finite" evil.

In "Cease to Exist," Gerry Carlin and Mark Jones offer a fresh analysis of the complex cultural matrix of the late 1960s that influenced Charles Manson and his "Family," particularly in relation to the "Satanic" murder of Sharon Tate and friends in 1969. Carlin and Jones argue that what is often dismissed as a spurious Mansonian occultism was in reality a coherent religious system of belief informed loosely by Christian eschatology, Eastern philosophy and more generally 1960s utopianism. In the years following the murder, a number of films sought to represent the Family directly and indirectly, often cashing in on the sensationalist media coverage and public perceptions of the occult in general. Ranging from sexploitation to "movie of the week" productions, Carlin and Jones demonstrate the degrees to which films were able to capture the complex range of beliefs at work in the Family. Carlin and Jones find that the films that most successfully make sense of the ideology that informed the Family's violence (which had a disturbingly positive rationale to "free" the minds of its victims), as well as the visceral and performative nature of the violence itself, are of the exploitation genres. Their essay is an exemplary case study in careful ideological analysis of the cultural legacy of religiously orientated violence.

Violence of an apocalyptic order comes under scrutiny in John Walliss's "The End is…a Blockbuster." Commenting on currents of millennial anxiety in Western culture at the end of the twentieth century, Walliss recognizes the playing out of apocalyptic fears in (particularly mainstream) cinema especially. Walliss shows that apocalyptic films valorize the everyday and embed the idea of human agency alongside or exclusive from divine agency. For

Walliss this represents a major shift from earlier cinematic figurings of the end of the world/world order, heralding a reversal of attitudes to the relevant values of science, technology and the threat of nuclear weapons especially. Walliss brings to bear socio-religious research on secularization and occulture to argue that recent apocalyptic films are typified by desacralization, and that their violence is directed towards the protection of the world as we know it. Indeed, Walliss demonstrates that the newly envisioned apocalyptic demise is conceived as a threat to our (read Hollywood's mainly American) status quo and the resourceful (again American) hero is the one to defeat that violent intrusion.

A group of film scholars from Winchester University conducted a case study of *The Passion of the Christ* with four stimulating papers. In "Counterfictional Suffering," Steven Allen theorizes as to the epistemological frame of reference with which viewers understand the figure of Christ in Gibson's film, particularly as this relates to the iconographical history of the Passion. Allen sets Gibson's claims to "authenticity" in the representation of violence against the film's highly rhetorical strategies in fictionalizing the event. Allen draws attention to the multifaceted ways in which viewers and critics have constructed ideas of authenticity and sees in the viewer's experience a constantly flowing comparative process in which viewers correlate the artistic tradition (esp. of the "old master" variety) with this visual retelling. Drawing on approaches to "counterfactual" history, Allen argues that Gibson seeks not so much to rewrite the Gospel accounts as to say "this is what could have been," and he is enabled to do so partly because of the viewer's inability to access anything like an "authentic" rendering of what the Passion actually was. In positing this "could have been" to the viewer, Gibson creates counterpoints with the collective memory of Jesus, particularly as it is rendered in art. This means that the appropriate category for Gibson's rationale is not so much counterfactual as counterfictional. The comparison yields the insight that Gibson's film is more interested in the pain of the flesh, with the artistic tradition showing more interest in the person of Jesus. In the end Allen manages to move refreshingly beyond the rather static authenticity debate expressed in recent religious and theological analyses of *The Passion*.

In his essay, "Controlling Passions," Shaun Kimber looks at the unusual way in which the certification of *The Passion* was contested and managed within the UK. *Passion* is the only film to have received an 18 certificate release concurrently with a 15 certificate. This was due to the pressure applied by Christian groups to allow the film to be screened to a younger audience. The film, re-released as *The Passion—Recut*, replaced the strongest violence with less violent material. Kimber takes the opportunity of this case study to enquire as to the nature of official as well as cultural forms of the regulation and classification of film violence in the UK. In doing so Kimber considers a wide range of cultural influences, including attention to the contexts of audience reception, production, marketing, distribution and forms of self-regulation. Kimber shows that the re-edited version of *The Passion* potentially alters the film's cultural meanings and the impact of its violence. The manner in which the cultural regulation of the film took place (through hype, debate, protest etc.) manifests, for Kimber, the discourses in British culture that were established well before the film's release. Kimber provides a fascinating insight into this historically unusual double-certification, foregrounding the ideologically complex tolerance of religious violence by conservative Christian groups.

In "*The Passion* as Media Spectacle," Oluyinka Esan investigates the powerful combination of the media and production and publicity values of *The Passion* in elevating it to the status of spectacle. Esan argues that part of the function of spectacle in mass media is to in effect disguise the spectacle's actual political and ideological significance. For Esan, spectacles are events constructed around a complex nexus of publicity and the multiple values of producers and audiences. As such, spectacles have a religious dimension in that they function as cultural rituals that reflect contestation over norms and values. In the end Esan demonstrates that cinema in particular offers a natural site for such contestation, and *The Passion* was a powerful example of the spectacle's ability to enlarge the capacity of audiences to accommodate violent imagery for the sake of spectacular religious ritual.

More issues of contestation come to the fore in Leighton Grist's essay, "Protest as Reaction." Grist charts the very different courses of the production, promotion and extraordinarily diverse reactions of the Christian right to Scorsese's *The Last Temptation of Christ* and Gibson's *The Passion of the Christ*. The two films, while similar stylistically, imbue very different meanings to violence. With its thoroughly human Jesus as its focal point, *Last Temptation* only sparingly offers a narratively legitimate violence, effecting inner turmoil. Gibson's entirely physical onslaught of violence, inflicted on a Christ sure of his divinity, is disturbingly less grounded in the narrative, appearing as vindictive and gratuitous for its own sake. Ironically, the vehement violence of protest demonstrated against Scorsese's film can be seen to reappear in the text of Gibson's, including an anti-Semitic dimension. Grist relates the accommodation of *The Passion*'s violence by Christians to a Freudian moral masochism in which the ego's desire for parental acceptance is substituted by punishment and the promise of future reward. Grist provocatively demonstrates that comparison of contexts of protest and production of both films yields numerous insights, some of which may be seen as deeply ironic.

Moving to an arena that is as much about spectacle as the cinema, two contributors offer their reflections on religion and violence in sport. In "The Religious Significance of Violence in Football," Rina Arya takes a fascinating look at not only the religious experience football offers to its fans, but the manner in which football relocates religious experience from ecclesial/institutional settings and, through transgression and violence especially, offers access to the sacred. Fans themselves imbue the football experience with religious significance, including concepts of sacred land and the use of sacred symbols. Arya sees at work elemental forms of religious behaviour, forms that reach across sectarian and other sociological divisions. Drawing on sociology of sport and of religion, Arya works with a distinction between the sacred and the profane, while understanding the two to be intrinsically linked. Football, with its attendant forms of ritual, constantly strides between the two, with ritual acting often as a protective barrier against the chaos of the sacred. Where ritual is transgressed in the form of violence (transgressing barriers of the body, of geography etc., with a shift from "staged" to real violence), the sacred can be understood to, in a sense, break through. Such violence performs an important function of sociological release and provides for working-class males especially the reassertion of identity in the face of the increasingly commercialized structures that dominate modern football. Arya shows conclusively that "football-as-religion" runs far deeper than its accumulated forms of ritual and symbols to touch on what Rudolph Otto long ago termed the "numinous" or "wholly other."

Our volume concludes with Hugh S. Pyper's foray into the distinctly peculiar world of World Wrestling Entertainment (WWE), "Cultivated Outrage." Pyper begins by mapping out the dynamics of the *lex talionis* (the Hebrew Bible's "eye for an eye" law of retribution) in relation to cultural and political understandings of outrage. By "outrage" Pyper refers to a state of emotion "beyond rage," but in the context of wrestling entertainment it is a state to inhabit with finesse and balance. In practice, vengeance (as part of a larger concept of justice) is rarely about the equal exchange of injuries, but rather the victim desires their excess of outrage to be answered. In the Bible, the execution of this component of excess belongs to God. But it is precisely that component, founded on non negotiable tenets of justice (law) between retribution and outrage, where WWE thrives: excess. The entertainment, the "spectacle of excess" (Barthes), relies on the audience's revulsion at the transgression of its own standards. As such, WWE operates with its own cosmic order, even to the degree that its wrestlers act out roles such as Islamic terrorists, all-American heroes and, in one bizarre instance, God himself. Long-developed melodramas with plot twists are acted out in the WWE universe, and when audiences witness the villains of that universe being "royally whupped," great satisfaction ensues, evidence of the successful way in which the WWE maintains a fine balance in its cultivation of outrage. Disturbingly, the WWE's world of "fake" and "believable" violence often spills out into real violence, with hardly believable narratives that are themselves steeped in religious ideas. Just as Arya demonstrates that football's religious dimensions run well beyond its ritual and symbolism, so too wrestling, also infused with religious imagery, plays out its violence in relation to deeply seated religious values.

Part One

In the Discourse of Terrorism

1 Seeing Beyond Fear of Terrorism on the Web

Jolyon Mitchell*

Introduction

In this chapter I investigate how the Web was used for the visual expression of non-violent resistance in the wake of the July 2005 bombings in London.[1] In particular, I will show how one website became a digital gallery for displaying and viewing responses to the attacks. I will look at the communicative ripples caused by this site, including the development of one other site which accepted the posting of more explicit religious imagery. These atrocities, which killed 52 people and injured over 700, inevitably provoked a wide range of responses. Every conceivable form of media carried the story, offering a host of interpretations. The revelation that these explosions were caused by religiously motivated and "home-grown" suicide bombers led to considerable soul searching in Britain. In both the international and local news media they received far more attention than the "daily" bombings in Iraq. Many religious leaders used sermons, radio broadcasts, television interviews and newspaper articles to condemn the London bombings.

It was the Web, however, that provided the opportunity for the most extensive and long-lasting form of popular response. With its open and easy access it became an ideal location for thousands of people to express their feelings about these suicide attacks and other forms of terrorism. In a few rare cases, some even took the chance to do what was very rarely permitted on the mainstream media: offer support for the bombings. In the cases that we are about to consider I will show how the Web became a place where a

*   Dr Mitchell is Director of the *Centre for Theology and Public Issues*, and Senior Lecturer in Communications, Theology and Ethics at the University of Edinburgh. A former BBC World Service producer and journalist, his most recent books include *Media Violence and Christian Ethics* (Cambridge University Press, 2007) and *The Religion and Film Reader* (co-editor, Routledge, 2007). He is currently completing *Inciting Violence, Promoting Peace: The Role of Religion and Media* (Routledge, 2011). He is co-editor of three monograph series.

vast number of people could express powerful emotions, including fear, anger and defiance, through a creative combination of images and words. These were often highly imaginative and sometimes comic expressions of non-violent resistance to terrorism. There are intriguing parallels to the responses after other terrorist attacks. For example, in 2001 following the September 11 attacks, "hundreds of thousands of people began posting online prayers, lighting virtual candles, and entering into religiously based dialogue in an attempt to cope with the tragedy" (Helland 2004, 33 and 2002, 297). There were also diverse reactions within "Cyber Islamic Environments" where a few extremists celebrated, while many others unequivocally condemned them on religious grounds (Bunt 2003, 67–123). This chapter will primarily consider less explicitly religious online responses to another series of terrorist atrocities.

There is a rapidly growing body of research into religious uses of the Web.[2] While several researchers have found that boundaries between religions and within religious traditions can be both asserted and blurred on the Web,[3] other researchers have claimed that increasing numbers of people use it as a space for defining and moulding their own identities,[4] as well as affirming old communities and forming new ones.[5] How to detect the presence of a "virtual community" or "community online," however, is a contested practice. Some studies have suggested that "virtual communities are nothing more than pseudocommunities," while others assert that "it is simply assumed too often that 'community' is present, without really specifying why or how" (Dawson 2004, 77). Probably the most extensive recent investigations into the relationship between community and identity in online religion are to be found in Heidi Campbell's *Exploring Religious Community Online* (2005) and Douglas Cowan's *Cyberhenge: Modern Pagans on the Internet* (2005).[6] Grounded in detailed empirical data, they provide nuanced accounts of how Christian groups and Pagan groups use the internet for both identity construction and community formation.

I will analyse how people from all over the world left their own distinctive visual marks on the Web as a way of expressing non-violent resistance against terrorism. I also ask the question: to what extent can this posting of images, and words, be described as the formation of a new online community of defiance? Or is this practice merely like using a supermarket noticeboard to pin pictures of a bike for sale or a lost cat? The only differences being: electricity, global reach and the seriousness of the subject. Or is this something between these two extremes? Perhaps it might be more accurate to see it either as a virtual art gallery which has few regulations and never-ending walls openly available to amateur digital artists or a virtual gathering point, with posted images becoming catalysts for debate and discussion. Even if it is not a fully fledged community does this collective enterprise go

beyond what Wellman and others have described as "networked individualism" (Wellman and Hogan 2004, 72–75) to become a network of resistance?
My contention is that to describe this either as the creation of a fully-fledged
online community or simply as an electronic noticeboard is to over-simplify
what is both a fluid and a social network built upon a set of practices, which
is better described, borrowing a Durkheimian phrase, as a "collective representation" in the face of shared trauma.[7]

In order both to test this thesis out and to understand this dynamic phenomenon it will be useful initially to set out a taxonomy of visual postings.
The aim here will be to establish a nomenclature for describing the different
ways in which primarily visual posting sites are used and function. Users
absorb, interpret, process, adapt and post their own images at these sites.[8]
What are the different uses that images are put to on the Web? We shall see
how they are used to defy, to console, to encourage, to explain and to
exhort. It will become clear that these images are put to a number of different rhetorical uses, from expressing heart-felt emotion to asserting identity.
In this context, we shall see how the visual signs of identity and the markers
of community become far less fixed and stable through their exposure in the
public domain of the World Wide Web. They are highly elastic signs. With
the advent of digital technologies, pictures and photographs have become
easy to manipulate and to send rapidly around the globe. In the age of sailing
ships, to transport a framed picture between continents would have taken
several weeks of costly and potentially dangerous travel, while today, for
those with access to the appropriate technology, it can be transported in a
few seconds across thousands of miles by no more than a few taps on a
keyboard and several clicks of a plastic mouse.

In this essay, I therefore examine a selection of specially created pictures
which were posted from all over the world to several websites to affirm
defiance against these attacks and other forms of terrorism. In particular, I
describe in detail the different kinds of images that were posted up on the
ground-breaking We Are Not Afraid site. I then consider how another more
explicitly religious site was used to affirm popular forms of non-violent resistance against terrorism. Some became the electronic home for photographs,
while others housed written opinion pieces or poems. Given that religious
beliefs were inextricably connected with these attacks it is neither surprising
that some users tried to employ religious imagery, nor, given the constraints
imposed by the site organizers, that others posted a vast kaleidoscope of
secular imagery to express their resistance. The merging of sacred and secular symbols is not a particularly new practice, but the use of digitally altered
photographs as non-violent statements against terrorist violence is more original. They clearly emerge from a diversity of social settings, where different
"doxas" and "sets of dispositions" are to be found.[9]

The Origins of the "We're Not Afraid" Site

"We're Not Afraid" rapidly grew into a website that attracted thousands of images of resistance against terrorism posted from all over the globe. Within two months it had received over 33 million hits. It began when Alfie Dennan,[10] a London-based Web developer, received a photo from a friend, Adam Stacey, showing how he had escaped the smoke caused by the bomb on the King's Cross train with a sock covering his mouth. Within thirty minutes of the London bombings on 7 July 2005, Dennan posted this photo on his Web log (or blog). In a little over two hours the BBC and other news organizations started to use this image. The result was that Dennan's Web log rapidly received numerous messages of support. Encouraged by these responses Dennan, along with several of his friends, set up a website on 7 July called "We're Not Afraid." Initially, it was simple images of themselves, their families and friends with the copy: "We are not afraid" imposed onto the digital pictures. Within days the site was overwhelmed with images at first from the UK, and later from all over the world.[11] With an estimated four million hits in the first few days of its existence the site swiftly snowballed into a global phenomenon. It is now possible to purchase, through this avowedly non-profit site, a wide selection of merchandise, including hats, mugs and T-shirts with "We are not afraid" emblazoned on the product. An exhibition of selected images was held in central London in the autumn of 2005. Even though the site itself is no longer actively maintained it still has over twenty thousand images, acting as a memorial to an extraordinary outpouring of non-violent virtual responses to terrorist attacks.

Images of Defiance

Many of the images were sent in as acts of defiance against the London bombers. In the first few days the earliest postings were often, though not exclusively, sombre. The founder of the site, Alfie Dennan, stares impassively out from the screen holding a piece of white A4 paper, simply written with a blue felt pen: "We're Not Afraid!" Not is double-underlined. The practice of posting images onto the Web as an act of defiance can clearly be seen in several of the pictures sent in by victims of the actual attacks. One survivor posted a picture of himself lying and bandaged in a hospital bed. On 12 July "Mark M. from Finsbury Park, London" wrote: "I was on the tube on the first carriage at Russell Square. I am not afraid." The words are almost overwhelmed by the striking photo of his face with small white medical tape on his forehead and cheek. The previous day a red-tinted picture was posted, showing a young woman with glasses looking down, with the words in black typed over the image: "Yesterday I lost my friend in London, today I am not afraid." Through such statements and depictions victims were able to assert their courage in the face of heartbreak. Other early postings included pictures of babies, children, pets and even more ironically large animals at the Zoo. Alongside pictures of suffering, images of innocence were used as non-violent statements of defiance.

It was not long before some contributors to the site became more adventurous and creative in their depictions. Tube signs and maps were adapted to incorporate the four key words. One woman is photographed sitting on the tube reading a paper; the headline is digitally changed to: "We are not afraid." Buses, taxis and even a yacht were also adorned by this simple statement. While the images of the vehicles were digitally changed to incorporate the statement, the yachtsmen claim to have actually painted the logo on the side of their boat for the Cowes race in the Solent (UK). Following the failed bombings on 21 July an old tube ticket is apparently embossed with the claim: "We're still not afraid." Like many of the submissions, this is a sophisticated piece of forgery as the typescript looks identical to the font used in the un-tampered parts of the ticket. The word "still" is to be found on a number of postings after the abortive 21 July attacks. Again the site became a space to express words of defiance in an original visual guise. Intemperate language is rarely permitted on the site, though some participants portray themselves literally "flipping the finger" or making a "V" sign to the camera. This non-verbal communication epitomizes the response to the attacks that is at the core of many of these examples of Web art.

Almost a month later a British man sent in the hazy photo of people in the smoke-filled tunnel walking down the tube line in semi-darkness, with only emergency lights illuminating their way to safety. The usual headline of "We're not afraid" is adorned with a series of eight exclamation marks. In the foreground a man is holding up a mobile phone while trying to capture the scene digitally. The merging of communication technologies and the ability of mobile phones to be used as cameras has turned every phone user into a potential amateur photojournalist. The phones themselves have become objects used to express defiance and resistance. One user sent in a picture of his Nokia phone, on which the following message could be seen: "We are still not afraid: we will never let terrorism dictate the way that we live. We refuse to live in fear. Terror will never win." In a further example of playful defiance, familiar Microsoft Window pop-ups were changed to ask the question: "Are You Afraid?" A boxed "No" makes the response clear.

Here then is an interesting qualification to the suggestion that this site was dominated by pictures of the self or those people or animals closest to the sender. Technological extensions of personality, redolent of McLuhan's theory about the "extensions" of humanity through media (McLuhan 1964) are also found posted at the We're Not Afraid site. These images of defiance draw upon a range of visual resources to make their point. The human face recurs again and again: sometimes smiling, sometimes angry and sometimes quizzical. Pictures of new media or other technological objects are rarer and often make use of additional words to reinforce the visual impact of the picture. Defiance takes on many guises and appears to be a driving force behind the posting of many of these images.

Images of Solidarity

Closely related to a rhetoric of defiance is an assertion of solidarity. Several contributors sent in images of the Twin Towers in Manhattan, sometimes in pristine condition and sometimes following the terrorist attacks. In one case, above the towers was not only the "We Are Not Afraid" statement, but also this list of cities: New York, Madrid, Moscow and London. The obvious attempt here is to locate the London attacks in a history of recent terrorism. In passing it is worth noticing which cities are excluded from this list and what an apparently Western frame is provided for understanding where terrorism is happening. Another, hauntingly picturesque, shot of a marina in the foreground and smoke billowing from Two Towers in the background is supplemented with the declaration: "This did not make us afraid. It made us more compassionate more loving & more unified!!!!"

Experience of terrorist attacks allows contributors to go beyond statements of sympathy to assertions of solidarity. In the highly visual world of this site, where as we shall see religious imagery is normally not allowed, numerous non-religious images are used to try and speak of peaceful solidarity. This could be described as an expression of civil religion, which emerges from the grass roots and where in this case the symbols of nation are intertwined with the symbols of faith.[12]

Images to Counter Fear

Many of these pictures reflect on the nature of fear and bravery itself. Some attempt explicitly to encourage the viewer's self-confidence. For instance, a man from Newcastle (UK) sent in a picture of a kitten looking into a mirror, who sees not itself, but a lion with a large mane. Consider the statement to the left of the mirror: "Look inside yourself. You are brave. You are strong. You are courageous." This sounds almost as if it has been taken from a "power of positive thinking" CD or book. The assumption here is that courage appears to come not from an external source but from within. At the bottom of the picture the claim of individual strength is qualified: "together we will be unafraid." Given that confidence is a fragile commodity, which terrorists aim to undermine, this kind of picture is a humorous visual reflection upon the belief that positive thinking can transform the timid viewer into a lion-heart. This makes an intriguing contrast with late medieval Western imagery which frequently shows several devotional figures kneeling in prayer, not before a figure of strength such as a lion, but beneath a suffering and bloodied semi-naked man. Nevertheless, vulnerable images have their own attraction and are also to be found all over the website. As observed earlier, the figures which are used almost like totems to counter fear are often children, partners or pets. They do not obviously suffer; and they are without obvious political power. Their charisma is heightened partly through their weakness and innocence in the face of terror.

Images of Popular Encouragement

Such encouraging sentiments are also to be found in pictures which appropriate images from popular culture. More specifically, the creative use of cultural icons is to be found in visual quotation from popular television programmes. For example, images from *The Teletubbies*, and characters from *The Simpsons*, are used several times. As if he is writing punishment lines, Homer Simpson's son, Bart, is pictured writing "We are not afraid" again and again on a school board. A shot from the popular British soap *Eastenders* title sequence, an aerial photograph of the city of London is adapted to read: *Not Afraiders*. These are two examples, chosen from many, of how television is used as a visual resource, which is mined for creative and rhetorical purposes. Several publicity posters from films are adapted. Three days after the first attacks in London a man from Milan adapted the famous picture of a large shark bearing teeth heading for a female swimmer, promoting *Jaws* (director, Steven Spielberg, 1975). He digitally scrawled in red either side of the shark two words: not afraid. The poster and opening titles from *The Matrix* (directors, Wachowski Brothers, 1999) are adapted to include multiple repetitions in green of: "We are not afraid."

From the early Middle Ages to the nineteenth century a common reference point for most Western viewers was biblical narrative. Frescoes, stained-glass windows and canvas paintings, unsurprisingly, drew upon stories from Jewish and Christian scriptures. These tales were known and repeated. Given the decline in scriptural knowledge and the global reach of cinema it is not surprising that films have become one popular resource for those making visual statements on the Web. Actual stills from films are used to good effect. Yoda, from *Star Wars*, is particularly popular. In small white capitals over a picture of the distinctively pointed ears of the cinematic character is the statement: "Fear is the path to the Dark Side. Fear leads to anger. Anger leads to hate. Hate leads to suffering." In large bold red capitals is the statement, mimicking the character's statement: "Not Afraid I Am."

Images to Provide Historical and Global Perspectives

A further rhetorical device is the employment of pictures from the past, thereby encouraging viewers to step away from the immediate and look backwards. Older pictures from London's history are drawn upon. For example, the famous image from the Second World War of St Paul's Cathedral surrounded by clouds in the Blitz is given the headline "We Fought Terrorism Before and We Won…" The bottom right corner has the adapted underground logo with the familiar four words. Famous paintings are also transmogrified. Munch's *The Scream* is adapted several times, most memorably with the figure now placed in front of the House of Commons and a red double-decker bus with the statement: "Smiling not Screaming."

The We're Not Afraid website provides valuable evidence for some of the visual resources people from all around the world reach for when the traditional forms of religious expression are made off-limits. Some scholars might describe this as an expression of "implicit religion," particularly if this term is understood with reference to "intensive concerns" for "commitments" that touch "human depths."[13] As we have seen, the majority of the images emerge out of people's closest circles of intimacy: close family, partners, or favourite pets. When faced by the threat of violence many people unsurprisingly use images of their "nearest and dearest." Beyond the intimate sphere there is evidence from the multitude of images provided, of the significance of friends, colleagues at work and of other members of a sports-team. These images speak of solidarity in the face of news of terror. The sphere of memory is drawn upon through the imaginative use of historical posters, family photos from tourist sites, trips abroad or postcards. The communicative environment also provides a rich source for contributors. As we have seen, images from popular culture, films, and the actual tools of communication are all woven together to create this vast digital tapestry. The presenting statement "We are not afraid," or more colloquially "We're not afraid," may in many cases actually be saying "yes we are afraid," but we will not change how we travel, who we care for or what we do. Given these sentiments it is not surprising that there are many pictures of people sticking out their tongues at the camera, and by extension at the viewer and at those who promote violence against defenceless women, men and children.

Images to Promote Understanding

The We're Not Afraid site celebrates the individual's creativity, sense of humour and right to express themselves, through creating a transitory virtual network. The comedy sometimes has an edge, as suggested earlier, with mockery of the terrorists being a common device. While the website organizers admit to welcoming "images of fearlessness from all people," such as firefighters or rescue crews, they will "not publish images of military or police personnel" if "there are guns visible or un-holstered in the image." The stated reason for this is that the team do not want "to send an aggressive message." They have refused several pictures of dead Muslims with the statement: "You should be afraid." They will not permit hateful, indecent or religious iconography. There are, however, several examples of pictures rich in religious symbolism. A Japanese Buddha with smiling children sitting in front, the vast statue in Rio of the arms outstretched Christ with a couple beneath, and the statue of huge praying hands from Tulsa Oklahoma all carry the usual statement but point towards different religious traditions. Alfie Dennan justified the use of these images, and not other explicit religious ones, on the grounds that the dominant theme was not religious and the sentiments could be expressed in any setting.[14]

There are a number of representations of Muslims in peaceful settings or poses. For example, several women in Islamic attire are pictured holding candles as are two walkers on a hill from Iran. In this case, as in some other postings, "We are not afraid" is translated, this time into Farsi. Perhaps most strikingly, a week after the July 7 attacks, a young Muslim woman posted an image of herself wearing a hajib with the unexpected words: "We are afraid." This is, according to the site's founder Dennan, the only picture out of over 20,000 posted with these words. Her explanation was as follows: "This pic is to highlight my concern as an INNOCENT muslim and to raise awareness about the increase in racial hate n [sic] crime because of the atrocity in london last week." As with many other comments the spelling, the sentences and use of capitals do not follow formal rules, sounding more colloquial than grammatical, while far more care appears to have been paid to the creation of the images.

The vast majority of the images found on this ever expanding site do not use explicit religious imagery. There are resonances with religious texts, such as the youthful faced man with the simple phrase that is also found in Psalms: "Fear No Evil." There are subtle visual allusions, which are redolent of belief in the afterlife, such as the picture of a woman walking towards a bright light emanating out of a tube tunnel.

Images to Promote Peace

In the wake of the London bombings and following the extraordinary success of the "We're Not Afraid" site several other sites were created. One of the most interesting was the Islamic site "Not in the Name of Peace" also set up only a few days after 7 July. The site's creator was a young British Muslim, Muhammad Ridha Payne. His opening statement to the site is passionate: "We need to show these maniacs that none of us think what they are doing is right, justified or Islamically based." Payne believes that "Islam has very clear guidelines as to what is right and what is wrong." He acknowledges that: "Of course we all feel aggrieved by actions in Afghanistan, Iraq and Palestine but this does not give anyone the right to kill further innocent people."[15] The site attracted far fewer images than "We're Not Afraid" and appears to have now been taken off the Web, but nonetheless the several dozen pictures posted make powerful points. Some seek to reassure viewers. For instance, the words: "Don't Panic I'm Islamic" surround a man, as he steps out of his British-looking house. He is wearing a simple black and white skull cap, pointing one finger and gently smiling. There is nothing threatening about his appearance. These images stand in sharp contrast to the more widely disseminated pictures found on extremist websites or in videos sent to television stations of masked men holding guns standing behind blindfolded kneeling hostages. There is nothing threatening in another image, a well-groomed, young, Asian-looking man, this time sitting on rocks with a harbour in the background: "Don't EXPLODE, STRIKE a POSE! ... because terrorism is never pretty." The comic twist here is found in several other postings such as one of a baby and the statement: "I want to grow up not blow up."

Images to Exhort and to Teach

There are more serious religious depictions, from individuals reading sacred texts to crowds praying to Allah. A young girl in a white robe kneeling on a prayer mat with supplicatory hands and an open Qur'an in front of her is accompanied by a phrase that through repetition emphasizes the name: "Not in the name [new line] the name of Islam." In a different picture, another young man is kneeling reading a Qur'an: "Seek knowledge not war." People in prayer are found in several other pictures. For instance, above two men kneeling with heads touching the prayer carpet of a mosque are the words: "the proverb says 'slaughter your ego with the dagger of self-discipline'"; below them three words are added: " 'not slaughter people'." In another picture of rows of men at prayer, nearly fifty Muslims kneel, and over the front row is the exhortation typed in white: "stop the slaying and get down to some praying." There is also a picture from Mecca with thousands of pilgrims at prayer with the white words "not in our names" superimposed in small letters at the bottom of the photograph. Among a number of Shi'ite Muslim young people whom I spoke with in Tehran about these sites (Iran, November 2005) it was this image which proved most popular. They were more critical of the images described above which identified terrorism with Islam, suggesting that these images should be addressed against "Talibanism," not Islam as a whole.

On the "We're Not Afraid" site several contributors had digitally daubed words upon a photograph of the new dividing wall in Israel, or at least a wall that looks strikingly similar to it. This image is recycled again on the "Not in the Name of Peace" site, but used for more explicitly religious reasons. The first line states: "Islam means peace." The second: "not in the name of Islam." The same sentiments are expressed on a skilful adaptation of a London street sign found on the "We're Not Afraid" site. The WAN team were so impressed they did something they very rarely do: comment on the image. "We received this terrific photo along with a link to an online petition which condemns terrorist acts committed in the name of Islam, which can be found and signed here. We urge people to check it out!" On the connected site a similar image is to be found, along with a quote from *The Holy Quran* (5:32) which is in English: "...to kill one person is like killing the whole of mankind... And to give life to one person is like giving life to the whole of mankind." Many of these images assert that "true" Islam is a peaceful and life-bringing faith. One overhead shot of a man apparently rapidly reading the Qur'an is overlaid with the claim: "Islam 'is a way of life' NOT 'a way of death.'" Life is in green and death is in red.

The colours are striking in many of these pictures. In another picture, five ethnically diverse babies, only in their nappies (diapers), clamber over a white long-haired woolly sofa towards a two-dimensional blue and green depiction of the world. Multi-coloured letters spell out "One World" while the globe itself simply has in black: "One God." In italics and in smaller letters is the catchphrase of the site: *not in the name of Islam, not in the name of peace.* Unlike images from the "hate" sites which position texts behind hostages, here the text is brought to the foreground, highlighting the peaceful intention of this posting.

While it is no surprise that images connected with Islam dominate this site, it is not confined entirely to images of Muslims. One posting has a picture of Pope John Paul II respectfully kissing a large green Qur'an in the presence of a Muslim religious leader. The heading is "united we can defeat terror." Another posting is a photograph of U2 playing at the Arrowhead Pond arena in Anaheim, California, on 1 April 2005. In the original picture, projected in red lines above the band, is the word "Coexist." This was created with a combination of normal letters and the major religious symbols of Islam (crescent in place of "c"), Judaism (star in place of "x"), and Christianity (cross in place of t). The inspiration for this powerful linguistic image was drawn from graffiti that the lead singer, Bono, saw somewhere in the Midwest of the USA. Notice how the added copy which frames the image reinforces what the picture itself communicates: "All GOD's people MUST and U2 can ... coexist!" Taken together, the use of the pictures of John Paul II kissing the Qur'an and U2 performing beneath this single word, partly created by religious symbols, are examples of how visual signs are recycled in new contexts to promote peace between religions.

Conclusions

In this paper I have described in detail the visual content of three websites created in the wake of the London terrorist attacks, and more specifically how images have been put to a wide range of rhetorical uses. As I have highlighted, the "We're Not Afraid" (WAN) site is an extraordinary Web phenomenon, which has now had over 20 million hits, and well over 20,000 images posted. This site has attracted participants and viewers from all over the globe. It has allowed people of many different countries, holding a broad spectrum of beliefs and using different symbolic sign systems, to protest against acts of terrorism. As we have seen, these protests take on many forms, with images used to express defiance, encouragement, solidarity and consolation. Both on this site and other less well-known posting locations, the images are used to promote peace, to teach tolerance, to encourage fearlessness, to mock the bombers, and even to satirize the contributors themselves. These practices can be described as unitive, generative and elastic. Such sites are not only uniting many different people in new independent associations, but also generating new patterns of global pictorial discourse, which are both elastic in their meaning and constantly changing. The WAN site initially became a space in which trauma, rage and grief could be articulated visually, though in the weeks and months that followed its creation the emotions expressed have widened. In some cases angry defiance has softened through the use of irony, satire and even celebration of what makes for the good life.

Sometimes contributors used the space to make sense of their own sufferings, with the text "We're not afraid" referring not only to terrorism but also to overcoming fears of cancer or domestic abuse. The site has extended beyond its original intention, with users stretching the meaning of the words and the images they send in. The "We're Not Afraid" site, and many of the images found there, also became catalysts for conversations in cyberspace. Some critical voices can be found circulating on the Web. A very small number of critics see WAN as being used for propaganda purposes, even implicitly supporting the military. Others claim, accurately, that there is no criticism of state terrorism.

Tragedy can strengthen ties of solidarity. Just as pictures of the devastation caused by the Asian tsunami (2004) and the earthquake in Haiti (2010) galvanized individuals and governments to offer aid, so news of the London bombings led to the expression of shared values, and notably on the WAN site an assertion of common humanity through the creation of pictures. But is the posting of images on a website merely resistance without action, a safe form of protest? My suggestion is that in the face of this violent storm people wanted to rally round and express their passionate feelings, and that by doing so they involved themselves in a dynamic action of solidarity. We have seen that this was a multi-layered response, where the people took expressive power to themselves. The silent lurkers on the Web were not quite so silent, articulating not necessarily what they felt, but what they wanted to feel: We are not afraid. The way in which the WAN site was used, according to its creators and explicit evidence on the site, illustrates how surfing the Web is a connected process in more ways than one, with users relying not only on search engines but friends' recommendations circulated by emails, text messages or mobile (cell) phone calls. Combined with television and newspaper reports they were guided to this new virtual gallery; they bookmarked it, they contributed to it and some then watched it grow on a weekly or in the early days on a daily basis. The discussion lists on the site illustrate that it also became a place of interaction. In this way websites become focal points, meeting places and resources for both friends and strangers. While not exactly caring networks of trust, for some people they even became spaces of visual cooperation and conversation, based upon fellow feelings, even though they inhabit very different cultural worlds.

What else then does this multi-faceted Web phenomenon demonstrate? First, many contributors to such sites have become adept at handling digital-image-producing technology. To make many of these images took time and effort, but this was not simply about users demonstrating their technological skills; many simply wished to communicate their own resistance to violence. Photos, paintings and drawings are adapted to make this point. Here is evidence of the democratization of communication among those with access to these technological resources. With the digitalization and subsequent convergence of phones, cameras and computers more and more people are becoming photojournalists and Web artists, skilled in creating their own icons. This partly explains how the simple claim that "We are not afraid" appears to have crossed over language barriers. For instance, following the Sharm al-Sheikh bombs (22/23 July 2005), which claimed at least 88 lives, hundreds of Egyptian demonstrators marched through the streets in protest, several carrying a banner. Written not in Arabic but in English were the words: "We are not afraid." The Web is not a formal community in the traditional sense of the word, but this visually composite site does provide the opportunity for cross-cultural discourse, at a grass-roots level of exchange.

Second, the site also appears to have provided the space for implicit or understated forms of religious communication. For instance, one picture on the predominantly non-religious WAN site shows ten middle-aged Catholic nuns. The words at the bottom of the picture explain who they are: "Indian Ursuline Missionaries working in Africa among Muslims and Christians." Here, inter-religious service is shown but not preached about. There is a sense in which co-existence is enacted at this site. This phenomenon goes beyond "networked individualism" (Wellman and Hogan 2004, 72–75) to a more cumulative form of interaction. From the debates on the Web surrounding the images it is clear that this practice is more than simply individuals connected through the network. Part of its power is that it temporarily brings together a global network of virtual resistance, far more expressively powerful than a single voice or even a peace demonstration. WAN is an example of a transitory and visually dominated network of resistance.

Third, the site appears to have inspired the development of more explicit religious sites, which have used the format to assert their own religious identities and communities as peaceful. It has allowed some Muslims tired of being portrayed as masked terrorists or merciless hostage-takers to show themselves in a different light: as peaceful, prayerful people and hospitable to other religious traditions. These amateur Web artists appear to be unified by a common desire to provide alternative responses to terrorism to those normally provided by the mainstream news media.

Finally, this raises important questions about how some people make use of the sign systems of their own religion and the symbols of popular culture to reinterpret their own fears for their communities, their families or themselves. Part of the draw of these sites is rooted in the fact that news about terrorism, or direct experience of terrorism, has the power to cause fear. The terrorist strikes are intended to provoke terror. Yet here is a form of mass popular resistance to such violence. Deep feelings can be aired. Emotions can not only be heightened, but also dispelled. These sites have the potential to act like a safety valve where people are free to express their fears, as well as their own creative and imaginative insights. This process is clearly often informed by a participant's residual anxieties. The conversations and postings around the images show how artistic creations and written interaction can sometimes sublimate or even dispel negative emotions. They thereby allow participants to use creative patterns of digital discourse to promote more peaceful forms of communicative interaction.

2 Violent Superwomen: Super Heroes or Super Villains? Judith, Wonder Woman and Lynndie England

Emma England*

The biblical heroine Judith of Bethulia is a female superhero. Circumstances surrounding her most famous act—the beheading of Holofernes—will be read together with the modern archetype[1] of the superhero, as given form in American comic books.[2] What is a superhero? According to B. J. Oropeza (2005, 5), superheroes share one or more traits: superpowers received by accident or chance, costumes indicating multiple identities, and absent parents. They experience a great tragedy as an incentive to becoming a hero, uphold justice before the law and, finally, mimic God with their noble origins and salvific abilities. Judith is the first of my superheroes; the second is Wonder Woman. The latter's solo comic has had the longest run of issues and been franchised into other media, making her the most successful female comic book superhero in history. My third and final figure to be "read" is, unlike the first two, indisputably "real" and located firmly within twenty-first-century vocabularies of violence. Lynndie England was arguably the most famous protagonist to come out of the 2004 Abu Ghraib prisoner abuse scandal, involving the torture of Iraqi prisoners by US soldiers. By adding her story at the end of my analysis of the mythical Judith and Wonder Woman, I hope to remove the possible "comfort-zone" associated with discussing the fictional as against the "real."

Focusing on the violence of these woman figures, the article will present "them" in a new and ambiguous light. This serves multiple purposes: it gives

*   Emma England is completing her PhD thesis at the University of Amsterdam on the Genesis flood narrative retold for children. Her article 'The water's round my shoulders, And I'm – GLUG! GLUG! GLUG!' is forthcoming in the Society of Biblical Literature's *In the Picture: Otherness in Children's Bibles*. She is on the committee for the European Association of Biblical Studies.

an opportunity to discuss a character from a sacred text within a cultural and political framework, opens the door that questions the reception of violence in society's icons, and seriously questions our presuppositions about the nature of a superhero, and indeed a supervillain. Finally, the characters are all woman figures, enabling the discussion of superhero characteristics from a specifically female perspective. Although there are hardly any universal differences between male and female superheroes, the similarities that superwomen share with each other are more numerous than the similarities shared with supermen. It is perhaps inevitable that these similarities are gendered and sexualized within their violent actions.

Judith's Story

Judith is a female character in an Apocryphal/Deuterocanonical book named after her. The earliest known version is in Greek. It is by an unknown author and may have been composed around 135–78 BCE (Moore 1985, 67–71).[3] Although scholars debate the matter, there is a broad consensus that the book is a work of fiction because of the numerous and apparently deliberate historical inaccuracies, such as Nebuchadnezzar being King of the Babylonians, not the Assyrians (Jdt. 1:1). In the narrative, Judith is a wealthy and pious widow (8:2-7) from the besieged town Bethulia. She reprimands the town elders and persuades them to accept her (undisclosed) actions before they surrender the town (8:9-36). Already, it is possible to see superheroic traits. She has absent parents, is God-like with noble origins, is suffering a tragedy and challenges the law makers to uphold justice. Before leaving the town to enter the enemy camp and meet Holofernes, the general of the besieging army, she prays to God (9:2-14), removes her widow's garments and makes herself "very beautiful." Thus we have our superhero's costume change. During her fourth night at the enemy camp Judith joins Holofernes for dinner, at the end of which she is alone in his tent "with Holofernes stretched out on his bed, for he was dead drunk" (13:2).

> [13:6]She went up to the bedpost near Holofernes' head, and took down his sword that hung there. [7]She came close to his bed, took hold of the hair of his head, and said, 'Give me strength today, O Lord God of Israel!' [8]Then she struck his neck twice with all her might, and cut off his head. (NRSV)

This action leads to the defeat of the enemy and salvation of Bethulia, and to Judith being praised by her town, the elders of Jerusalem and the High Priest (15:8-10). Throughout her life she remained a chaste widow; despite the desire of many, "she gave herself to no man" (16:22). During her lifetime and "for a long time after her death" (aged 105) no one "spread terror among the Israelites" (16:25). And so we can see Judith as a saviour, a God-like figure—a superhero.

Wonder Woman's Story

In contrast to Judith, we know considerably more about the history of Wonder Woman but her narrative is infinitely more complex. She was originally created by the psychologist, and inventor of the lie-detector, William Moulton Marston, and first appeared as a supplementary story at the back of the eighth issue of *All-Star Comics* in 1941. The fictional character is predominantly, but not exclusively, presented in three volumes totalling 569 issues:[4] 1942–1986, 1987–April 2006 and June 2006–current. These span nearly seventy years of development, not counting the retroactive continuity, crossovers, alternate universes and re-imaginings in different media. My concern lies with the comic-book version. This in itself not only requires a severely edited summary of her life to date but also a disclaimer: I can only present some of the major events in her timeline. Therefore I am largely ignoring re-imaginings and storylines completely outside of the three-volume narrative, in addition to stories where the title "Wonder Woman" has been given to characters other than the original Princess Diana.[5]

Wonder Woman and Diana Prince are pseudonyms of Princess Diana, an Amazonian woman from Paradise Island (renamed Themyscira in Vol.2, Iss.1,[6] 1987). She was created from clay by her mother Queen Hippolyte and given life by Aphrodite (Vol.1, Iss.1, 1942). Many of her early comics described her as "beautiful as Aphrodite, wise as Athena, swifter than Mercury, and stronger than Hercules" (first cited in *All-Star Comics* 8, 1941). Wonder Woman has superheroic powers: strength and flight being two of many, as well as God-like noble origins. One day, the US Army Intelligence Officer Steve Trevor (with whom there are various romantic sub-plots, particularly in Vol.1) crash-lands on Paradise Island and is near death. Princess Diana restores him to health and Aphrodite announces that an Amazon must accompany him to fight the terror of the Nazis. By means of a tournament, Princess Diana wins the right to leave her homeland and her mother (note the absent parent motif: the mother becomes absent but the father never even existed) and travels to "Man's World," specifically "America, the last citadel of democracy and of equal rights for women" (*All-Star Comics* 8). She was awarded gifts by the Olympian Gods including the Lasso of Truth, an indestructible lasso that can bind the strongest of people and Gods, including Superman and Ares. Anyone bound by it is compelled to tell the truth. Her indestructible bracelets, which deflect projectile weapons, are Wonder Woman's other

best-known gift from the Gods. Having moved to "Man's World" Diana Prince
worked as a nurse Lt. for the US Army and as an assistant to Steve Trevor,
while Wonder Woman joined the Justice Society of America (JSA) as its first
female superhero (*All-Star Comics* 12, 1942). She worked as the secretary
before the JSA was disbanded (in retroactive continuity). Wonder Woman
co-founded, together with Batman, Superman and others, a similar and longer-
lasting group, the Justice League of America (JLA), an organization of superheroes established to defend the earth (*The Brave and the Bold* 28, 1960).
Following various heroic acts the JLA and numerous other heroes join forces
with Wonder Woman to stop the destruction of the world as caused by the
sorceress Circe (*War of the Gods* 1-4, 1991). During this cosmic battle Circe
kills Wonder Woman by devolving her into the clay from which she was
created (Iss.3, November 1991) only to be re-created out of the clay by her
mother the following issue (December 1991). Eventually, she becomes the
first DC Comics (DC) comic hero to kill a human, Maxwell Lord, whom she
killed in order to prevent the destruction of the world and free Superman
from his mind-control (Vol.2, Iss.219, 2005). For this crime she is indicted
before a grand jury but is later exonerated (*Manhunter* 26-30, 2007). Wonder Woman therefore supersedes the law, has the ability to save and is a
superhero.

Superheroic Violence

Our two entirely different superheroes are set in very different time-periods,
yet share striking similarities. They both leave their homes to defend humanity: Judith sacrifices herself by putting her purity and life in danger by leaving
Bethulia and entering the enemy camp (10:10-11) while Princess Diana leaves
Paradise Island for "Man's World." Both characters commit murder. Both
characters even have a "side-kick": Etta Candy is Wonder Woman's primary
sidekick, particularly in the early years. In stark contrast to Wonder Woman
she is short, rather plump, childlike and bumbling. Of course, Judith's equivalent is the maid/servant/slave (i.e. 8:7, 16:23)—she is left to her own devices in the Bethulian camp and has no obvious control over her destiny.
There are of course differences between the superheroes. It would be hard
to justifiably claim that Judith was ever a secretary or that Wonder Woman
has permanently, irrevocably died. It is important to accept that there are
such differences but, for the most part, it is the similarities which are of
significance here, specifically those relating to violence.

Before looking at the violence itself, it is relevant and necessary to ask
why violence was committed. The initial and obvious answer is because

each character had the proverbial "baddie" or "villain" to defeat: specifically with Judith, and most frequently for Wonder Woman, tyrannical dictators. Ares, the God of War (later renamed Mars) is perhaps her deadliest foe; he is after all immortal. He recurs in all three volumes of Wonder Woman and affects the DC universe as a whole. In the Volume 2 version of her creation,[7] Wonder Woman has to fight Ares who has declared that the Amazons will not succeed in their goal of spreading peace and strengthening the Olympian Gods through worship. Ares tries to start World War III by manipulating the United States and Russian army into full readiness for simultaneous nuclear attacks, thus destroying humanity. By binding Ares in her Lasso of Truth, Wonder Woman persuades Ares that if he causes WWIII humanity will be destroyed and there will be no one left to worship him, and no God can exist without worship (Vol.2, Iss.1-7, 1987). Judith's enemy, Holofernes, may not literally be a God or from another realm but he is a military man—a warmonger much like Ares. He is an alien of the national kind and gives Godly status to his commander Nebuchadnezzar, and he undoubtedly threatens the integrity of the heroine's home.

We could also argue that Holofernes is almost a traditional comic book villain, particularly if the reader is aware of textual geographical and historical inaccuracies. Even without such knowledge it is easy to demonstrate the irony. Judith, for example, says to Holofernes "I will say nothing false to my lord this night" (11:5).[8] Of course she doesn't—her Jewish God is her lord not this self-important supervillain. With the book and the protagonists' speech littered with such ironic statements Holofernes comes across as a bit of a "dimwit." He is destroyed by his own weaknesses. Perhaps he believes he has "trapped" Judith by persuading her to be alone with him, but his own desire for sex, fuelled by his weakness for wine, ensures that he himself is trapped. His own self-entrapment serves to exacerbate the irony within the narrative—just like his comic book counterpart. Ares is trapped by his own plan and weakness—the success of his plan would lead to his own destruction, suggesting that his own ability for chaos is simultaneously limited by stupidity and his unceasing desire for chaos.

A further similarity between the villains is the devastation they actually, and potentially, cause their victims. As a resident of Bethulia, Judith is a victim. If Holofernes is successful she would probably be raped and enslaved and her faith would be suppressed. Anyone that doubts this should read ch. 2, where Holofernes' campaign of terror becomes clear: he is a violent aggressor who "ravaged" and "plundered" (2:23) and "killed everyone who resisted him" (2:25). Likewise, anybody who thinks a comic character can't be raped and murdered hasn't read *Identity Crisis* (2004), where Sue Dibny is raped in retroactive continuity and later tortured to death over the space of many issues.[9] Apart from my own assessment of why the superheroes have to fight the supervillains, they both explain why they fight. Wonder Woman frequently does so in the form of narration, to explain why she is doing things. On one occasion, she is holding up a wall and narrates, "I am caught in a defining moment of my life…holding back the chaos…as mankind falls inexorably toward death" (Vol.2, Iss.151, 1999). Judith explicitly states her reasons for generating violence in a hymn of praise "before all Israel," speaking of the actions of the enemy against *her* people:

> ^{16:4}He [The Assyrian] boasted that he would burn up my territory,
>   and kill my young men with the sword,
>   and dash my infants to the ground,
>   and seize my children as booty,
>   and take my virgins as spoil. (NRSV)

Judith also says to the town elders that if Bethulia is captured "all Judea will be captured and our sanctuary will be plundered; and he ['the Lord our God' 8:16] will make us pay for its desecration with our blood" (8:21). Judith is defending her people, faith and God. The latter two aspects, it could be argued, are the primary motive for her violent actions as Judith is repeatedly presented as a very pious Jew. That her faith is challenged, and would be more so under the control of Holofernes, is undoubtedly a major factor in her actions. What of Wonder Woman though?

Princess Diana in all her guises is regularly witnessed praying to her Gods, the Gods of Olympus: "Oh, Gods of Olympus! Though I love *paradise*, I yearn for *more* from my life…I yearn for a *purpose*!" (emphasis comic's own, Vol.2, Iss.1, 1987). The religion is not recognizable as anything "actual" as it is a fictionalized version of the Greco-Roman pantheon,[10] but the Gods are significant and recurring. These Gods, like Wonder Woman herself, change shape and character over the course of the ages but ultimately they interfere with, control and help Princess Diana and her associates as well as the world. Indeed, a recurring theme is the changing nature of their role in humanity's lives as other Gods replace them. What has this to do with the violence in Wonder Woman you might ask? Aside from Ares causing wars there are instances where Gods are at war; the most obvious of these is in the four-issue *War of the Gods* (1991). The primary (and ultimately defeated) antagonist, a sorceress named Circe, declares "I am brewing a Holy War." Considerable violence stems from Wonder Woman in this issue. Not only does she destroy Circe but also the God Hectate whom Circe worships. And how does she do it? By binding Hectate's spirit with her lasso (Issue 4). Interestingly, this violence is also done to herself—she sacrifices herself believing her death will save the world from Circe because of the curse that connects them in life and death (she was wrong).[11] This is one difference between Judith and Wonder Woman—Judith potentially and figuratively sacrifices herself but never actually does so. Nevertheless if self-sacrifice is a superheroic trait both characters are superheroes. At least so far.

Wonder Woman kills and violently subdues Gods and monsters in her story, but what of humans? The main violent act of each character is the murder of a man. Judith decapitates Holofernes with his own sword (13:8) and Wonder Woman snaps the neck of Maxwell Lord. These murders may have been justifiable, if there is such a thing as "justifiable homicide," but either way, both women chose to kill their opposition. There are other similarities relating to the despatch of the supervillain. Wonder Woman broke the neck of Maxwell Lord. She snapped it, quite literally with her bare hands. Only one step removed from this, Judith decapitated her enemy with his own sword; with all her might, she wielded it against his neck twice. These are very immediate, very violent and very gruesome deaths. They are both extremely graphic; in Wonder Woman's tale the visual is key. The image is accompanied by no words but a single sound: "KRK" (Vol.2, Iss.219, 2005). Re-reading the Judith narrative in this light, we can almost hear the self-same sound and we *can* "hear" the fall of the sword and the slicing through the spine. This is helped by an alternative translation of the text offered by Carey Moore: "Then she struck at his neck twice with all her might, and chopped off his head" (Moore 1985, 222). The onomatopoeic nature of Moore's choice of "chopped" highlights the physicality and sound of the action. So too do artistic representations of the decapitation, the most depicted scene from Judith's life. Many of the representations are just as graphic as the depiction of Wonder Woman, with blood spurting from the neck instead of the grizzly sound.[12]

Just as Judith's violent act is re-imagined, so too is Wonder Woman's. The next issue of *Wonder Woman* (Vol.2, Iss.220, 2005) re-imagines it; this time she is narrating it as a past event with her own justification for it: "I made my decision. I stand by it as the proper one." In this image the murder is seen from the side, as opposed to the original where Maxwell's death is shown from the front. In the original, Wonder Woman kills Maxwell from behind but not so here—she stands in front of him. Another difference is that Superman takes a more active role, running towards Wonder Woman trying to stop her, whereas he looks a bit vacant, almost stupid, in the original. This, of course, connects to the repercussions Wonder Woman faces (more on that below). There is even a third retelling in *Infinite Crisis* 1 (2005). In this re-imagining Superman is telling how the murder was broadcast on television; the single image duplicates the actual murder in the original but at a wider angle. The only major motif present in all three depictions is the binding of Maxwell Lord.

As we have already seen, Wonder Woman does not just commit the one act of violence. She regularly beats, batters and murders. This violence has become increasingly graphic, so much so that even Princess Diana herself states, "In a world filled with violence I seem to be reverting to it more and more" (Vol.1, Iss.244, 1978). This statement can almost be read as a metafictive commentary on her decline into violent villainy. What about Judith though? She is a war leader, correctly predicting that the enemy army will flee upon discovering the death of Holofernes. Rather than merely letting them live, run and tell the world of the strength of Bethulia, she gives the order for all able-bodied men to chase the soldiers down: "they will flee before you. Then you…will pursue them and cut them down in their tracks" (14:3-4). This is hardly the action of a forgiving hero. Instead it reflects the nature of a vengeful villain. The reactions to the violent actions differ greatly within the narratives. Batman and Superman ostracized Wonder Woman after the killing of the human Maxwell Lord (but not for numerous murders of non-humans). She was being judged by her male counterparts whereas Judith was praised. What might this say about the narratives? Certainly, in both stories the superwomen are praised for killing the "other," in Judith's case, the foreigner, but in Wonder Woman's, the Gods and monsters but *not* the human. In this case the human, at least with regard to murder, is not regarded as "other." Does this say anything about their respective location in time and place? Does it suggest a particular change in morality, or that there is a case for justifiable homicide during war and as self-defence but not for punishment? Are Batman and Superman's extremely negative reactions to her a commentary on capital punishment? Perhaps the gender of the killers was relevant. For Judith the very fact that she was a woman is key to her narrative, with the recurring theme "by the hand of a woman" (i.e. 13:15). God is so powerful he can defeat his enemies even through a mere woman.[13] Conversely, Wonder Woman exists in a more equal world where it has to be shown that no one, irrespective of their gender, should get away with murder, particularly as the heroic murder of humans had thus far been a taboo for DC comics. Finally, did Wonder Woman's colleagues react negatively, perhaps as a get-out clause for the male (and better selling) superheroes while the Bethulian men remain blameless in the narrative?

Sexualized and Gendered Violence

The violence in both narratives is sexualized and gendered. The female super-protagonists are sexualized in their attire and actions and stereotypically gendered in their reliance on men. Like their male counterparts, female superheroes rarely fight crime as anything other than their "superhero alter-ego"—even though they are fully capable of doing so when in their civilian clothes. Unlike male superheroes, their civilian identity is also an alternative, uniformed image. For Judith, this is as a widow in widow's garb—clothing wholly defined by her relationship to a (dead) man. For Princess Diana, this is as Diana Prince (note the masculinizing reduction of her title) acting the *assistant* to the *man* she regularly saves when wearing her Wonder Woman costume. Her costume is a sexualized item in and of itself, becoming increasingly more revealing throughout the ages. The skirt gradually became hot pants and then high-cut knickers, all the while her breasts became unfeasibly large for any one to be able to run with, much less fight (see Fig. 1, also Daniels 2000 and Robinson 2004). When Judith is introduced she is wearing her everyday attire: she has "put a sackcloth around her waist and dressed in widow's clothing" (Jdt. 8:4-6). In preparation for entering the enemy camp Judith is presented differently; she "made herself very beautiful" (Jdt. 10:4). Both characters are depicted, within their narratives and reimaginings, wearing what is considered the sexy dress of the day. They also use sex in their enemy-defeating escapades. Wonder Woman even uses bondage as a punishment, and in turn, is frequently in chains herself.[14] This is because of the dubious understanding of bondage in William Moulton Marston's personal philosophy: "A bound or chained person does not suffer even embarrassment in the comics, and the reader, therefore, is not being taught to enjoy suffering" (Daniels 2000, 20). What a delicious irony: all the killings listed here (and many more besides) include binding by the so-called Lasso of Truth, which by its very nature controls, captures and subdues. Invariably, these images are incredibly sexualized turning the binding into sadomasochism. The original version of the killing of Max Lord demonstrates this. As can be seen in Figure 1, the dead Max is still bound as Wonder Woman stands over him. We, as the viewer, are on the floor with Max as we follow the lasso up her artificially extended leg, across her thigh to her genital region. From here the viewer's gaze ends in her hand with the lasso hanging, like a flaccid penis simultaneously emasculating and feminizing her after her typically "male" action.

Judith is similarly depicted. She uses her sexuality to deceive Holofernes into being alone with her. Perhaps the most obvious example is when she reclines on lambskins in Holofernes' tent (12:15-16). This deception enables her to commit what has been frequently interpreted as a sexual act—killing him on his bed. By violently attacking the head both characters can be seen as acting in a traditionally masculine manner while also committing an act of castration, if Freud's theory is to be believed (1963, 212–13).[15] If this is the case, the women are moving beyond saving their people, and even punishment, into the world of revenge—a trait more readily associated with supervillains than superheroes.

Fig. 1. From "Wonder Woman" # 219 © 2005 DC Comics. All Rights Reserved

Beyond this, female superheroes have a problem. They are not permitted, for whatever reason, to be fully independent heroes in the way that
supermen are. They end up being helped and invariably rescued by a male
superhero. Often these superheroes have the role of conferring legitimacy
on the female either through narrative techniques (Robinson 2004, 85) such
as telling the story or through explicit actions. Even the name "Wonder Woman"
was given to her by a man, Steve Trevor. She heals him and identifies herself
as "just a woman," to which Steve says "My Wonder Woman." Thus, as
Robinson notes, it is her capacity to heal, not to fight, which names her
(2004, 28). Many of the major moments of Wonder Woman's career (her
joining the JSA, death and resurrection) occur outside of her solo comics and
within stories of multiple characters. This is common in comic book narratives as the industry maximizes revenue by spreading a key story across many
individual characters' issues to self-publicize and increase sales. However,
with Wonder Woman there seems to be an excessive amount of this exacer-
bated by the seemingly constant inclusion of Superman in Wonder Woman's

comic. This is to such an extent that the last issue of the second volume of Wonder Woman, issue 226, is a crossover tale with Superman!

Judith does not escape this indignity. Legitimacy is conferred upon her by the elders granting her permission to enact her plan and leave Bethulia. Then there is Achior, an advisor to Holofernes. He is sent to Bethulia to suffer its population's fate, ultimately converting to Judaism. Within the structure of the narrative Achior effectively swaps places with Judith in location and role: Achior moves from the enemy camp to Bethulia and becomes a peaceful friend to the Jews whilst Judith becomes a "warrior" in the enemy camp. Whereas Achior's role-change is permanent, Judith is gradually domesticated and resumes her original role as "pious widow" (Levine 1992, 26; Roitman 1992, 31–45). Wonder Woman experiences a similar fate. In Volume 3 Princess Diana rejects her role as Wonder Woman while defending her murder of Max Lord in court. Instead she becomes a secret agent with Donna Troy taking on the Wonder Woman role. This suggests that female superheroes never quite have the same heroic certainty as male superheroes.[16] At the very least their identity as superheroes is limited and ambiguous. At worst their extreme violence opens the door to them being labelled "supervillains." This label can be applied by reference to a "real" and political supervillain.

Lynndie England: The Villainy of Superhero Violence

The violent connections between our "fictional" superheroes are clear, but what about the "real" Lynndie England mentioned earlier? Born in 1982, she lived in a trailer park in Fort Ashby, West Virginia where she worked as a supermarket cashier. Aged 17 she joined the US Army as a reservist, to pay for college.[17] Before being called up, she worked in a chicken processing plant, where she met and married a colleague. While in Iraq she met and fell in love with a man 15 years her senior, Charles Graner, with whom she has a son. According to an interview with Lynndie in *Marie Claire*, she was smitten by him and did everything he said (McKelvey, n.d.). He took his camera everywhere, taking photographs of her, including in sexually demeaning positions. This pattern of willing submission carried through to their work when they were transferred to Abu Ghraib, an Iraqi prison. She was only 20 and was assigned as a clerk but ended up guarding prisoners. Graner claimed that he told Lynndie to pose for photographs with humiliated Iraqi prisoners (Edgar 2005).[18] An example can be seen in Figure 2. Lynndie England was convicted by a military jury on one count of conspiracy, four counts of maltreating detainees and one count of committing an indecent act. Judge Pohl asked the sentencing panel to consider her "age, family and financial difficulties,

Fig. 2. Lynndie England, Abu Ghraib Torture (copyright free)

mental condition, military awards and victims" (Edgar 2005). She was sentenced to three years in jail and a dishonourable discharge. Her actions can define her as a supervillain as she was an alien in another land and, many would argue, an oppressor, violating the land and the peoples where she was based.

The photograph in Figure 2 is immediately similar to the image of Wonder Woman (Fig. 1). In both, the "victim" is bound and the lead/lasso is held by the protagonist. The connection between the images provides a stark "wake-up call" that when Wonder Woman binds her enemies it is as a form of torture for the retrieval of information. It causes suffering, degradation and humiliation, as well as forces changes in behaviour (as in the case of Ares) of those that are bound. What can this have to do with Judith? Look at the third and final image. In it we can see a graphic depiction of a modernized Judith, binding, humiliating and torturing Holofernes in a similarly brutal fashion to the others. The horror of the act is cruelly depicted; urine runs down the victim's legs. The image clearly reflects scenes from Abu Ghraib—even Judith has a cigarette dangling from her mouth as Lynddie does in many of the photos of her. The theme of the phallus seen in Wonder Woman's lasso is also carried through in the other images. Judith's phallus is planted, firmly erect, between her legs. The explicitly phallic nature of the bondage is interesting as a reflection of the known sexual activities of the women. Despite the fact that both are presumed not to be virgins and both have an ambiguous relationship with sex, both remain essentially aloof of physical sexual activity.[19] Conversely, Lynndie, as a mother and in her relationship with Graner, was openly sexually active, but her phallus is distanced from her, pointing away from her. Further, hers is the least gendered of the images. Her female shape is the least emphasized, her breasts neither bare nor heaving. Her image is the least stereotypically "titillating" but she is, nonetheless, a sexual being wielding a phallus. All three images are simultaneously confrontational in their subconscious sexuality, but tepidly sexy in their stereotyped sexuality of women, breasts and bondage. Perhaps this is to make the images consumable for all audiences.

In the images, the women's actions are brutally framed for public consumption. Lynndie's action was probably intended for a small number of sympathetic eyes but ended up being seen by the whole world for what it was—a violent oppression. Wonder Woman's murder was created for us, the reading/viewing public, but even within her own narrative it was broadcast to the world as a violent act helping not only her friends to disown her

Fig. 3. Heidi Popovic, *Judith with the Chainsaw*, 2007 (unpublished sketch, copyright Christian Pölzler)

but leading to the public who loved her to fear her. Likewise Judith's act has been shown for what it truly was, a cold-blooded murder, in the countless images of her and within her own narrative. She publicized her action by displaying Holofernes' head on the parapet (14:1). These acts are a form of communication, but what is it they are saying? This will inevitably depend upon the reader but one may question the nature of the "other" as victim, situated in time and place. Whereas Judith is fully supported in her attack of the foreigner, Wonder Woman is completely rejected for hers and Lynndie is supported within her own environment but utterly rejected outside it. What do these complex variations say to you about the possible hypocrisy in understanding our heroes? What does it say about humanity, that the only character wholly rejected for their most violent action is the cultural, the unquestionably fictional? Or does this say more about the dehumanizing nature of war? Further, to me, the public nature of the actions suggests that all three women have fallen into their own trap. Even if their intentions were good, their violent self-entrapment causes pain and humiliation, and they have been shown wanting by the very actions intended to help. This irony places them within my framework of a supervillain.

Now that the tables have turned on Judith and Wonder Woman, it is only fair to do the same for Lynndie, but how can we possibly understand Lynndie England as a superhero? By removing her from these infamous images we can look at the woman, the true (American) superhero. She left her home to save her home (and did so as a woman in a man's world). She had absent parents in her new territory where she wore a costume—her army uniform seen in the self-same photos which declare her a supervillain. Lynndie upholds justice by policing in Iraq and by superseding the legal system for what can be perceived as "the greater good." She is, by Oropeza's definition, as presented at the beginning of the article, and in comparison with Judith and Wonder Woman, a superhero.

This is hard for me to accept but it is the logical and necessary conclusion: ultimately the three women are all supervillains as well as superheroes. This leads one to question how superheroes, particularly of the "real" kind, can become supervillains. What is it that makes this happen? It also questions the morality of the violent superheroes and the extent to which they are idolized icons in Western (particularly American) society. This idolization manifests in many ways but even the frivolous is disturbing, whether it is a child adoring Wonder Woman (as indeed I did) or more alarmingly as something to be explicitly mimicked. There is a disturbing phenomenon called "doing a Lynndie," seemingly begun by the now defunct website Bad Gas (Kirkpatrick 2004). It involves finding a preferably unknowing "victim" and pointing at them, copying Lynndie. In the photograph they copy, Lynndie gives the "thumbs-up" to a nude row of male prisoners, each with a bag over his head (again, the head is targeted) as a form of bondage. A simple Google search for "doing a Lynndie" yields nearly 30,000 results (as of June 2010). What does this say about the interaction between people and "characters"? Is there a difference between people's reactions to actual events or comic books, or does the reaction of Lynndie simply mean that people really "don't give a shit"? For my part, I am hoping that the latter is the case rather than people being pleased and excited by one human torturing another. This article makes an uncomfortable point; it challenges the common understanding of typically idolized sacred and cultural heroes. Perhaps more difficult to accept is the emotionally and intellectually disturbing request, implied in the analysis of Lynndie, that asks you to think about dehumanized political figures in an overtly positive way in order to make a fair and more ambiguous analysis. By doing so we can begin to fairly think about many of the seemingly unanswerable questions I have asked about society's superheroes and supervillains.

Part Two

In Cinema

3 Biblical Epic and the American State: The Traitor and Sanctified Violence in *Esther and the King* (1960)

*Jo Carruthers**

The relationship between the Hollywood biblical epic and the Cold War narrative of the battle between freedom and despotism, with religion signifying American values against godless communism, is well attested (see, for example, Lev 2003 and Wright 2007). Raoul Walsh's *Esther and the King* (1960) is certainly a product of self-consciously patriotic America, enacting an exploration of treason through the stance of the godly Esther against the traitorous "prince" Haman. This essay explores the significance of the film's commentary on the "traitor" both in the context of the Cold War itself and in relation to the reception history of Esther in which a focus on the traitor has been common. Finally, it will consider the film's performance of the tension between the religious adherent's loyalty to God (indispensible to the State because of its function as a signifier of American "freedom") and the State's insistence on absolute national allegiance.

Esther and the King, starring Joan Collins and Richard Egan, falls in the shadow of the 1959 *Ben-Hur*, which won a number of Oscars (including Best Picture, Cinematography, Director, Best Actor and Best Supporting Actor). It is based on the biblical story of Esther, a Jewish girl who is chosen to become queen to King Ahasuerus, ruler of the Persian empire from Ethiopia to India. When prime minister Haman is offended by the Jew (and Esther's uncle) Mordecai, he manipulates the king into ordering the slaughter of the whole empire's Jews, neither man knowing Esther herself is Jewish. Through a series of convoluted plot twists, Esther saves her people through risking her

* Jo Carruthers is a RCUK Academic Fellow in the department of English at the University of Bristol. She is the author of *Esther Through the Centuries* (Blackwell, 2008) and various articles on the reception history of the book of Esther. She is currently writing *England's Secular Scripture: Islamophobia and the Protestant Aesthetic*.

life in approaching the king to petition him and denounces the "enemy" Haman.

It has become a near truism of film criticism that the Hollywood biblical epic of this era is a faintly veiled commentary on American politics and that, as Peter Lev points out, the "blending of religious and political discourses are both characteristic of Cold War America" (Lev 2003, 164). At a time when the Soviet Bloc identified itself primarily through atheistic modernity, the portrayal of "religious subjects" far from being a simple assertion of American piety could, as Melanie Wright suggests, "serve as an association of loyalty to the American way of life" (Wright 2007, 57). Although many of these biblical epics are set in the ancient world of despotic rulers and continent-wide empires, in these films religion signifies democratic values and they enact the victory of American-style "freedom" over Soviet-style totalitarian rule. The 1956 *The Ten Commandments* even explicitly states in its prologue that "it is about whether humanity will be ruled by a dictatorship or by the laws of God," God's laws here implicitly synonymous with American political policy. Peter Lev spells out the application: "the Pharoah's reign can be viewed as a representation of Russian Communism, and the Hebrews as the free and democratic West," citing Moses' final speech: "Go, proclaim liberty throughout the lands, unto all the inhabitants thereof" from Lev. 25:10 as indicative of this blend of Israelite-American democracy (Lev 2003, 164).

This interpretation of *The Ten Commandments* is easily mapped onto *Esther the King* in which the Jew, Simon, the fiancé of the girl Esther (Joan Collins) is King Ahasuerus's "loyal Judean," whose military success is highlighted alongside his piety as he thanks the king for the empire's highest military honour with "May my God bless you, sire." We are introduced to Esther as the voice of "God's laws" in the film's second scene, which opens on a man hanging in Esther's village, the soundtrack's dissonant chord invoking the melodrama of terror and wrongdoing. Whilst the character Nathan explains that Haman "demands an example for all who cannot pay their taxes," Esther asserts that such governance "offends the will of God," and orders Nathan to cut the man down (the emphasis that it is those who *cannot*, not *will not*, pay underlines the unfairness of the tax system). Nathan's traditionally prophetic voice (his name evokes the prophet from 2 Samuel 12) is overpowered by the godly voice of Esther. Like *The Ten Commandments'* prologue, this early scene sets the film up as a battle between despotism—what Mordecai later calls "the cruelties of Prince Haman"—and a fair and just rule established on the laws of God. That the law of God is associated principally with home politics is clear with this early emphasis on taxation. When Esther becomes queen of the Persian empire, she immediately influences the king to change tax law so that Haman's fixed levies are replaced by a system of proportional payment,

bringing the Persian Empire in line with American—and thereby God's—
principles.

A story of court intrigue, the Book of Esther becomes drastically rewritten
in Raoul Walsh's Hollywood epic. For example, Esther's death-defying approach to the king becomes trespass of the law that women must not speak
at court. The most notable diversion from the biblical story, as far as this
essay is concerned, is the setting up, from the film's beginning, of Haman as
a traitor. Even as the king marches back from military victories in Egypt, the
film presents Haman in his first scene in the bedroom of Queen Vashti.
Staring at his reflection in a hand mirror, taken from the queen's dressing
table, he boasts of his "services" on the king's behalf in his absence, and
declares that he will be "the next king of Persia." A self-serving minister,
Haman's disloyalty and passivity are coupled with an unmanly vanity that
contrasts strongly with the muscular and military king who is absent from the
palace only because he is risking his life on his people's behalf. The film's
opening 90-second spectacle of the returning army frames the film with the
marvel of the empire's military force and the spoils of war, aligning Ahasuerus's
empire with the technological spectacle of Hollywood. In so doing the film
subsumes Persia within the greater might of America. As such, the vain and
domestic Haman is constructed as anathema to modern America,
simultaneoulsy valorizing military prowess and muscular patriotism.

Although Haman's status as traitor is a common one in the reception
history of Esther, it is one based upon speculation regarding the story, at best
implicit in the biblical text. Beginning with rabbinical writings of the second
century onwards, commentators interpret the minister's attempt to slaughter
the Jews as treason—Esther's (difficult to interpret) denunciation of Haman
can be taken to imply that Haman's actions harm not merely herself and the
Jews, but primarily the king. The *Targum Rishon* (one of two expansive Aramaic rabbinic translations dating no later than the sixth century) fills in Esther's
speech, making overt what it sees as implicit indications of Haman's treason:
"the adversary is the wicked Haman who sought to slay you (yesterday) in
the evening in your bedchamber, and to dress himself today in royal garments, to ride on your horse, and to lower the golden crown upon his neck,
to rebel against you and to take away the kingdom from you" (Grossfeld
1991, 75). When Haman is accused and the king storms out of the room, he
throws himself, literally, on the queen's mercy. His unseemly submission to
Esther, read by the king on his return as an attempt on her chastity, is
for many further evidence of treason, following the logic that a sexual con-
quest of the queen precedes an attempt on the king's life (see Carruthers
2008, 239–41).

Such interpretation becomes explicit in *Esther and the King* and Haman's
treason is against the State, not simply the person of the king. Haman steals

from the king's treasury, threatening the empire's economic stability and causing heavy taxation. His attempt on the king's life threatens not only the king but the population as a whole because Haman has been proved a cruel, despotic ruler in the king's absence. Haman not only sleeps with the king's queen in his absence, but also tries to set up his own concubine as the king's next queen as a step towards usurpation. Although Haman does attack the king, he is vilified because of his mistreatment of the empire's population: his is a crime not merely against a leader, but against the State as an abstract principle. His hanging of those who "cannot" pay their taxes represents his mistreatment of the population and it is this that rationalizes his execution at the film's end. Such an unsubtle characterization suggests that this film is not primarily about the queen's bravery (as the story of Esther is often understood) but is instead a portrait of the machinations—and, importantly, the fall—of the traitor.

By subsuming American values within religious discourse, and vice versa, such biblical epics assert American political positions to their home audience through a highly authoritative framework which inherently sanctifies those politics. As such, violence against the traitor is sanctified as a fulfilment of God's "will." Such a close relationship, however, necessitates that proposed American values need to *seem* compatible with religious principles. That the traitor is unforgivable is a familiar concept to the post-9/11 rationale of violent counter-terror performed, for example, in the successful American series *24* with its repeated violence against those who threaten State security. The punishment of the State-enemy is a modern-day axiom. This was not always the case, as intense defence of this position in the reception history of Esther demonstrates. That *Esther and the King* works so hard to defend its portrayal of an unforgivable enemy also suggests that it was a concept not wholly accepted in 1960 Protestant-dominated America. In fact, the portrayal of an unrepentant, consistently "evil" Haman contradicts the Protestant narrative of repentance and salvation, and the film works hard to portray treason against the State as an unforgivable sin. An aporia is produced as democratic values—which assert the supreme importance of choice and self-autonomy—are set over a narrative that sets the villain beyond choice, beyond repentance and thereby beyond mercy. It is a triumph of a quasi-apocalyptic rationale of a cosmic war of good and evil over a more nuanced religious discourse of repentance and forgiveness, as epitomized in a parable such as that of the Prodigal Son.

Absence of mercy towards Haman is a problem that is confronted directly in Thomas Brereton's 1715 dramatization of the Esther story in which Haman calls upon "Christian" forgiveness: "I find 'tis vain to fight your God, and live:/ But does he teach you never to forgive?" (44). The implicit theological problem of *Esther and the King* becomes explicit here. That such lack of forgiveness is personally distasteful to Brereton is clear in Esther's distance from revenge, as it is the king (as head of State) not her that denies mercy (45). Sir Bernard Crick, Emeritus Professor of Politics at Birkbeck, on an article on Tyrrancide (a concept that has obvious overlaps with this concept of the unredeemable enemy), suggests that "Much of our thinking about the relationship of ethics to politics was shaped by long or half-forgotten theological dispute and debate about the justification of killing tyrants" (Crick 2006). It is the tail-end of this now "long-forgotten" theological dispute that *Esther and the King* enters into.

In 1646, in a sermon on the Book of Esther before the House of Commons during the English Civil War, the Protestant minister Richard Heyricke denies mercy towards the enemy of the State: "as for Apostates that are false to their Covenant and to your State, let not your eye pitty them, let not your hand spare them, execute justice to the enemies of the Commonwealth, shew mercy with favour to your friends" (Heyricke 1646, 30). Heyricke's assertion here is articulated in a context in which treason, in legal terms, was changing from being conceived as action against the body of the king only to that of action against the State as an abstract principle. Although many date the emergence of the concept of the "State" to Hobbes' *Leviathan* in 1651, this sermon indicates that such ideas were circulating prior to *Leviathan*'s publication and more importantly, they were emerging directly alongside changing concepts of treason (see Orr's *Treason and the State*, especially 32 n. 11 and chapter 2, "Sovereignty and the State").

In 1647, only a year after Heyricke's sermon, the commentator John Mayer reflects on the scene invoking apocalyptic imagery:

> Mystically, by Haman's coming with the King to the feast, we may understand the wicked communicating with the Lord in the Eucharist, but it is to their own judgment and damnation. Haman's petitioning to the Queen upbraided, as an oppression of her, shewed that the petitions of the wicked suing for mercie at the last day, shall be so far from prevailing, as that they shall be taken for oppressions, the great Judge being hereby provoked to wrath the more. (Mayer 1647, 68–69)

Drawing on Puritan Calvinistic principles of predestination—in which the fate of the elect and damned are predetermined and unchangeable—lack of mercy towards the State enemy is justified by reference to God's own lack of mercy towards "the wicked" at Judgement Day.

Contemporary politics in the wake of terrorist action against the State rationalizes and makes appealing the identification of personified evil (for example in Osama bin Laden) and consequential violent counter-terror. In the same way, William Beveridge, Lord Bishop of Asaph, in 1704 defended counter-terror in response to the Gunpowder Plot of 1603, the attempt to blow up king and parliament. He even claimed the Plot supersedes the averted genocidal threat to the entire empire of Jews and calls it "such a Conspiracy, and such a Deliverance, that the like is scarce to be met with in any History, sacred or prophane, except in this Book of Esther; where we have also a clear Precedent for making a Law for the Publick and Solemn Commemoration of such a Deliverance every Year" (1704: 16) and later repeated his claims "that in some things the Copy Exceedeth the Original" (18). As chosenness is mapped onto Protestant England, Esther's Purim also becomes a standard for annual celebration on England's Bonfire Night, November 5th. We find in his sermon a God-ordained, pre-emptive strike: "GOD had so ordered it, that the King's Mind was altered, Haman disgraced and hanged, Mordecai advanced, the former Decree revoked, and another granted, that the Jews might defend themselves, and with the assistance of the Magistrates and Officers in every Province, destroy all that were *ready* to destroy them" (17–18, my emphasis). Preaching on Esther 9:27 and 28 at Laura Chapel, Bath on Guy Fawkes' Day in 1848, Edward Tottenham links the story of Esther, and its festival Purim, to two historical events: the "horrible and wicked" Gunpowder Plot, "executed against the king and the whole state of England, for the subversion of government and religion established among us" and the arrival of William III on the same date "for the deliverance of our Church and nation from Popish tyranny and arbitrary power" (1848, 4). Tottenham's logic is undermined as he simultaneously challenges Jewish acts of "revenge" against Haman whilst defending punishments of State traitors through allusion to this same Haman. At Purim, as celebrated in Jewish communities, he claims, there is "much that is objectionable. There is often great intemperance, and a spirit of revenge displayed, not merely in the record of Haman's cruelty ... but in the curses they pronounce on him" (13). In a nuanced—yet not altogether successful—negotiation of the notion of forgiveness, he condemns the Jews for their violence and curses, yet limits forgiveness to "personal injury" (15) and unquestioningly condemns the Roman Catholic Church for its encouragement of treason against Britain (17). Normative Protestant logic is inverted as mercy demands violence not forgiveness.

Commentaries in the nineteenth century defend violence against the enemy of the State rationally through privileging the importance of protecting the innocent. George Lawson reasons:

> A worse curse may have come upon Esther, if she had neglected the opportunity afforded her by God, for securing the peace of Israel by the destruction of Haman's creatures. They were a race of vipers. Their venom was not diminished. If they had not been crushed, they might have found an opportunity to sting the man who had brought destruction on their companions in wickedness. (1804, 210–11)

Thirty years later, the commentator Thomas M'Crie asserts:

> It is a dictate of common reason that it is lawful to repel force by force, and to take arms against those that come in hostile array. The tendency of the opposite doctrine, in the present state of human nature, would be to bind the hands of the innocent and peaceable, and expose them as a helpless prey to the turbulent and the mischievous. It is warrantable to employ carnal weapons against carnal violence as it is to use spiritual weapons against spiritual violence. (1838, 256)

M'Crie's choice of language here suggests that "human nature" is so depraved—again following mainstream Calvinist logic—that it even becomes animalistic as the "turbulent" and "mischievous" become hunters, and the "innocent" their prey. The inherent carnality of such action, and the dehumanizing of the individuals involved demands "carnal," that is violent, non-spiritual, response. For Alexander Symington, in his 1878 commentary, it is, again, the defence of the innocent that impels violence against the traitor: "Esther has a tender heart; but she is not a fool ... [I]f the righteous execution of one wicked man can save them, justice and mercy both forbid her to plead for that man" (151). Somewhat illogically, mercy, here, demands a lack of mercy for particular individuals.

It helps, of course, that the religious discourse of *Esther and the King*, like many of the Hollywood biblical epics, is suitably vague, meaning that such theological problems are less apparent. By making Esther into primarily a romantic tale, the narrative of violence and lack of mercy is removed from any explicit doctrinal context and becomes more insidious precisely because it is a stealth narrative, not necessarily apparent enough to provoke thoughtful reflection. Nonetheless, the film engages with constructing defence of counter-terror precisely within the tradition outlined above. It does this by delineating legitimate versus illegitimate violence, and particularly the legitimate use of State violence, sanctifying violence against the traitor. Echoing Lawson, M'Crie and Symington, *Esther and the King* sets up the defence of the weak as an exemplary reason for State violence (in which treason is an act against the State, conceived as an abstract notion of "the people") and in doing so sets up a "Victim Triangle" of Jews-as-Victims, Haman-as-Victimizer and the State-as-Rescuer that legitimizes State violence against Haman. As the early modern Protestant writers reflected a Puritan sense of predestination in their logic, so the assertion of unforgiveness in *Esther and the King* is testament to the Puritan basis of American society in which the doctrine of predestination is based on the religious status of individuals being eternally static, despite their seeming transience and flux from a human perspective. In a doctrine that bases salvation on God's intervention, humanity is split between the elect and the damned and, although only God knew who belonged where, it was an unchangeable status, the "damned" lacking the God-given grace to authentically repent. At the foundation of democratic America is an essentially undemocratic worldview that denies personal choice. This aporia, an unpickable knot of logic, influences the structure of American values and politics, making the mixture of ostensible choice and latent stasis a familiar tenet of modern politics, and especially the politics of the "enemy." It is a contradiction evident in *Esther and the King*.

Violence not only pervades the film but is structured in such a way to identify legitimate and illegitimate forms. Haman's hanging of the Judean is clearly illegitimate, although "legal," whilst the king's (and his "loyal Judean's") State violence is not only legitimate but celebrated. Other scenes enact the bifurcation. The king's camaraderie and sense of equality is underlined in a scene of wrestling training with his soldiers in which the men, ostensibly at least, wrestle as equals. Bare-chested, cheering and laughing, the men practise democratic violence. When the king thinks a soldier has let him win, he orders another soldier to throw his opponent to teach him not to hold back: an act of apparent fairness is enacted through violent punishment ordered from above, hereby legitimizing State-ordered violence in the guise of fairness.

After the first queen, Vashti, is deposed for adultery, the law requires that all virgins be gathered for the king to choose a replacement (it is from this "crop" that Esther is plucked). Haman's government violently seizes the women in a set of short scenes in which shrieking women are stolen, notably from sites in which they are employed in "honest work," in field, seashore and village. The scene of Esther's seizure is designed to be especially distasteful as she is forcefully stolen at the wedding altar from her groom, Simon, who nonetheless, and legitimately, knocks a soldier unconscious as he battles to retrieve his bride. The defence of the weak as the exemplary reason for violence is reiterated as the king leaves a wrestling session and finds the guards stealing three women from the harem (under Haman's orders, who wants to remove the most beautiful to make way for the candidate under his influence). The king takes on the three guards single-handed, his act of prowess celebrated in the adoring and grateful looks of the women. As the frame through which morality, and God's will, is articulated, Esther's gaze legitimizes the king's violence on her behalf; it is in fact the scene that sparks Esther's interest in this man who is clearly not merely heroic (Esther is too morally refined to be so easily impressed), but noble.

As well as constructing a binary of "legitimate" and "illegitimate" violence the film also portrays its key characters within a triad of Victim, Victimizer and Rescuer. Expanding Stephen Karpman's construction of the "Victim Triangle" in his paper "Fairy Tales and Script Drama Analysis" (1968), Michael Ovey outlines the triad of Victim/Victimizer and Rescuer as a scheme of victimhood in which victim status "indicates moral innocence," in which victims may speak with "unique authority" precisely because of the wrong done to them. In this nexus, the Rescuer is also "cloaked with innocence and righteousness" and can "enjoy the benefits of non-accountability" (Ovey 2006). That the Jews are victims is underlined not only in the first scene in which one of their number is hanged, unfairly, for not being able to pay taxes, but also in Mordecai's invocation of the Shoah. Simon's attack on the soldiers who steal away his bride, Esther, results in soldiers attacking Jewish villages, a collective punishment in contravention of article 33 of the 1949 Fourth Geneva Convention and as such in opposition to American democratic values. In his response to the news, Mordecai reflects: "from one spark a Holocaust," painting the scene of State revenge as a precursor of the twentieth-century Shoah, a memory only fifteen years old at the time of *Esther and the King*. In doing so Haman's government becomes associated with Hitler's. *Esther and the King* is an especially Jewish film, rather than "Judaeo-Christian," devoid of the Christian iconography that suffuses *The Ten Commandments* (1954), for example (see Nadel 1993). It is this Jewishness that functions to further enhance the typology of victimhood.

In *Esther and the King*, Esther and the Jews are Victims, Haman the Victimizer and various figures—but mainly King Ahasuerus—act as Rescuer. It is a triad set against an ideal of peace that, through invocation in the mouth of Mordecai, becomes associated almost entirely with the empire's Jews (the king often acts nobly, it seems, only because of the influence of the Jewish Simon, Mordecai and then Esther). At a war conference with Ahasuerus and Haman, in which an attack on Greece is debated, Mordecai declares: "I dream of the day when there will be an end to war," and hopes for "building instead of destroying." He points to the Jews as an exilic people "seeking always for some haven of peace." As they articulate the film's morality, both Esther and Mordecai are presented as innocents in need of protectors. Esther is rescued by the king when stolen from the harem by Haman's guards, and when Haman rashly orders the destruction of the Jewish people, whilst the king is away at Persepolis, the film dwells on the figure of Mordecai in a prison cell. Praying through Psalm 23, "The Lord is my Shepherd," when he comes to the line "he prepares a table for me in the presence of my enemies," the camera pans to Haman, the subject of the verse, positioning him as the subject of the psalm and of God's vengeance. The disenfranchised Mordecai, loyal and yet unfairly imprisoned, is set against his victimizer, Haman, sitting unlawfully on the king's throne. In the scenes of attack that ensue, Mordecai comes so close to death that his neck is in the noose, a passive figure who offers no resistance to the soldiers, in need of the military might of the king and his soldiers.

The logical outcome of the structure of the "Victim Triangle" is to construct a Victimizer who is beyond the mercy of the Victim or Rescuer. Responding to Karpman's Victim Triangle theologically, Michael Ovey warns: "Encouraging people to think that they, as victims, do not need mercy [in other words, that they are in a privileged realm, beyond criticism], can encourage ... the thought that they need not show mercy" (Ovey 2006). Further, the biblical story and the film, in personifying evil in a single character follows what David Keen, Professor of Complex Emergencies at LSE, has called the "fantasy of finite evil." When one is reassured of "being certain about the source of the threat," of "an apparent if arbitrary solution," then the solution of limited violence is appealing. It is Keen's assertion that such logic "underpins a violent approach to counter-terror" (2007). The film solves the problem of illegitimate violence in Esther through the annihilation of evil in the person of Haman, a solution familiar to modern politics.

Finally, the film engages with a further contradiction at the heart of America's assertion of religious piety as indicative of American democratic values alongside Cold War paranoic demands of citizen loyalty. Philip E. Jacob's 1955 article, "Religious Freedom—a Good Security Risk?" explicitly articulates the quandary. Jacob admits the centrality of religious freedom to American self-identity: "Freedom of religious belief and practice have been accepted as so integral a part of the American political and social heritage that to challenge its 'loyal status' appears heretical" (41). Nonetheless, he argues that such religious freedom is a "bad security risk because it dares to condemn and resist, with all the force at its command, the actions of government which it holds to be wrong" (40). Devotion to a "higher law" enables dissention, as can be seen in Esther's vocal denunciation of Haman's policies throughout *Esther and the King*. She demands that the hanged are taken down, contravening the law, and stands up against him in the king's court, breaking the law and risking her life, in the name of her God and justice.

It is a problem that the film tackles perhaps because its Jewish emphasis means that its characters are simultaneously American and Other, enabling a distanced exploration of dissension, as personified in the exotic, yet homely, Esther. In the film's second scene, as Esther implicates the king in the government's cruelty, her fiancé, the war hero Simon, outlines a principle of Jewish identity in which State loyalty is separate from either private worship or place of birth:

> We were born in Persia. Our home is where we live. We worship our own God. But Ahasuerus is our king.

The principle is clear: religious devotion leads to and enables loyalty to government. As such, the film constantly underlines that such religious fervour will always be in the service of—and not to the detriment of—a "righteous" state as represented by Ahaseurus and indicative of America itself. Simon's devotionally-inspired patriotism contrasts with the "prince" Haman, who as vain and traitorous is the antithesis of Simon: Haman is geographically, culturally and religiously suspect. He is even portrayed as a drug-user and believer in superstition: he is frequently pictured taking his "Eastern potion" and throws lots to the Babylonian God.

Esther and the King stands in a trajectory of a defence of State violence that emerges in the early modern period alongside the emergence of the nation-state; a logic that still resonates today. Clothed in the vapid epic of Hollywood romance, the story of Esther provides a sanctifying narrative in the service of State violence, simultaneously endorsing the righteousness of violence against the traitor and the violent imperative of righteousness itself.

4 Cease to Exist: Manson Family Movies and Mysticism

Gerry Carlin*
Mark Jones*

In early August 1969, less than a week before the Woodstock festival, the decade of peace and love was brought to a premature end by a weekend of brutal murders in the Hollywood hills. Starlet Sharon Tate, 26 years old and over eight months pregnant with film director Roman Polanski's baby, three of her friends of varying degrees of celebrity, and three less well-known victims, were butchered in the apparently inexplicable Tate-LaBianca slayings. While there was early speculation that the killings were drug-related or even mafia-arranged, these rational explanations were soon superseded by dark whispers of Satanic rites and occult practices—as *Newsweek* reported, there was speculation "that the murders resulted from a ritual mock execution that got out of hand in the glare of hallucinogens" (King 2000, 222). These rumours were fuelled by the strange filmographies of Polanski and Tate, by malicious gossip, and by crime scene leaks. If you cross Polanski's *Rosemary's Baby* (1968) with Tate's alleged initiation into witchcraft (Greenfield 1970, 16), add embellishments to the physical evidence, and scrutinize it through "occulted" vision, then it is easy to echo Dennis Wheatley's assertion: "[t]hat it was a Satanic killing I had no doubt from the first account of it" (Wheatley 1971, 272).

Resisting occult lines of enquiry, the police (incompetently) pursued drug and organized crime connections. When the perpetrators were finally apprehended, though, they would prove to be even more bizarre than the gossip columnists could have desired. In the documentary *Witness: Charles Manson—The Man who Killed the Sixties* (1994), Vincent Bugliosi, chief prosecutor and

---

*   Gerry Carlin is Senior Lecturer in English at the University of Wolverhampton. He has published on modernism, critical theory, and aspects of 1960s popular culture.

*   Mark Jones is Senior Lecturer in English at the University of Wolverhampton. He has published on science fiction, horror films, popular music, pornography, and aspects of 1960s popular culture.

author of the subsequent bestseller about the case, *Helter Skelter* (1974), would later describe Charles Manson and his "Family":

> Here you have this little guru, 5 feet 2 inches tall. He gathers around him a bunch of kids from average American families—you'd never expect them to be mass murderers—and convinces them that he's the second coming of Christ and the devil. Ultimately he gets them to kill total strangers. This is an extremely bizarre, strange case.

Closer examination, however, reveals that Manson and his philosophy, while apparently outlandish, were actually rooted in the broad cultural matrix of the 1960s. Although he was incarcerated for the first part of the decade, Manson spent a lot of time, as did many others, independently preparing for something like the spiritual awakening of the summer of love. His interests and reading while imprisoned had included popular music, the Bible, science-fiction novels, popular psychology, hypnotism, occult lore, mysticism and Scientology—the last being important as a body of belief and practice from which Manson would borrow or "squirrel" ideas of karma and reincarnation, and phrases like "coming to Now" and "cease to exist" (Sanders 1972, 28–31; Bugliosi 1974, 144; Smith and Luce 1971, 256).

Manson started gathering his Family of followers soon after his release from prison in 1967, and they soon developed a semi-nomadic lifestyle. As the leader of a communal group, Manson fulfilled many of the mediatized stereotypes of the 1960s cult guru; principally, this consisted of a project to psychosexually "deprogram" his followers through group sex, psychedelic drugs and a philosophy of ego-death—an eclectic mixture of mysticism, communalism and pop psychology. While the Family was at first little different from other communal groups in late 1960s California and elsewhere, by early 1969 Manson had started preaching a science-fictional apocalyptic doctrine he called "Helter Skelter." This told of an imminent race war in which armed black revolutionaries would rise against rich white middle-class "pigs," assume the reins of government, fail and descend into chaos, and ultimately allow the Family of chosen ones to emerge from their hiding place in a "bottomless pit" located beneath a lake in the desert (an idea gleaned from both biblical prophecy and Hopi Indian legend) and rule a transformed world— an armoury and a fleet of vehicles and equipment were being stockpiled in readiness. Syncretic interpretations of the Bible and pop music foretold this event: Manson extensively used the Book of Revelation and The Beatles' *White Album* (*The Beatles* 1968), especially songs like "Helter Skelter," "Piggies," "Blackbird" and the sound collage "Revolution 9." Indeed he considered The Beatles to be the "deadly locusts" and "Angels" of the apocalypse foretold in Revelation. One of the pretexts for the killings was to catalyse the race and class war that would bring Helter Skelter into being in a fusion of popular culture and millenarian prophecy (Bugliosi 1974, 238–45; Sanders 1972, 147–50).

Evidence that the Family considered themselves to be carrying a grandiose future design into history would materialize itself in different ways, not least in Manson's consistent pose, and treatment by others, as a possible reincarnation of Christ—his final arrest report named him as "Manson, Charles M., aka Jesus Christ, God" (Bugliosi 1974, 128). Several who encountered him in the Haight-Ashbury in 1967 saw him as a charismatic Christ-like figure, and Family members would casually insist that Manson "was just a hole in the infinite through which love was funnelled… Charlie is Jesus Christ" (Watkins 1979, 29–30; see also Gilmore and Kenner 1971, 33–39). In the socio-cultural upheaval of 1967–69 the Family, with Manson at its spiritual heart, aligned themselves with something like the original Christian impulse. Manson kissed and washed feet, asked people if they were "ready to die" and granted eternal life. He was also "crucified" in staged rituals by a Family who came to see themselves, mystically and politically, as a reincarnation of the early revolutionary Christians, struggling against a tyrannical Establishment and moving into a new world (Sanders 1972, 35). Family member Susan Atkins declared that "We were tuned into God—at least Charlie was, and the rest of us through him. But we believed we had to fight to survive" (Atkins 1978, 114).

Early in Family history, in late 1967, Manson was employed by Universal Studios as an advisor on a projected movie about the modern-day return of Christ (Sanders 1972, 44–45). Manson's knowledge of early Christian history, or biblical theology, was probably nugatory, but his role was apparently to provide a Christ-like perspective on the contemporary world (Felton and Dalton 1970b, 32). While this signals an attempt on the part of the producers to lend counter-cultural authenticity to the project, and a recognition that Manson expressed the appropriate "guru-effect," he was apparently more concerned with filling the film soundtrack with his own compositions (Gorightly 2001, 78). Around this time Manson did record in Universal Studios, though nothing emerged from this until later bootlegs. Listening to these recordings now it can be seen that long before either Helter Skelter or the Tate-LaBianca murders, and only a few months after Manson's release from prison, the kernel of Family philosophy was already in place, expressed in both Manson's lyrics and his extemporaneous asides. A major aspect of the Family ethos was communal performance, and the dialogue preserved between the tracks shows just how uncomfortable Manson was in a studio booth without intimate Family support—"I wish you'd all come in here! Why don't you just let that thing ride, c'mon in we'll chat awhile man" (Manson, *Unplugged*, n.d.)—so the sessions produced nothing releasable. Similarly, the film project collapsed, partly, as Manson himself acknowledged, because his knowledge

of the Bible and emulation of Christ were outweighed by his jail-house rac-
ism: the film was to feature Christ as a black man in the American South, and
Manson "couldn't buy that concept" (Manson 1986, 136). The failure of
these projects perhaps intensified the urgency Manson felt in disseminating
his message, and a further opportunity was soon forthcoming. In 1968 the
whole Family were suggested as the subject of a film to be produced by
Terry Melcher, Doris Day's son (Melcher, along with his partner actress Candice
Bergen, had been the previous tenant of the house where the Tate killings
took place). The Family had met Melcher through their association with Dennis Wilson of The Beach Boys, whom the Family lived with for a while and
where Manson met and impressed the likes of Neil Young, John Phillips of
the Mamas and Papas, and others. Pseudonymous producer "Lance
Fairweather" (probably Gregg Jakobson) "would say to him, 'Charlie, you can
do so much more with your music and with film than you can ever fucking
do running around in a bus with your girls and preaching the stuff' " (Felton
and Dalton 1970b, 33). The Hollywood documentary also collapsed. While
Melcher intended a portrayal of peace-loving hippies, Manson wanted a
visual explication of his emerging apocalyptic doctrines. Notoriously, though,
rumours persist that the Family used stolen cameras and film to shoot their
own extreme home movies. Though some elements of Mansonian lore come
from esoteric sources, much is lifted from popular—and even trash—
culture, and from the mass media, and the new messiah would strive to
promulgate his message using these communicative forms.

The closest Manson's early message came to the awareness of a mass
audience was with his song "Cease to Exist." The lyric promises true being in
return for total submission and renunciation: "Cease to exist/Just come an'
say you love me/Give up your world/Come on you can be…/Submission is a
gift" (Manson, *Lie*, 1970). The Beach Boys recorded a version of this song,
changing the lyric to "cease to resist" and renaming it "Never Learn Not to
Love." It was issued as the B-side of the single "Bluebirds Over the Moun-
tain" in 1968 which got to 61 in the US charts, and is included on The Beach
Boys' LP *20/20* (1969). As one writer notes, "a year before he became world
famous, Charlie had the rare distinction of being the first satanic killer with a
record on the US charts" (Lachman 2001, 329), but Manson disliked The
Beach Boys' slightly modified version and has suggested that changing the
lyrics to his song was a contributing factor in Dennis Wilson's untimely death
(Gorightly 2001, 137–38). Manson's message of universal love through ego-
extinction is turned by The Beach Boys into a romantic love song, essentially
individualizing a communitarian ideal.

The idea that love and some form of death are compatible, and even a
special form of communion, is an undercurrent of the popular cultural tides
that washed the 1960s. In 1966 The Beatles released *Revolver* which, with

hindsight, was the envoy for their impending role as mediators of a new, psychedelic, counter-cultural consciousness. The final track on the disc, "Tomorrow Never Knows," is an experimental song that opens with droning sitars, reversed sound effects and a chanted injunction to "turn off your mind, relax and float downstream," followed by a repeated assurance that this "is not dying." The lyric continues with instructions to "lay down all thought" and "surrender to the void" (*The Beatles* 1966). The central ideas are lifted from the work of Timothy Leary, the iconic spokesman of the "acid" generation whose experiments with mind-altering chemicals began at the Harvard School of Psychology (MacDonald 1997, 164). Leary and his colleagues would become extremely influential in the mid-and-late sixties as their eclectic borrowings from a range of religious and mystical sources sought to give both a procedural and philosophical basis to the idea of LSD as a liberating modern sacrament. John Lennon took the lyric for "Tomorrow Never Knows" from *The Psychedelic Experience: A Manual Based on the Tibetan Book of the Dead*, where the chemically generated journey away from the ego, self and delusion and into self-transcendence was grafted onto Buddhist teachings on the transition from life to death, and the focus shifted from the dead to the tripping: "With your ego left behind you, the brain can't go wrong... Whenever in doubt, turn off your mind, relax, float downstream" (Leary et al. 1964, 14).

If egotism is the problematic condition, then perhaps it might be best to have never formed one. As the earliest study of the Family suggests (it was researched before the murders) from the outset Manson promoted the innocent, "unprogrammed" condition of childhood as an ideal—"Charlie used the words of Jesus, 'He who is like the small child shall reap the rewards of heaven'"—and fostered the belief that "infant consciousness was the ultimate state" (Smith and Rose 1970, 116–17). As both Leary and Lennon recognized, that which maintains adult self-consciousness, the process that generates it out of the condition of childhood, is rational thought itself: "What [Christ] is saying is 'Don't think.' He who thinks is lost, because if you have to think about something, to doubt it, you're lost already" (Felton and Dalton 1970a, 29). Mansonian philosophy exhibits an extreme reaction against selfhood—its past and its moral burdens—in favour of the "now" of pure being, a transmoral world outside history, thought and language. Family members aimed to extinguish the self, to become void in order to merge with the group and the undifferentiation of existence. Tex Watson, the Family member with most blood on his hands, described Mansonian teaching thus:

> *Everything was one*, [Manson] said. The programming which our personal histories had built into us put barriers between us and the realization of that oneness, kept us broken in separate fragments torn from our connection with the Whole. We kept seeing "you" and "me," when in reality there was

only "it," the *one*. The only way to break down those barriers between ourselves (or the fantasy of self) and true oneness, true unity, was love... (Watson
1978, 72)

This dissolution through love first required the death of the ego, but when
applied to the world outside the Family it became translated into a theology
of death-as-love-as-liberation. Initially, only the first and last elements of this
equation were perceived, and they were understood politically. The *Los
Angeles Times* from 2 December 1969 reported that "The suspects slew
their victims, police believe, both to 'punish' them for their affluent life style
and to 'liberate' them from it" (Schiller 1970, 48–49). Such statements gelled
with the anti-materialist revolutionary rhetoric of the time, and would lead to
groups such as the Weathermen and other revolutionary figures and underground publications to voice initial support for the Family and their opposition to "rich pigs" (Bugliosi 1974, 221–22). The more complex cosmic
communalism of Family theology, however, is encapsulated in Susan "Sadie"
Atkins's notorious statement when a cellmate asked her whether killing a
pregnant woman bothered her: "I loved her, and in order for me to kill her I
was killing part of myself when I killed her... You have to have a real love in
your heart to do this for people" (Bugliosi 1974, 85).

The fundamental Family doctrine decrees that love effaces all moral categories; Manson testified that "I told them this that in love there is no wrong"
(Dwyer 1995, 215). As an early commentator remarked,

> If the ultimate truth ... is that "All is One" and "One is All," and that in this One
> all the opposites, including good and evil, are eternally reconciled, then have
> we any right to blame Charles Manson? For seen from the point of view of the
> eternal Now, he *did* nothing at all (Zaehner 1974, 72).

The Family's nondualist philosophy, usually dismissed as cultish claptrap, and
seen as derivative of such sinister and sensational pop cults as the Ordo
Templi Orientis, Process Church of the Final Judgment, and the Church of
Satan, is actually a coherent theology, and identifies the Family with mystical
Hinduism, but also with heretical Christianity. The (theo)logical conclusion of
Mansonian universality is that if all opposites are united in the one, then
Manson can be both God and the Devil, as he testified in court (Dwyer
1995). He even heals the fractured image of the biblical Christ—"As 'God'
he could be both the Christ of St John who is love and the Christ of the Book
of Revelation who wreaks terrible vengeance on the unrepentant wicked or,
in Charlie's peculiar mythology, 'rich pigs'" (Zaehner 1974, 62).

This complex theology was maintained within the Family through the apparatus of an active religious community. Correspondences can be identified
between Family theory and praxis and those of any other functioning religion: a mythology (both miraculous and eschatological); structures of ritual

and taboo; sacred texts (Book of Revelation, *The Beatles*); doctrinal exegesis; ethical structures (complete altruistic devotion within the group). For the group, communion was a constant reinforcement of Family values, and its principal constituents were acid and song. "Each night the Family would eat together, smoke a little grass or hash, often drop acid. Then after the meal we'd all sit in a circle to listen to Charlie sing his songs and preach to us" (Watson 1978, 72; see also Watkins 1979, 62–64). As noted above, it was notoriously difficult to satisfactorily record Family music in the studio because its prime function was to support a communal ritual. Some indication of this remains in contemporaneous materials, and in particular in the footage and soundtrack of *Manson* (1973). Filmed largely before and during Manson's trial, it features the non-incarcerated Family members enacting ritualized group interactions, including dancing, bathing, communal embracing, and singing, to a soundtrack of Manson's music.

This representation of communal unity has developed an iconic function in most attempts to dramatize the Family, and is typically used to signify a singularity of mind and purpose. It features in both "canonical" *Helter Skelter* TV movies (1976, 2004). The first is a virtual blow-by-blow retelling of Bugliosi's book, focusing on the investigation and trial. The later version fills out their characters, deeds and philosophies. Although by 2004 it was less contentious to attempt to display the pre-murderous Family communitarianism positively, neither "movie of the week" can adequately approach the religiosity of the group experience. Both recirculate Mansonian folklore—for example, Manson allegedly breathing life into a dead bird—but they avoid such explicit religious imagery as the Family's staged crucifixions. In the same year as the second *Helter Skelter*, Jim VanBebber's *The Manson Family* would feature a much more intimate approach to the Family's religious culture. Using recurring shots of Satanic figures, psyschomimetic imagery and an extended sacrificial blood-orgy initiated by the mock-crucifixion of Manson, the film attempts to both literally and symbolically represent the sacramental aspect of the Family. A mixture of recreated documentary and fake "found" footage, it intermittently presents itself as incorporating the "lost" Family home movies, specifically fleshing out the rumours of the infamous "snuff" films (as described and so named by Ed Sanders in *The Family*). Framed through the device of a contemporary documentary filmmaker in the process of editing authentic footage, it is able to draw on thirty years of visual and literary depictions and renderings of Familial discourse. Most crucially, unlike the mainstream TV movies, VanBebber uses the modes and sensibility of exploitation cinema, which since 1969 has firmly established the iconography of the Mansonian guru.

Although there was an already extant cycle of counter-cultural massacre movies which predated the Manson murders, the schlock sex-and-horror genres responded swiftly to integrate Mansonian themes and figures. Some extant biker/hippie/sex and murder movies merely had to change their titles or modify their marketing to exploit the Manson theme more effectively: *Angel, Angel, Down We Go* (1969) was renamed *Cult of the Damned* after the Tate-LaBianca killings hit the press; *Satan's Sadists* (1969, aka *Nightmare Bloodbath*) was a biker film whose publicity cashed in on the news coverage; *Love Commune* (1970, aka *Ghetto Freaks, Sign of Aquarius* and *Wages of Sin*) featured what appear to be added scenes of a black mass (see Kerekes and Slater 1994, 9–11). Mansonist gurus and associated ritualistic elements would also leach into other horror sub-genres—the vampire film (*Dracula A.D. 1972*, 1972; *Deathmaster*, 1973); virally-infected and zombie killers (*I Drink Your Blood*, 1970; *Children Shouldn't Play with Dead Things*, 1972); ancient evil rising from other dimensions (*The Dunwich Horror*, 1970). It was most useful, though, in rape and torture films. *Wrong Way* (1972), an almost unwatchable jeeper/biker/hippie soft porn "roughie," features a condensed Manson Family, complete with bus, teenage girls, and a hieratic guru. When two girls wander into their camp whilst they are burying a previous victim, Freak (the Mansonian figure) determines to kill them, but first informs them: "We shall now reduce you to sexual beasts. When your ego is annihilated, we shall all be united." Most infamous of the Manson rip-offs is *Snuff* (1976), filmed as *Slaughter* in 1971. The original film utilized a hippie guru and his violent female acolytes, while the extended release print added a supposedly real filmed murder sequence, again exploiting the myth of the Family home movies.

Snuff typifies the sensationalization of the ritualistic apparatus of Manson and the Family. Some exploitation films, though, would engage more thoroughly with the group's theatrical theology and ideology, and could approach a more faithful rendition of the cultic mindset and violent performativity. The most intense evocation of ritualized and cinematized torture and killing is found in Roger Watkins's *The Last House on Dead End Street* (1977, but filmed in 1973). It is awash with allusions to the Manson murders and their context, including an ex-jailbird murderer and his female associates, and their classy, kinky victims. Terry Hawkins—the cult killer—is a director of pornography, and is commissioned by his future victims to produce a film which will transcend the banality of the genre. He does so through a sequence of grandiosely theatrical "snuff" films. As with the re-enactment of Family home movies in *The Manson Family* and the allusion to them in *Snuff*, Watkins fills in yet another piece of lost Family lore, hinting at the rumoured pornographic films found at the Tate residence and films made by the Family "with quite a few recognizable Hollywood faces in them" (Sanders 1990, 403–405). Hawkins, in a classical theatrical mask reminiscent of the bearded Manson, presides over the murders as both film director and high priest. The sequence of murders becomes increasingly ritualized and eventually Satanic in staging, accompanied by an eerie choral soundtrack, and culminating in the final victim being forced to fellate a cloven hoof protruding from a woman's jeans. Though principally a metafilmic commentary on cinematic perversity, the leader's gnomic pronouncements ("the unclothed answer is me"), and the excessively ritualized evisceral "sacrifices" allude to a debased if fundamentally unrepresentable religiosity. Watkins has testified to the central influence of Sanders's *The Family* on the film (Kerekes and Brottman 2002, 104). It seems that with Mansonian murder even the most straightforward slaughter movie ineluctably becomes a transcendent ritual.

The Manson Family's heretical Christianity is confronted directly in *Sweet Savior* (1971, aka *The Love Thrill Murders*). It features ex-teen idol Troy Donahue as Moon, the charismatic leader of a commune of Jesus freaks. His father, we learn through flashbacks and Moon's nightmares, was an evangelist preacher, but the pseudo-Satanic blood-drinking and sex initiation of a naked girl that opens the film tells us how mutated this evangelism is, while key phrases echo documented Family pronouncements: "A world of pigs that twisted your mind, mutilated your soul"; "I am you… you are us… I am God's earthly messenger. In his name I declare you a member of this family." These, and other details such as writing on the commune walls and readings from the Book of Revelation, bind the narrative closely to the Family and the Tate murders. Moon's group have been hired as "freak" sexual entertainment at a party hosted by a young pregnant actress whose film-director husband is away in Rome—he had once hired Moon and his group for one of his films. The commune arrive at the house in a van with "Jesus is good" and "God lives" painted on the side. After drugs and a ritual breaking of inhibitions (the repetition of obscenities) the sexual frolics begin. Predictably, the night ends with the ritualized slaughter of the partygoers, fulfilling Moon's earlier statement "If God says it's alright, then everything is justified." It is a concise summation of Mansonian theology. As Tex Watson stated at his trial, "There was no wrong. Everything was perfect. It was perfection, the flow and the oneness, and there was no mistake. Manson was a perfect being, to me more like Christ and we were totally him then" (Nelson 1991, 88). The righteousness of the group's actions is made believable through the establishment of a justified disgust for the victims' decadent and degenerate lifestyle, making this exploitation quickie perhaps the most effective evocation of the Family's belief system's specifically Christian elements.

The millenarian framework of Family belief, though, can only be echoed successfully in apocalyptic science fiction. In 1971 *The Omega Man* depicted a near-future, post-holocaust world in which the "last man on earth" is besieged by a population of biological warfare victims. They are psychotically anti-technocratic, ascetically theocratic, and call themselves the Family.

Significantly, in an apparently "Helter Skelter"-inspired scenario, infection has turned their skins ashen white. The identification of the film with a religiose counter-culture is firmly established in the opening scene where Charlton Heston is first seen watching *Woodstock* alone in a cinema. It is reinforced at the film's close when he is symbolically crucified by the Family. Only one year after the trial, this film extrapolates Family doctrine to produce an imaginative evocation of an apocalyptic Mansonian future.

It appears that only in exploitation and genre cinema can the problems posed by the Family be informatively addressed in ways that seriously engage with their extreme theology and ideology. This is perhaps appropriate as so much of the Manson mythos and the Family's formative experiences come from the popular media—Manson's oft-quoted trial statement, "I am only what you made me. I am only a reflection of you" (Dwyer 1995, 217), is perhaps more accurately focused by Family member Brenda "Nancy" McCann who insisted that "We are what you have made us. We were brought up on your TV. We were brought up watching *Gunsmoke, Have Gun, Will Travel, FBI,* and *Combat*" (*Manson* 1973). This commonality of mediatized socialization, shared between the Manson Family and "straight" society, is only ruptured by the power of Family love and belief. In commentaries there has consistently been a lack of acknowledgement of the Family's ideological motivations, many of which have also been a feature of other revolutionary, religious and millenarian groups and movements throughout history. The Family shares with these groups elements of mystical illumination, the redemption of the chosen, the recovery of primal innocence, antinomian ideals beyond good and evil and the transcendence of dualities (Nielsen 1984, 330–34; see also Nielsen 2005, 94–95). Few sociological and criminological interrogations of the Manson murders account for the central importance of these phenomena. Their reluctance to do so is mirrored in mainstream representations, which similarly fail to engage with transcendent belief as a legitimate factor in Family exegesis. The impossibility of effectively communicating the religious experience and its associated communality mean that versions of the events of August 1969 will always present them as monstrous, anomalous and inexplicable, rather than what they perhaps were: the (theo)logical outcome of a commitment to 1960s utopian ideology. As Family member Catherine "Gypsy" Share stated, as she sat surrounded by the remnants of the Family in the Spahn Movie Ranch in 1970:

> "Give up everything and follow me," Christ said, and we have given up a lot to follow *our* dream… There are no couples here. We are all just one woman and one man. "All you need is love." We were the only ones gullible enough to take The Beatles seriously. We were the only people stupid enough to believe every word of it. (Felton and Dalton 1970c, 38)

5 The End is...a Blockbuster: The Use and Abuse of the Apocalypse in Contemporary Film

John Walliss*

The closing decade of the twentieth century witnessed an outpouring of millennial fears and expectations quite unprecedented in the modern world. In an era in which Francis Fukuyama (1993) was celebrating the post-Cold War "end of history" and arch-postmodernist Jean Bauldrillard (1995) was declaring ironically that the year 2000 would not happen—time's arrow having gone into reverse at some point in the 1980s—many, even if they did not embrace a Christian eschatology, still looked towards the transition from 1999 to 2000 (or 2000 to 2001 depending on their position) with a sense of trepidation. This was not, of course, a free-floating anxiety. A number of events that took place, or issues that emerged, in the 1990s played on fears of an apocalyptic dénouement to the century whether by the effects of extreme weather conditions, the AIDS epidemic, ebola and other viruses, the Y2K "Millennium Bug," variant CJD (Creutzfeldt-Jakob disease), or the actions of some "apocalyptic cult" such as the Branch Davidians, Aum Shinrikyō or the Order of the Solar Temple (see, for example, Dunant and Porter 1996; Wojcik 1997; Walliss 2004). Indeed, to take just the last example, such was the concern among law enforcement agencies that the shift from 1999–2000 would herald a literal explosion of outbursts of violence by apocalypti-cally-minded groups that several, most notably the Federal Bureau of Investigation (2002, 28) and the Canadian Security Intelligence Service, produced reports for their agents on what the FBI report, *Project Megiddo*, referred to as "individuals or domestic extremist groups who profess an apoca-lyptic view of the millennium or attach special significance to the year 2000."

*   Dr John Walliss is Senior Lecturer and Director of the Centre for Millennialism Studies in the Faculty of Arts and Humanities, Liverpool Hope University, UK.

As would perhaps be expected, these apocalyptic fears were also re-flected within popular culture, most notably within film. Simultaneously tap-ping into and feeding from the general sense of *fin de siècle* anxiety, Hollywood treated cinema audiences to a number of films dealing with apocalyptic "End of the World" scenarios such as alien invasions (*Independence Day*), giant meteors (*Deep Impact, Armageddon*) or super-viruses (*12 Monkeys*). Other films, most notably the Kevin Costner films *Waterworld* and *The Postman* had as their backdrop a world that had been ravaged by environmental and/or geo-political collapse. Not to be outdone, Satan himself, in the form of Gabriel Byrne, attempted in *End of Days* to escape his eternal prison and bring about the end of the world by producing a child with a human woman between 11pm and midnight on the eve of the millennium.

The shift into a new century and calendrical millennium has not witnessed a significant slowing down of film releases either drawing on the idea of the end of the world as a motif (for example *Donnie Darko*) or explicitly dealing with "end of the world" scenarios (e.g. *28 Days Later, The Day after Tomor-row*, and *The Core*). Indeed, 2000 saw the release of *Left Behind: The Movie*, an adaptation of the first volume of the series of "rapture" novels of the same name written by Christian premillennialists Tim Lahaye and Jerry Jenkins. Drawing on the authors' interpretation of biblical endtime events, *Left Behind* revolves around the pre-millennial "rapture" of the Elect up to Heaven and its aftermath for those literally "left behind" during the Tribulation. This has been followed by two more sequels, *Tribulation Force* and *World at War*, both of which focus on the post-Rapture world where the antichrist runs the United Nations, enforcing a universal religion on the world, and where a small number of remnant Christians (the so-called "Tribulation Force") try and oppose him. More recently, *Right at the Door* has drawn on contempo-rary, post 9/11 fears about terrorist attacks to present an apocalyptic vision of the terrifying aftermath of a radiological "dirty bomb" attack on Los Angeles. At the time of writing, the sequel to *28 Days Later* (*28 Weeks Later*) and *Sunshine*, also by Danny Boyle, are on theatrical release

In this article I intend to present an analysis of both the use and abuse of the notion of the apocalypse within contemporary cinema through a critical engagement with the recent work of Frances Flannery-Dailey (2000), Mervyn Bendle (2005) and Conrad Ostwalt (1998, 2000, 2003). In particular I will explore Ostwalt's and Flannery-Dailey's claim that contemporary apocalyp-tic films are characterized by what the former refers to as a "desacralization of the apocalypse," wherein the traditional notion of the apocalypse is secu-larized and placed within the sphere of human agency. Thus, rather than presenting a traditional image of the apocalypse as a divine event largely outside of the sphere of human agency, films such as, for example, *Arma-geddon* or *12 Monkeys* not only locate the cause of the apocalyptic event within the natural world (e.g. a comet or a supervirus), but also show how it may be prevented through human agency. In doing so, I will critique Bendle's claim that, in contrast to films produced during the Cold War that dealt with the possibility of nuclear holocaust, contemporary apocalyptic films are hall-marked by an attitude of scorn and ridicule towards the everyday. This, I will show, is invariably far from the case. Rather, I will argue that without excep-tion contemporary apocalyptic films are characterized instead by a valoriza-tion of the everyday wherein, in an almost Durkheimian way, the contemporary social order (understood typically as male and north-Ameri-can) is reaffirmed and celebrated.

Before doing so, however, I should like to spend a brief moment clarifying what I mean by "apocalyptic films," particularly as in much of the literature the term has typically gone undefined and remained implicit in its use (see Stone 2001; Broderick 1993a, 252). The term "apocalypse" has its root in the Greek word *apokalypsis* meaning "revelation" or "to unveil" (O'Leary 1994). Within biblical and religious studies it is typically used to refer to a genre of Jewish and Christian literature which relate visions of the end of time/the world and the emergence of a new and perfect social order. This genre would include texts such as the Old Testament Book of Daniel and the New Testament Book of Revelation, as well as other non-canonical texts such as the Apocalypses of Thomas and Adam or the Revelation of Esdras, all of which present prophecies "unveiling" the shape of the future. However, within popular usage the term is used much more broadly to refer to any form of immense cataclysm or destruction; typically involving the whole planet (i.e. "the End of the World"). Thus, for example, fears of an all-out nuclear war or planetary environmental disaster may be understood as being "apoca-lyptic" in nature, even where they are not linked to any biblical eschatology or a sense of an unveiling of history (Wojcik 1997). The reason for this being that such events involve—in a manner akin to those described in apocalyptic texts—the cataclysmic destruction of all human life and/or the planet.

In this article, my use of the term "apocalypse" and "apocalypse films" will stay closest to this latter understanding of a cataclysmic destruction of humanity and/or the earth. This, after all, is the one that will be deployed by both the producers and the audiences of such films (its use is thus justified from an emic perspective).[1] However, I will show how many films typically draw on several if not all of these overlapping understandings of the term; how, for example, a film may deal with the "end of the world," present its plot as a form of cautionary tale of what could happen in the future (a poten-tial "unveiling"), and quote or make reference to real or invented apocalyptic texts. In doing so, I will explore some of the possible tensions or problems that may arise. To this end, my article will be structured in three sections. In the first, I will briefly outline Ostwalt's thesis of the "desacralization of the apocalypse" within film. Following on from this, in the bulk of the article, I will develop and explore this thesis in relation to several of the films outlined in the introduction. Finally, I will discuss some ways in which contemporary apocalypse films invert both the central characters and the message of apocalyptic texts.

Ostwalt on the "Desacralization of the Apocalypse"

In several recent contributions to the study of religion and film, Conrad Ostwalt has drawn our attention to what he has termed the "desacralization of the apocalypse" within contemporary film. Taking as his initial starting point the notion that contemporary culture has undergone some degree of secularization, Ostwalt (1998, 4) argues that this has led not to the decline of religion (the position of, for example, Steve Bruce 2002), but rather to a blurring of the boundary between the sacred and the secular wherein, for example, "cultural forms perceived to be secular might very well address religious questions and tap the religious sensibilities outside of recognizable religious institutions."[2] Equally, religions may themselves adopt popular cultural forms in order to communicate and make their message relevant to modern, secular audiences (see, for example, Ostwalt 2003, 57–87; Forbes and Mahan 2005, part 2). In particular, he argues that this blurring of the sacred/secular boundaries "has assisted in creating a new apocalyptic myth…more palatable to contemporary popular culture"; a myth characterized by a fundamental desacralization of the traditional understandings of the apocalypse (Ostwalt 2000, 20). The process of secularization thus results, Ostwalt claims, in the co-opting of the apocalypse by popular culture, so that, for example, film makers may now raise the spectre of the end of time in much the same way as Fundamentalist preachers, albeit with different motives. Indeed, going further he argues that such films may actually function religiously in that by confronting audiences with the possibility of imminent world destruction, they thereby "help viewers come to grips with human contingency" (Ostwalt 2000, 1). Apocalypse films may thus operate for contemporary audiences in much the same way as *La Danse Macabre* and *momento mori* tombs once did for medieval and Renaissance Europeans (see Clark 1950; Binski 1996).

Nevertheless, Ostwalt argues, this new apocalyptic myth differs in significant ways from its biblical forerunner. First, as noted above, within apocalyptic films there is a toning-down of the fatalism that one finds in apocalyptic texts. Where, for example, the Book of Revelation presents an account of the apocalypse as both supernatural in origin (brought about by God and with supernatural agents as the central *dramatis personae*) and as essentially unavoidable for either the living, or, indeed, the dead, contemporary apocalypse films reject this and posit an end that is both natural and, crucially, *avoidable* through human agency. In other words, whereas the wrath of God cannot be averted by humans, the same is not true of asteroids, superviruses or alien invasions. The contemporary apocalyptic myth thus represents an example of what Daniel Wojcik (1997, 211) refers to in his typology of apocalyptic orientations as *cataclysmic forewarning*, "in which apocalypse is said to be imminent but avoidable through human effort" and where "predictions of potential disastrous scenarios...are presented with the hope of motivating people to act to avert possible catastrophes and save humanity from approaching, but not inevitable, doom."

This links with the second and third characteristics of the new myth highlighted by Ostwalt (2000, 3); that "the cinematic apocalypse depends on a human messiah...to rescue humanity from those elements that threaten annihilation," and that although such films remove "the divine element from the apocalyptic drama" they still maintain "religious symbolism, imagery [and] language." As I shall discuss in more detail below, just as apocalypse films have secularized the potential causes of apocalyptic destruction, so too have they found a saviour in a non-supernatural form. Indeed, not only do such films secularize the apocalyptic hero, but, I will argue, in doing so they typically invert the apocalyptic hero by presenting him (and it is typically a male) as both a defender of the existing social order and as fundamentally flawed. However, despite removing the divine presence from the apocalypse, many of the films I will discuss below do not shy away from drawing, both overtly and covertly, on the language, symbolism or ideas found within apocalyptic texts. In some cases apocalyptic texts themselves—or texts invented by scriptwriters which sound suitably "apocalyptic"—may also be quoted within the films and form plot devices (see Denzey 2004).

Fourth, as an arguable reflection of the cultural hegemony enjoyed by science, not only do apocalypse films "allude to the idea that religion has trivialized the apocalyptic threat," but they also typically find a solution to this threat through science. Religion is, of course, invoked. However, the real solution to the apocalyptic threat facing humanity is invariably found within these films in some combination of science and technology, not in miracles or divine intervention. Finally, pulling all these points together, Otwalt argues that within contemporary Western society, popular culture has become the most effective purveyor of "of our culture's eschatological consciousness" and that this has resulted in the emergence of "secular eschatological imagination" that simultaneously feeds into and is influenced by forms of popular culture, such as films.

Discussion

There is much of merit within Ostwalt's analysis, although I would argue against his latter assertion that popular culture has become the most effective purveyor of apocalyptic ideas. The years since 9/11 have witnessed, particularly in America, a resurgence of apocalyptic ideas and rhetoric linked with the "War on Terror" and the Bush administration's religio-political agenda (see McLaren 2002; Lifton 2003; Urban 2006). This is not to deny either the role of popular culture in influencing contemporary apocalyptic sentiments, or the emergence of a secular eschatological imagination, but rather to highlight that, in America at least, the religious eschatological imagination has not gone away, and that in many ways it currently enjoys a more hegemonic political (and possibly also cultural) position than its secular equivalent (see Gribben 2006 on the "mainstreaming of prophetic expectation" in the late twentieth century).

Equally, while I would accept the general thrust of Ostwalt's thesis regarding a postmodern blurring of the distinction between the secular and the sacred, I would argue that a more nuanced understanding of the process of secularization is needed to grasp the role of religious ideas within popular culture (it is also a matter of intense debate whether it is possible to argue that the USA is a secular society—certainly the statistics would point to a different conclusion! See Baylor Institute for Studies of Religion 2006). For this, two potential avenues of theorization offer themselves to us. First, we may return to Peter Berger's (1990 [1967]) classic distinction between, on the one hand, the secularization of society and, on the other, the secularization of consciousness to argue that, irrespective of the status of religion in the wider society, the prevalence of religious ideas within popular culture may be seen as evidence for the continuing fascination—or at least curiosity—that religious/spiritual ideas still hold for individuals. Or, on a mundane level, it may equally be true—and I would argue that it certainly is—that, as Wright argues, the foundational nature of the Bible and Christianity within the West make them almost a taken-for-granted set of ideas hardwired into culture (Wright 2007). Consequently, even if they do not accept a traditional Christian eschatology, for example, audiences will still understand and react almost instinctively to apocalyptic imagery and language. Indeed, it could be argued that, within a culture steeped in Christianity, it is impossible to talk about the destruction of the planet and/or mass destruction of humanity and *not* invoke on one level or another the spectre (and it is often only a spectre) of Christian apocalypticism. As Will Self (1998, xiv) observes in his introduction to the Canongate edition of the King James translation of the Book of Revelation:

Our sense of the apocalypse is steeped in the language of *Revelation*. In this century the star called Wormwood *has* fallen, and the sea has become as black as sackcloth of hair, and the moon has become as blood. We have heard the silence—about the space of half an hour—that accompanied the opening of the seventh seal, yet we are still here.

Second, we may draw on the more recent work of Christopher Partridge (2004; 2005) on what he terms "occulture" and, more specifically, his notion of "eschatological re-enchantment." Echoing to some extent the sentiments of Ostwalt, Partridge (2005, 2) argues that Western societies are currently witnessing "a confluence of secularization and sacralization," where old forms of religion are drying up and being replaced by new non-Christian spiritualities. These new spiritualities, he argues, are both resources of and resourced by popular culture, or, more specifically, a "reservoir of [hidden, rejected, and oppositional] ideas, practices and methodologies" that he terms "occulture." Occulture, then, is simultaneously "the spiritual *bricolour*'s Internet from which to download whatever appeals or inspires," as well as being "the well from which the serious occultist draws" and "the cluttered warehouse frequently plundered by producers of popular culture searching for ideas, images and symbols" (2004, 85). More specifically for our purposes here, occulture may be seen as a source for the apocalyptic themes, motifs and texts that the producers of popular culture may dip into at will to create new cultural products (be they films, novels, or song lyrics); products which then, in turn, become part of both the language of popular culture and the reservoir of occulture (see Partridge 2005, chapter 7).

Having examined briefly some of the potential shortcomings of Ostwalt's thesis, I now turn my attention to expanding upon his notion of the "desacralization of the apocalypse." First, I would concur with him that contemporary apocalypse films represent a secularization of the apocalypse through their focus on both natural—typically "man-made"—disasters as the agent of cataclysmic destruction and the way in which they show how these may be prevented through human agency. As noted in the introduction, within these films the supernatural element is almost completely removed so that the agent of destruction becomes, for example, superviruses (*12 Monkeys, 28 Days Later*), giant meteors (*Deep Impact, Armageddon*), geopolitical collapse (*The Postman*), or some form of environmental catastrophe (*The Core, The Day After Tomorrow, Waterworld*). Similarly, destruction is averted, or at least mitigated against through the actions of heroic individuals (typically heroic north Americans).

This is not to say that supernatural—or at least non-human—agents of destruction or salvation are not also presented, but they appear much less often—specifically only in two films: *Independence Day* and *End of Days*. Indeed, *End of Days* is noteworthy among its peers for its exclusive focus on the supernatural as both the agent of potential destruction and, indeed to some extent, salvation. In contrast to, for example, the heroes of the films listed in the previous paragraph who avert catastrophe through their human efforts, the hero played by Arnold Schwarzenegger in *End of Days* ultimately comes to rely on faith. Indeed, as Walsh (2002) notes, this is in many ways the central theme of the movie. When we are introduced to Schwarzenegger's character (Jericho Cane) he is shown as someone who has lost what faith he has in God after his family are murdered during a burglary. Later in the film when he is offered assistance by a shadowy group of Catholic clergy who are attempting to subvert Satan's plans, he retorts in a classic Schwarzenegger action hero way by telling them that "between your faith and my Glock 9mm, I take my Glock." However, at the end of the film, shortly before his final confrontation with Satan, Cane, who has fled to a church, is shown contemplating the church's religious images and statues before throwing his machine gun to the ground and praying "please God, help me. Give me strength." Finally, Cane draws strength from statues of Jesus and St Michael in order to overcome the possession of his body by Satan and throw himself onto the latter's sword, thereby forcing Satan back to Hell. The journey of Cane's character through the film is thus for Walsh (2002, 7), one from anger to faith, or from being "an action hero…to a prayerful believer," albeit one who ultimately has to rely on violence in order to defeat his foe.

That said, however, it is only at the end of the film that we are shown Satan as a supernatural entity—as a dragon (arguably an allusion to Revelation 12–13). For most of the film he is shown in human form; albeit a form with some degree of supernatural abilities. Similarly, the audience is not shown divine entities saving the day, but rather have to rely on the—albeit heavy-handed—symbolism of Cane contemplating religious iconography accompanied with choral voices. Indeed, the only "good" spiritual beings presented in the film are Cane's own deceased wife and child who appear right at the end of the film after Satan is vanquished and Cane lies dying. In this way, for all its supernatural elements, the film ultimately conforms to the standard narrative of the apocalypse film genre whereby human agency—albeit with spiritual strength—is able to triumph over the forces that seek to wreak destruction on humanity.

Linked with this privileging of human agency, apocalypse films also place a strong emphasis on science and technology as the means whereby their respective apocalyptic catastrophes can be averted or, at least, mitigated against. Both are, however, nevertheless typically presented in an ambivalent light, not least because they themselves are more often than not the cause of the catastrophe. In this way, apocalypse films may be seen on one level at least as one manifestation of contemporary cultural unease about science within the West (see, for example, The Wellcome Trust 2000;

National Science Board 2004). However, when examined more closely, the films do not appear to be critiquing science *per se*, but rather, as Susan Sontag (1967) noted four decades ago, the *misuse* of science or even the ways in which, in spite of their best intentions, the fruits of scientists' labour may backfire or bring with them unintended consequences.[3] So, for example, in *28 Days Later*, the virus that drives those infected with it to become filled with insane rage was, the film's opening scene reveals, initially created by scientists attempting to create a suppressant for rage and violence. Its release, we are shown, and the subsequent breakdown of civilization are the result, not so much of the direct actions of scientists themselves, but rather a group of animal rights protestors who unwittingly free the infected animals from an experimentation facility.

This trend is, however, best illustrated in *12 Monkeys*, where scientists are presented as both the heroes and villains of the film, with one set of scientists in the future sending a convict, James Cole, back in time to the present day in an attempt to stop a supervirus being unleashed by, it turns out, a "rogue" scientist. However, here again, the villain is not so much the scientists themselves who developed the virus, but rather the rogue scientist who seeks to use it. As with *28 Days Later*, the message of the film is thus that it is the misuse of science, and not science itself, that is potentially dangerous, if not cataclysmic. Indeed, it is noteworthy that although the central character in *12 Monkeys* is James Cole, the ultimate hero of the film is arguably the lead scientist from the future who, it would appear, (possibly) succeeds where Cole does not. Thus, in the film's penultimate scene, after Cole has been gunned down by security at the airport, the rogue scientist is shown taking his seat on the plane next to a female passenger; the lead scientist from 2035 who, possibly knowing that Cole would fail, has seemingly travelled back in time in order to thwart the release of the virus. The question of whether she is successful is not answered in the film and, indeed, the whole film offers itself for multiple interpretations, but the final lines of dialogue in the film, which are hers, would suggest that she is: "Jones is my name. I'm in insurance."

This ambivalence does not extend, however, to one particular manifestation of the (mis)use of science and technology: nuclear weapons. In contrast to innumerable films from the 1950s through to the late 1980s which presented nuclear weapons as a negative force (see Evans-Kasastamatis 1999; Winkler 1999; Shapiro 2002; McCrillis 2002), within many contemporary apocalypse films they are presented in a much more positive light. In particular, whereas in films ranging from *The Day the World Ended* (1956), *On the Beach* (1959), to *Threads* (1985) and *When the Wind Blows* (1987), nuclear weapons were presented as the actual cause of global apocalyptic destruction, the chief protagonists in films such as *Armageddon, Independence Day,*

The Core and *Deep Impact* utilize them in order to *avert* the destruction of the earth and/or humanity.[4] In *The Core*, for example, several nuclear warheads are detonated at the earth's core in order to restart the earth's rotation and thereby avert environmental disaster; at the climax of *Independence Day*, the hostile alien craft are destroyed by nuclear strikes; while in *Armageddon* and *Deep Impact* a meteor is defected from earth's path by detonating warheads beneath its surface. Indeed, in the latter film the warheads take on almost a semi-divine status when the mission to detonate them on the meteor is named the "Messiah Mission."

Again, as was the case with science and technology more broadly, this shift in the way in which nuclear weapons are presented may be linked with a distinction being drawn within the films' narrative between the technology itself and its (mis)use. Thus whereas earlier films presented nuclear weapons in negative terms by explicitly linking them with their military use (which was always framed as a misuse), within these latter films, a clear distinction is drawn between their use for positive ends (saving the world/humanity) and negative ones (destroying the world/humanity). So, for example, during the press conference accompanying the launch of the mission to destroy the meteor in *Armageddon*, the US President, after introducing himself "not as the President of the United States, not as the leader of a country, but as a citizen of humanity," waxes poignantly on how:

> for the first time in the history of the planet, a species has the technology to prevent its own extinction. All of your praying with us need to know that everything that can be done to prevent this disaster is being called into service. The human thirst for excellence and knowledge, every step up the ladder of science, every adventurous reach into space, all of our combined modern technologies and imaginations, *even the wars that we have fought have provided us the tools to wage this terrible battle.* (emphasis added)

This notion that nuclear weapons are simply "tools" that can be redeployed to more positive ends is also expressed in *Deep Impact* where a voiceover (provided by TV news coverage) accompanying the launch of the mission describes how "with the help of Russian engineers, a technology that was designed to propel weapons of mass destruction will power the ship that will intercept the greatest threat that our planet has ever faced." However, the film that arguably best exemplifies this distinction between positive/negative use is *The Core*, where it is revealed the earth's core has stopped revolving as a direct consequence of a clandestine military project for producing earthquakes known as Project DESTINI (Deep Earth Seismic Trigger INItiative). In this way the central theme of the film is the (positive) use of one form of destructive military technology to undo the (negative) actions of another.

As well as presenting nuclear weapons in a positive light (or at least a morally ambiguous one), contemporary apocalypse films are also characterized by extremely positive portrayals of religion. This is particularly the case in the Hollywood films where one finds a highly sentimentalized form of religion presented, typically at the moment of gravest crisis and then at the point where the disaster is averted. So, for example, in *Deep Impact* after announcing on a live television broadcast that the "Messiah Mission" has failed in its attempt to completely destroy the approaching meteor, the US President (accompanied by syrupy music) concludes by telling his viewers:

> I wish...no, wishing is wrong, it's the wrong word now. That's not what I mean. What I mean is; I believe in God, I know a lot of you don't, but I still want to offer a prayer for our survival, mine included, because I believe that God—whomever you hold that to be—hears all prayers, even if sometimes the answer is no. So may the Lord bless you, may the Lord keep you, may the Lord lift up His divine countenance upon you, and give you peace.

However, it is also found in the British film *28 Days Later*, albeit in a more subtle way. In the scene where the central character, Jim, returns home after discovering about the viral outbreak to find his parents dead after having taken their lives we hear a lone voice singing the hymn *Abide with Me* on the soundtrack. Later in the film in a similarly emotive scene *Ave Maria* is played. According to the film's director, Danny Boyle, the two pieces were used to signify to the audience "the history or the culture of the past in Britain that had gone."[5] In this way, religion becomes a signifier for a cultural memory of a happier and more secure (pre-apocalyptic) age.

In contrast, apocalyptic beliefs, where they are presented at all, are typically presented in a much less positive light and are invariably dismissed either implicitly or explicitly within the narrative of the film as outlandish or strange. In the director's cut of *Independence Day*, for example, after the alien spacecrafts have obliterated a number of world cities, an apocalyptic "end of the world" preacher (complete with a crucifix painted on his forehead) is shown amid the rubble and carnage, Bible and a "the time has come REPENT while you can" sign in hand declaring (in suitably King James Version-sounding English) to those trying to escape that "the end hath come! He's spoken his word and the end hath come!" Similarly, in *Armageddon*, when Bruce Willis's character asks a NASA employee why the public has not been informed of the approaching meteor, he is told that "If news of this got out there'd be an overnight breakdown of basic social services worldwide; rioting, mass religious hysteria, total chaos, you can imagine; basically the worst parts of the Bible." Finally, in *End of Days*—arguably, as I noted above, the most "religious" of the recent apocalypse films—cultural fears of what might take place on the transition to the new millennium (here defined as from 1999–2000) are similarly dismissed in a radio call-in:

Caller: I'm trying to figure out what everyone is predicting here. Is the world going to come to an end at exactly 12:01 on New Year's or...

Host: I tell you what, lady, I think you should play it safe: not quit your job yet. I'll tell you something else, in two days this place is going to see the wildest party ever. We're gonna be there with the first 100 callers, we're gonna make the most noise, and we're gonna be the craziest, and if the world comes to an end what the hell? We're all gonna be together, and if it doesn't, then we'll all have the best night...

The one film that breaks from this view, however, is *12 Monkeys*, which presents a more nuanced image of apocalyptic prophecy by raising the question of whether such prophecies may be inspired by (fore)knowledge of events. This theme runs throughout the film through its treatment of time travel and madness, but is expressed most explicitly in a scene in which the heroine, the psychiatrist Dr Kathryn Railly (played by Madeleine Stowe), is shown giving a public lecture in 1996 entitled "Madness and Apocalyptic Visions." During the course of the lecture she quotes Revelation 15:7 ("One of the four beasts gave unto the seven angels seven golden vials, full of the wrath of God, who liveth forever and ever"), which she then links to several historical visionaries who predicted that humanity would be wiped out by a plague of some sort. One of these is a World War One soldier who, after being hospitalized with a shrapnel injury, claimed to have come from the future "looking for a pure germ that would ultimately wipe mankind off the face of the earth, starting in the year 1996." This is greeted with chuckles from the audience, who clearly believe such prophecies to be symptoms of madness. However, shortly before this, the audience (who of course are already aware of the aftermath of the virus's release) had seen James Cole transported back in time to the trenches where he had met the soldier shown in Railly's slide presentation. Indeed, the soldier, it is revealed, is one of Cole's accomplices, José. Later, after discovering from the police that Cole has a World War One bullet lodged in his leg, Railly realizes that the larger photograph from which her slide is cropped shows Cole reaching towards José; an image that the viewer would also recognize from the previous scene. Later in the film, after Railly has come to accept Cole's claims, they are shown walking past an "end of the world" street-preacher who is quoting Revelation 16:17 to his listeners ("Then the seventh angel poured out his vial into the air"). As Cole walks past him, the preacher stops and shouts at him, "You! You! You're one of us!"; the implication being that he, like Cole and José, has also been sent from the future to warn humanity of the virus. Finally, the viewer is able to link this passage and Revelation 15:7 with the vials containing the virus which are shown being released in the airport at the end of the film. In this way, as Flannery Dailey (2000, 20) notes, the view that apocalyptic prophecies are strange or outlandish, if not manifestations of insanity, is reversed within the film narrative and "true sanity is equivalent to knowing the apocalyptic future." Indeed, going further, prophecy becomes not so much a revelation of the future, but rather a statement of what, from the perspective of one from the future who has travelled back in time, has already occurred (what Railly refers to in her lecture as "The Cassandra Complex"—"in which a person is condemned to know the future but to be disbelieved, hence, the agony of foreknowledge combined with the impotence to do anything about it.").[6]

Contemporary "Apocalypse Films" and the Inversion of the Apocalypse

Contemporary apocalypse films, then, are characterized by a fundamental desacralization—if not inversion—of the apocalypse. In contrast to texts such as the Book of Revelation, which present apocalyptic scenarios as supernatural events, outside the scope of human agency, and, indeed, as necessary events within sacred/human history, the films I have described both secularize and invert it in their narratives so that the apocalyptic event becomes both natural or human-made in nature and avoidable through human agency. Indeed, as I noted above, in general these films are dismissive of apocalyptic beliefs, painting them as weird or outlandish; the province of "the end is nigh" preachers and other social misfits.

However, perhaps the most fundamental inversion of the apocalypse within these films concerns the latter's posture vis-à-vis the current social order. Whereas apocalyptic texts are inherently critical of the contemporary social order and look toward a time in the not-too-distant future where it will be replaced with a divine order ("a new heaven and a new earth" to quote Rev. 21:1), these films are in contrast characterized by an explicit valorization of the contemporary social order. As Walsh (2002, 13) notes in his discussion of *End of Days*:

> Revelation envisions the present evil age divinely interrupted and replaced by a new divine age and kingdom. By contrast, *End of Days* envisions a demonic interruption, ruining an American present and ushering in a kingdom of evil. *End of Days* is comfortable with the American present and wishes to preserve it against a monstrous foe (a pattern reminiscent of Cold War horror and science-fiction movies). Jericho's death is not the apocalyptic-engendering death of the hero of Mark or of the martyr heroes (including the lamb) of Revelation. Jericho's death restores normal life.[7]

This theme of preserving the existing social order against apocalyptic threats—whether they be meteors, aliens or superviruses—is, as we have seen, the central plot within the majority of the films that I have discussed above (indeed, according to Sontag, it is one of the central features of the science-fiction genre). This is seen perhaps most clearly in *Deep Impact* where, in addition to the plan to destroy the approaching meteor, the US Government also initiate a plan, in the words of the President, "to ensure the continuation of our way of life." This is a network of caves underground in Missouri designed to hold a million people (including "200,000 scientists, doctors, engineers, teachers, soldiers and artists" as well as randomly selected individuals) "for two years until the air clears and the dust settles." These caves, he goes on, again drawing on biblical imagery, are "more than a dormitory. It's our new Noah's Ark," and will also contain seeds, seedlings, plants and animals so that the survivors can start over again in the post-apocalyptic world.[8]

However, we also find this valorization even, if not more so, in films which are set after the cataclysmic destruction of the current social order. Here, though, in contrast to the heroes and heroines seeking to defend it, we find it valorized instead through its absence vis-à-vis the chaos of the post-apocalyptic present. This is particularly the case in films such as *Waterworld* and to some extent *28 Days Later* where the central plot of the film is the quest by the chief protagonists for something approximating the old order (understood as "the answer to infection" and the mythical "Dryland" respectively). However, the film that I would argue exemplifies this trend is *The Postman*. Based on the novel by David Brin, and set in a post-apocalyptic USA of 2013, *The Postman* stars Kevin Costner as a drifter who finds a United States Postal Service uniform and a sack of old letters while looking for shelter from a storm in an abandoned jeep. Initially using the uniform as a way to bluff his way into an armed township, the drifter/Postman tells those inside that he is a representative of the "Restored United States of America" (the motto of which is "stuff is getting better every day") and is greeted as an almost messianic figure. Realizing the hope that he brings, the Postman sets about recreating a makeshift postal service and, in doing so, battles and ultimately triumphs over a local warlord, General Bethlehem (who is painted as an anti-American, far-right, Feudal lord). The central narrative of the film is thus an explicit paean to American idealism and a sense of shared norms and values—or what Brin (1998, n.p.) refers to as "the gracious little things that connect us today." According to Brin (1998, n.p.),

> *The Postman* was written as an answer to all those post-apocalyptic books and films that seem to *revel* in the idea of civilization's fall. It's a story about how much we take for granted—and how desperately we would miss the little, gracious things that connect us today. It is a story about the last idealist in a fallen America. A man who cannot let go of a dream we all once shared. Who

sparks restored faith that we can recover, and perhaps even become better than we were...watching Kevin Costner's three hour epic is a bit like having a great big Golden Retriever jump on your lap and lick your face, while waving a flag tied to its tail. It's big, floppy, uncoordinated, overeager, sometimes gorgeous—occasionally a bit goofy—and so big-hearted that something inside of you has to *give*... that is, if you like that sort of thing.

For these reasons, I would disagree with Bendle's (2005, 30, 31) claim that in contrast to earlier Cold War films where "everyday life was represented as invaluable in its innocence and simplicity, something whose loss in a nuclear war would be irrevocably tragic...[within more recent films] everyday life is scorned and even vilified." In particular, I find particularly questionable his claim that:

> contemporary cinema offers extremely misanthropic representations of the apocalyptic near future and communicates a fear and hatred of everyday people. The masses are depicted as mindless, barely functional vermin, ready to tear each other apart in a desperate rage for survival. Accompanying this is a depiction of the heroes and survivors being readily transformed into effective killers, capable of butchering large numbers of people who, perhaps only hours before, may have been their friends, allies, or even family members (Bendle 2005, 41).

Rather, I would argue that through its defence against catastrophe or through characters seeking out its approximation in the post-apocalyptic world, contemporary apocalypse films not only valorize everyday life but also, in an almost Durkheimian way, reaffirm it (Durkheim 1961). While all of the films focus, as would be expected, on the broad impact (potential or actual) of the apocalyptic disaster, through, for example, the destruction of cities, they also draw viewers' attention to how these disasters are played out and experienced on an everyday level, through personal losses and triumphs, the difficult choices made and so on. These films are, in other words, as much about the tragic breakdown of the repetition and taken-for-grantedness of the everyday ("normal life") as they are about the actual or potential destruction of whole societies (see Lefebvre 1971; Felski 1999–2000). This, again, in many ways is to be expected—viewers after all will find it easier to identify and have an emotional connection with "everyday" characters like them making difficult decisions or responding to huge turmoil than they would with, say, the decisions made by a President. So, on one level at least, the focus on the everyday is one technique whereby film-makers may pull their audiences emotionally into the narrative of the film.[9] However, on another level, I would argue that the films may also be seen as a symbolic reaffirmation of the everyday; an everyday which is presented as being under threat from catastrophic events, but which ultimately survives in one form or another.

This valorization of the existing social order/everyday links with the final way in which contemporary apocalypse films invert the message of apocalyptic texts, such as the Book of Revelation. Although some commentators have pointed to the heroes of apocalypse films as examples of "Christ figures" or "Messiahs" (in the sense that they are saviours or ones who sacrifice themselves for others; see Flannery-Dailey 2000),[10] if they are Messiahs or Christ figures then they are fundamentally different to those found within apocalyptic literature in several crucial ways. Primarily, whereas the Lamb/Messiah of Revelation is a violent, countercultural character (one who actually destroys the existing social order), the hero of apocalypse films is, as we have seen, one who defends or seeks for an approximation of the existing order. Moreover, whereas the Christ figure might traditionally be understood within both apocalyptic literature and more widely as a perfect individual (or even superhuman—*Superman* or otherworldly—*The Day the Earth Stood Still*—Koslovic 2002, Etherden 2005), the hero within apocalypse films is typically presented as human, all too human or, indeed, flawed in some way.[11] So, for example, in *Waterworld*, the Mariner is a mutant with webbed feet and functional gills who is almost killed at the first Atoll he visits because of this. James Cole in *12 Monkeys* is a criminal who is introduced to the scientists as having "a history…violence, anti-social, six repeated violations of the Permanent Emergency Code, insolence, defiance, disregard of authority—doing 25 to life." Similarly, although *Independence Day* is bristling with several leading males, arguably the real hero of the film is Russell Casse, a single-parent, Vietnam veteran who lives in a trailer, works as a crop duster and who believes, much to the bemusement of everyone else, that he has been abducted by aliens, and who ultimately sacrifices himself to destroy an alien spacecraft at the climax of the film. Finally, as noted above, the character played by Arnold Schwarzenegger in *End of Days* is presented at the beginning of the film as a down-on-his-luck ex-police officer whose life has fallen apart and who is contemplating suicide. Hardly the stuff that Hollywood heroes—or, for that matter, messiahs—are typically made of![12]

Conclusions

Films, as a form of cultural expression, have always mirrored the times and the cultures in which they were produced. From the Cold War paranoia of films such as *The Invasion of the Body Snatchers* and *The War of the Worlds*, through to the nuclear Mutually Assured Destruction of *Dr Strangelove*, *WarGames*, and *When the Wind Blows*, film makers have both reflected and given voice to the cultural issues, events and neuroses of their day (O'Leary

2000). Indeed, in many ways films such as these *cannot* be understood without reference to the context in which they were produced.

The films that I have discussed in this chapter were all released in a period of approximately nine years (1995–2004); a period of time spanning both the build-up and transition to the new calendrical millennium as well as the attacks of 9/11 and the subsequent "war on terror." They cover a period of time characterized by heightened anxiety and tensions concerning global warming and other natural disasters, "super bugs" and pandemics, as well as fears of terrorist actions, possibly involving Weapons of Mass Destruction. More broadly, from a geopolitical point of view, they cover a period of time following the fall of the Berlin Wall and the apparent victory of liberal Western democracy and a shift from a focus on a distinct, bounded enemy (the "Red Communism" of earlier films) to a series of diffuse military/political threats (such as the infamous "axis of evil" or "Islamic Radicalism"). It has also witnessed—whether as a manifestation of a Lyotardian "postmodern condition" or not—a growing cultural ambivalence about the benefits of science and technology and of experts and expertise.

These themes were all played out in various ways in the films that I have examined in this chapter. Each of them revolves either around some form of threat to the existing social order which is countered or at least mitigated against through the use of science or technology (often the technology of nuclear weapons decried in earlier films) or around attempts to restore some (often idealized) portion of that order. These threats are on the whole either natural disasters or human-made in form, rather than the outcome of, for example, nuclear hostilities between nations. Each of them valorizes human agency and self-sufficiency, showing how everyday—even apparently flawed—human beings (albeit typically North Americans) may rise to challenges and overcome great adversity. In sum, each of them is permeated with both a highly sentimentalized attitude towards the status quo and a sense of optimism towards the future and human powers. Threats may come and go, they tell us, but humans will rise to them and the everyday world will continue as normal; the apocalypse is neither now nor nigh, nor is it preordained. It is, instead, just another series of problems for human ingenuity coupled with science and technology to address.

Part Three

A Case Study: The Violence of
The Passion of the Christ

6 Counterfictional Suffering: Authenticity and Artistry in *The Passion of the Christ*

*Steven Allen**

Before beginning my analysis of Mel Gibson's *The Passion of the Christ* (2004), I wish to reassure the reader that the inclusion of the notion of fiction in my title is not a provocative attempt to question the historical existence of Jesus or the Christian record. I have no wish to enter into the populist debate engaged in by Lee Strobel in *The Case for Christ* (1998) and by his opponent Earl Doherty in *Challenging the Verdict: A Cross-examination of Lee Strobel's 'The Case for Christ'* (2001). Nor for that matter am I engaging (directly) with the academic study of the historical Jesus (see Crossan 1991; Dunn 2003; Meier 1991; Sanders 1985, 1993). I am not a biblical scholar.

The *raison d'être* for the chapter is to explore the frame of reference we use to understand the depictions in the film. Historical knowledge remains vital therefore, because it is through examining its intersection with cultural imagery that I seek to map out how an audience makes sense of the film. Inevitably, my study makes some generalizations regarding the audience. The homogenization has the drawback of denying individual experiences; personal interpretations are vital to a full understanding of the reception of the film, not least because these views gained wide currency through the numerous website forums that flourished after (as well as before) the film's release.[1] Reactions and comments embodied variations heavily dependent upon different devotional practices as well as beliefs (or lack of). However,

---

* Dr Steven Allen is a Senior Lecturer in Film Studies at the University of Winchester. His research into Australian and British cinema, as well as animation, focuses on the representations of landscapes, memory/history, and the body. His publications include articles on Will Hay, the seaside in British cinema, sound in Tex Avery's cartoons and animating the horrific. He is currently working on a book exploring the depictions of pain as pleasure in mainstream cinema and is co-editor (with Dr Laura Hubner) of a forthcoming collection of essays examining the relationships between cinema and the visual arts.

there is a productive (and positive) rationale in my approach, in that it sets out a theoretical framework for the epistemological engagement with a media product that was seen to offer a radically different and yet simultaneously familiar representation of the Passion. I seek to theorize the process, and understand the cinematic representational strategies in terms of their convergence with and divergence from the pictorial depictions Gibson (2004) and his cinematographer Caleb Deschanel (in Bailey and Pizzello 2004) have claimed influenced them.

To understand fully the shifts in representational strategies, I will focus on how the film was seen to offer a more authentic representation of Jesus' suffering than traditional visual representations, such as paintings, frescoes and devotional images. From a film studies perspective, I aim to show how the cinematic text establishes an exchange with our collective reservoir of imagery of the Passion: a strategy that promotes a respectful borrowing from the paintings of grand masters to aggrandise the movie, but which relies on cinematic sleight of hand to juxtapose a different set of representational strategies. In summation, it depends on comparative artifice to convey a sense of authenticity.

Much debate surrounding the film has centred on how "real" the film is, with the notion of realism including historical accuracy, fidelity to the Bible, and graphic bodily destruction. What appears to be at stake is legitimacy via authenticity. Mel Gibson evidently believes *The Passion of the Christ* to be authentic. In an interview with *Christianity Today* he stated "the Scriptures are the Scriptures—I mean they're unchangeable… And I think that my first duty is to be as faithful as possible in telling the story so that it doesn't contradict the Scriptures" (Neff and Struck 2004). Stephen Prince (2006), by contrast, has questioned the realism of the violence in the film by critiquing the historical accuracy of the torture scenes, and pinpointing how the promotional strategy was unusual in that it did not highlight the 135 digital effects within the film (a familiar marketing point), and so instead encouraged a conception of authenticity rather than manipulation. He consequently sees the realism as illusory, stating, "I am assuming that fidelity to the historical record constitutes one basis for realism in a historical drama like *The Passion of the Christ*. Deliberately diverging from this record takes us toward the stylistic domain, toward the artifice of cinematic fiction, and away from realism, at least in terms of its historical constituent" (2006, 14–15).

In the foreword to an accompanying photographic account of the production, Gibson distances his work from such criticism by stating the film "is not meant as a historical documentary nor does it claim to have assembled all the facts. But it does enumerate those described in relevant Holy Scripture. It is not merely representative or merely expressive" (Gibson 2004). In effect, he maintains that a correlation to the Scriptures is sufficient, whilst

simultaneously allowing leeway for deviation. Such a stance only partly ne-
gates Nicholas P. L. Allen's (2005) criticism, which charges Gibson's amal-
gamated vision with ignoring the contradictions across the Gospels, and with
moving away from realism towards stylization, both in respect of individual
elements, such as the use of Church Latin and the avoidance of Greek, and
with regard to what he sees as excessive, indulgent cinematic violence.[2]
Reviewers also frequently focused on realism, but much more positively. To
give just one example, Brett Willis (2004) states, "Gibson is giving us a look
at what that blood sacrifice actually was."

How one judges authenticity is evidently multifaceted, but a unifying factor is the comparative process: a strategy of counterpointing the film with
what is already known or believed. The historical record for Jesus is one that
has been subjected to much greater influence than most histories, thus prompting James D. G. Dunn to argue: "The only realistic objective for any 'quest of
the historical Jesus' is the Jesus remembered" (2003, 335). The historical
Jesus is therefore only accessible as the Jesus of collective memory. Although
Dunn is making the link between the historical man and the subsequent faith
(as he surveys trends in historical narratives as indicators of a collective memory
of Jesus), I wish to extend that arrangement to see how the representations
in *The Passion* are authenticated by the spectator via a wider interplay of
shared remembrances.

The historically legitimate Jesus that Gibson seeks to portray is not only
moulded via Gospel accounts, non-biblical sources, classical paintings, previous films and so forth, but is understood through them. In particular, the
imagery is judged against the story of Jesus, and I do mean story, although it
can never be totally divorced from an ingrained sense of historical fact, as the
story, complete with images, is part of the prevailing culture in the West. We
come to the movie with pre-formed visions of the last days of Jesus' life. Our
images are taken from previous films such as *King of Kings* (Nicholas Ray
1961) and *The Last Temptation of Christ* (Martin Scorsese 1988), with much
of the critical commentary on *The Passion* drawing attention to this (see
Chattaway 2004; Grist 2010; Prince 2006). It is noteworthy that Prince suggests "[t]he film's graphic violence was judged to be 'realistic' in comparison
with the pre-existing cinematic tradition of sanitized and oblique depictions
of crucifixion" (2006, 14). Furthermore, Prince sees such a strategy for reading the film as masking the heavily stylized violence and its visual effects. In
many respects, I align myself with his argument. However, Prince is primarily
concerned with the technical process, so whilst noting the compositional
and editing strategies, he discusses these in terms of setting up effects, and
disguising their artifice. The "realism," he therefore argues, results from the
adoption of current cinematic techniques, which, because of their contem-
poraneousness, appear more real: "the viewers' mental frameworks

themselves derive from cinema" (2006, 22). My problem with this being a sufficient explanation is that we mostly experience the depiction of Jesus not through cinema, but via art (whether this is religious icons or greetings cards). For this reason, I contend we must pay greater attention to another regularly referred to counterpoint, the old master, notably those by Caravaggio, Grünewald, Mantegna and Pacher, with almost all studies of the film pinpointing the relationship.[3] The frequency of the comparison is unsurprising, with the publicity for the film highlighting the intertextuality, including Gibson stating, "I began to look at the work of some of the great artists who had drawn inspiration from the same story" (Gibson 2004) and the "Background Info" on the US version of the Official Movie Website proclaiming "Gibson asked cinematographer Caleb Deschanel ... to make the movie look like the paintings of Italian Baroque artist Caravaggio" (Icon Productions 2004). Inevitably, the parallels with iconic images of Jesus not only suggest pictorial pleasures, but also work functionally, as the reference to art legitimates the re-presentation of the story. However, I wish to suggest a more integral relationship, whereby the spectator is positioned to make sense of *The Passion of the Christ* through an overarching dialogue between the film and art.

In an interview for *American Cinematographer*, Deschanel states that "I felt like I was seeing the iconography of my childhood—all of the representations that I eventually came to know as art—unfold onscreen in an excoriating way" (Bailey and Pizzello 2004). Comments such as this, as well as the promotional strategy mentioned earlier, helped foreground a relationship with paintings. Undoubtedly, there are aesthetic links, not least the film's look, with its sharp contrast of light resembling the painterly qualities of Caravaggio. In addition, individual shots reference the classical works, for example Diane Apostolos-Cappadona pinpoints Michelangelo's Vatican *Pietà* being reworked in the film with Mary on the ground (2004, 106). The application of the iconography of Catholic art prompts David Morgan to state, "[r]ather than invent new visual forms for conveying the intensity of Jesus' suffering, Gibson relies on pictorial motifs from the fourteenth to the seventeenth centuries" (2004, 85). The comment is slightly misleading though, as Morgan continues by seeing the iconography providing "coherence and recognizability" to "allow Gibson interpretative room to vary, invert, or accent the representation" (86). The reinterpretation begins to become apparent when one recognizes the lack of correspondence between the mediums of painting and cinema.

By centring on the look of the film being similar to paintings (mostly through lighting, facial features, and isolated compositions [see Bailey and Pizzello 2004]) we ignore how we look at, or view, a film, with it being orchestrated very differently to how we view a painting. Two crucial distinctions are, of course, stasis/movement and single/multiple images. The commonalities between the two depictions are therefore conjured up both textually and inter-textually, but are emphatically denied by other dominant features of the film. However, it is not that one aspect of representation is privileged over the other; rather it is the activation of the contrast that is of note. In essence, it is not that we are seeing moving paintings, nor that we are seeing something distinct, but that we are watching a constantly comparative process, which challenges our accepted notions of the events. Through oscillating between similarity and difference, I believe we should not be in search of realism but the suppositional: it could be like this, but it could also be like that. *The Passion of the Christ* offers the viewer a reformulation of what might have happened to provoke an engagement with the depicted suffering. Before expanding on this, it is important to situate the methodology I am employing.

My argument is modelled on the line of reasoning called "counterfactual history." This is a methodology that sets out to understand the past by deliberately falsifying it, and so prompting debate. It is a *"what if"* type of history, for example "What if there had been no American Revolution?" (Clark 1997) and "What if Germany had invaded Britain in May 1940?" (Roberts 1997). Formerly regarded as unacademic, or as E. H. Carr once called it, "a parlour game" (1964, 97), counterfactual history has recently become more prominent (see Cowley 1998; Ferguson 1997a; and Sobel 1997), whilst broader discussions of counterfactuals, causation and the possible have prospered in metaphysics and, in particular, modal logic studies. In respect of history, Niall Ferguson (1997b, 83) has argued that rather than dismissing counterfactuals as speculation without validity, we should see the hypotheses in terms of plausibility. Infinite possibilities are reduced to the plausible to facilitate an exploration of a possible course of events. Furthermore, Martin Bunzl (2004) argues that the causal claims of the historian implicitly involve the counterfactual; in effect, the defining of a cause involves an assessment of what might have happened under a different course of events. That the world could have been different leads to a basic configuration of a "possible world." David Lewis contends that:

> It is uncontroversially true that things might be otherwise than they are. I believe, and so do you, that things could have been different in countless ways… I therefore believe in the existence of entities that might be called "ways things could have been." I prefer to call them "possible worlds" (1979, 182).

Although having a different ontological status to the actual world, the possible world is grounded in the actual world, retaining historical figures, physical laws etc., thus enabling it to facilitate an exploration of the contingency of historical events.

Such theoretical grounding has enabled alternate histories to be applied, even if not fully accepted, and these histories say much about how we remember the past, but also about contemporary changes such as the breakdown in determinist thinking, and the recognition of alternative voices. However, the central aim of counterfactual history is to provoke debate: if "X" had happened instead of "Y," might "Z" not have happened. It relies on inserting a false historical element, but equally, depends on our knowledge of what did happen in the actual world to give the divergence meaning.

Gibson's film works not by falsifying the past by, for example, Jesus surviving the crucifixion and reaping vengeance on his tormenters. Nor can it categorically contradict the punishment someone like Jesus would have received for his "crimes"; there are, after all, few spectators who have any frame of reference from the actual world to judge how accurate the violence inflicted upon him is, nor can assess the validity of Jim Caviezel's reactions to his supposed wounds. But the film still relies on a counterfactual quality for its evocation of suffering. And here I am using factual not in a sense of accuracy or realism in the abstract sense, but as a comparative term: the counterfactual arises from the divergence from our collective reservoir of imagery of the last days of Jesus' life.

The almost relentless assault that forms the basis of the film contradicts our previous experiences of its representation. Realism debates would suggest that the graphic violence sets out to reveal the falsity of past depictions, but I would contend that the cultural weight and pervasiveness of the previous imagery makes Gibson's film function as a *"what if"*: what if Jesus was beaten like this? And ultimately, what if he suffered such torment, doesn't his pain mean more? The point is not to say this is how it was, but to say this is how it might have been. The film stimulated discussions because of the representation of pain and its difference to previous depictions. We have got to where we are today by assuming it was like "A" (where "A" is the accustomed pictorial version) but if it were like "B" (vicious assault) then perhaps we should not be at point "C" (the present), but at point "D" (what exactly point "D" is will depend upon personal ideology and interpretation of the film, but evidently a familiar response is a greater sense of religious devotion). *The Passion* therefore invites the audience to change that future, a future that in fact is the present, and stretches onwards after the film has ended.

As we have seen, counterfactual history has to be plausible but different. In the film, plausibility, in part, is derived from the historical figures and cultural contexts, but also, somewhat bizarrely, comes from application of factually inaccurate detail. The Latin cross (instead of the Tau cross), a loinclothed Jesus and other accepted iconography function as sites of the familiar. The counterfactual, or more accurately, the counterfictional, comes from obliging us to contrast the images with the works of Caravaggio, Mantegna, Masaccio and other artists. It is noticeable that several reviewers make links to Matthias Grünewald's Isenheim Altarpiece (c.1512–16), but although one of the most vividly disfigured and tormented depictions of Jesus, Gibson appears to make no reference to it. Apostolos-Cappadona sees this as possibly ironic (2004, 103), but a more productive answer might point to Gibson's need to oppose *The Passion* with previous depictions and so assert the film's counterfictional status. To acknowledge a previous representation of intense suffering would undermine the film's counterfictional status.

The function of the counterfictional strategy becomes clear when we consider the representation of pain. Current cultural practices place much emphasis on the authenticity of pain. We can think of body modification, dangerous sports and the resistance to cyberspace as a legitimate field of human experience. Pain, an intense sensorial response, is regarded as more authentic than thought. The film's opening quotation from Isaiah points towards the importance of conveying pain: "He was wounded for our transgressions, crushed for our iniquities; by His wounds we are healed"; the more wounded Caviezel appears, the greater the sense of healing. The graphic contrast of the wounds in the film to those in traditional iconography equates to Gibson's expression of our sins. Representational conventions, such as the bearded Jesus, which only emerged from the late fourth century onwards, act as touchstones, anchoring the film's representations to established iconography, thus enabling it to generate its meaning, couched in an authenticity of pain, through counterfictional history. Let me further demonstrate this by way of an example: the scourging sequence.

In *Iconography of Christian Art*, Gertrud Schiller states that "[t]he image of the Flagellation of Christ is common in the west" with "about 1000 among monumental paintings in Italy," and that the imagery "probably stemmed from psalter illustrations" (1972, 66). Its status of being predominantly a devotional image, in particular in relation to Catholicism, means that such images are less well circulated than the crucifixion, especially in respect of wider culture. The lack of comparative imagery means that for many spectators the whole sequence runs as counterfactual history.[4] Even knowledge of the Bible prevents an expectation of the prominence the scourging has in the film, not least because it receives scant mention, but also because only John states it is the sole original punishment (John 19:1).[5] The sequence therefore has a limited prior basis in the collective memory. It is as if the film is showing you what previous depictions had dared not show, and so the scene is pervaded with pseudo-honesty.

Not only does the scourging connote authenticity, but it is additionally a principal event, lasting for nine minutes and twenty seconds from first lash to the last, including a 50-second flashback.[6] The importance of depicting the suffering is confirmed by the duration of the assault being extended via the inclusion of slow-motion shots. Gibson attempts to induce the notion of pain through three counterfictional features that distinguish it from traditional imagery. Firstly, somewhat counterintuitively, we are not allowed to linger on the suffering. Instead, Gibson utilizes 179 shots, with an average duration of just over 3.1 seconds each. The latter figure tells only part of the story, as there are only six shots in the flashback sequence, and numerous reaction shots of the crowd, in particular of Mary, are held for longer. Of the beating, many shots are only a fraction of a second in duration. Allied to this, several shots, somewhat appropriately, are whip pans (rapid turns of the camera), often matching the whipping movement, but which blur the action and create a visceral response for the spectator. The brisk edits and camera movements deny us the contemplation we normally experience when viewing a painting. Instead we are subjected to a visual and visceral assault. Apostolos-Cappadona notes that because cinema is based on movement, "the participative encounter available through a Byzantine icon is inconceivable with Gibson's movie. The lines between art and film do not blur" (2004, 108). However, although I have argued for the clash of modes of representation facilitated by the disparities between the two mediums, I believe Apostolos-Cappadona overstates the necessity of the division, as film is not just about movement, it is also about stasis, and more especially the combination of the two. Pacing is a fundamental part of editing, and even subtle shifts to longer shot durations can provide a significant impression of the pictorial, whilst director Peter Greenaway has shown the possibility of coalescing cinema and painting via the tableau. Gibson therefore chooses not to pause for contemplation.

Secondly, the shots in the scourging sequence are mostly close-ups and medium shots, denying us a full view of Jesus' body. Such images contradict our experiences of Jesus in art. Concentrated on the fragmented body, the brutalized features connote flesh rather divine or even human presence. And thirdly, shots cut away to the guards and people watching, but the sound of the whipping continues, sometimes featuring visually as a blurred element in the background. These shots link to us bearing witness to the beating, drawing attention to our passive spectatorship. Furthermore, as much as we may wish for the visual respite, the sound draws us back, emphasizing the continuing assault, and I would argue, encouraging us to want to see it, if only because we know we will have to return to it before it may end. In an art gallery housing paintings depicting the torture of Jesus, we are empowered to look away, and our senses will be secure, but here there is no such respite (film being both an aural and visual medium), and instead we are obliged to confront our complicity. The sequence, via its unflinching graphicness, is centred on connoting pain.

When watching the film, most evangelical Christians and non-believers will draw upon a limited visual repertoire of the Passion. Comparisons made with high art and popular culture's reproductions will have a greater counterfictional status than those made with devotional and meditative texts and images, which Amy Hollywood notes "are often excruciating, elaborating in seeming endless detail on the cruelties Christ sustained" (2004). The more widely circulated and recognizable paintings have a different emphasis to that of the film, as pain is not pivotal. The figure of Jesus is more removed and less corporeally human, a treatment related to there being less focus placed on a physical assault. For example, in a painting such as Caravaggio's *The Flagellation of Christ* (1607), in contrast to the physical destruction of the body there is stoicism, a passive resistance. Moreover, the perspective of the painting is different, being from a distance equivalent to a medium long or long shot, giving a full view of the body, and highlighting the presence of Jesus rather than the cuts and scars. Indeed, there is little sign of wounds, and when they are shown, as in Michael Pacher's *The Flagellation of Christ* (c.1498), they are not destructive but indicative of suffering. Gibson's version blatantly heightens the display of bodily annihilation, but our appreciation of the extent of the damage comes from the film's foregrounding of a comparative framework to comprehend the imagery. I am certainly unconvinced we can interpret Jesus raising himself from his knees to take an additional beating as a realistic portrayal; it is, after all, an act of bravado familiar from countless Hollywood action films. Instead, it functions as a *"what if,"* designed to contrast with previous interpretations that form the historical Jesus of our collective memory.

Gibson's willingness to construct a whole scene centred on the flagellation aligns him with the late Middle Ages Christian meditative strategies. Amy Hollywood argues that the violence of the Passion "plays a crucial role in eliciting memory and emotion" (2004), and Gibson regards the whole film as "contemplative in the sense that one is compelled to remember (unforget) in a spiritual way which cannot be articulated, only experienced" (Gibson 2004). That the relationship to memory works in a counterfactual/counterfictional manner becomes clear when we note the justification for the "creative licence" employed by the medieval author of *Meditations on the Life of Christ*:[7]

> Thus when you find it said here, "This was said and done by the Lord Jesus," and by others of whom we read, if it cannot be demonstrated by the Scriptures, you must consider it only as a requirement of devout contemplation. *Take it as if I had said, "Suppose that this is what the Lord Jesus said and did"* (Bonaventure 1961, 5 [emphasis added]).

Just as the writer in the Middle Ages has asked, Gibson requires the spectator to imagine this is how Jesus was beaten. And to be able to enter into this "possible world," he makes reference to what has already been experienced (classical and cinematic representations), and so anchors our understanding in the pseudo-actual world.

A similar analysis can be applied to the crucifixion sequence, which, although much more familiar and so not such a radical departure from our cultural memory, still works counterfictionally. Amy Hollywood argues that in the "final moments of the film, the images become more and more static, increasingly resembling medieval and early modern religious paintings, sculptures, wood cuts, and manuscript illuminations derived from and often used as pictorial aides to the meditation on Christ's Passion" (2004). The comment is juxtaposed with a previous observation that the "crucifixion occurs in a flurry of jump cuts" (2004). Let me tease out the full implications of the change at the film's closure. What Gibson does for the majority of the movie is deny the spectator the reflective contemplation that he shows the diegetic onlookers experiencing. Again it utilizes conventional (although historically inaccurate) imagery such as nails in the palms, and spurting blood from the side wound. However, the meditative contemplation and beauty embodied in pictures such as Velázquez's *Christ Crucified* (1632) and El Greco's *Christ on the Cross with Landscapes* (1605–10) is destroyed. Gibson instead attempts to impart pain via cinematic stylization such as slow motion and close-ups. In addition, a striking difference between paintings and the film relates to stasis, both within the frame and across shots. Firstly, Caviezel's body is constantly being jarred as he is nailed to the cross, and this accentuates his body, his corporealness, not his pictorial divinity. Secondly, the rapid edits, especially those including close-ups, prevent us from fixing the suffering with our gaze. We get the impression that Jesus is suffering, but never dwell long on individual actions. The visual jolts involve us in the physical jolts portrayed by Caviezel, and so we are engaged in a visceral and emotional response. The consequence is a supplementary layer of authentication. Citing Jody Enders (2006, 189), Alison Griffiths states, "[w]hen a viewer's 'authentically powerful emotions feel like historical fact,' … we will most likely get sucked into mistaking representation for reality" (2007, 26).[8] Our visceral engagement, I contend, is made to feel like historical fact because of the counterfictional relationship foregrounded by the film.

That Gibson is able to frame the debate in terms of pain, whilst disguising its lack of authenticity, is largely due to its counterfictional structure. In accordance with counterfactual history, Gibson constructs a *"what if"* scenario. But the falsification is not in terms of its historical accuracy. Rather it breaks with familiar iconography to fraudulently claim it is authentically representing pain. It is not just that it is a different representation to those we are familiar with, but that the film prevents our contemplation. The film does not allow us to meditate on the image as we would with a painting, but instead we are obliged to reflect on how the film is different from what we have seen before: how it contradicts our cultural memory. The difference is read as authenticity. The tableau of stasis becomes frenetic fragmentation, devotional distance becomes brutalized minutiae, and contemplative reflection becomes synaesthetic convulsion/revulsion. Individually, and possibly even collectively, such techniques have a validity of use, but to aggrandise the techniques in respect of authenticity is spurious. Rather they remain a *"what if."* Gibson's challenge is he believes that past images have caused complacency, yet he needs to retain their cultural gravitas (as they are central markers of the historical Jesus) to give his film status and meaning. Rather than admit to the counterfictional structure, he attempts to situate the film alongside the images he simultaneously denounces. The bind is that for counterfactual history to work, it requires anchoring elements for plausibility. And this is where we return to the problem of a historical Jesus—there is no such thing, only the Jesus that is mediated through cultural images, stories, theology and so forth. Gibson poses a *"what if"* indebted to these remembrances, but simultaneously wants his film to operate outside this framework so that it "is not merely representative or merely expressive" (Gibson 2004). That Gibson attempts to construct *The Passion* as both actual world and "possible world" points to why so many critics have focused on its misleading claim to realism. In his search for authentic pain, Gibson finds the suffering to be relative.

7 Controlling Passions: The Regulation, Censorship and Classification of the Violence in *The Passion of the Christ* within Britain

*Shaun Kimber**

This chapter explores the British regulation, censorship and classification of the violence in Mel Gibson's *The Passion of the Christ* (2004). Here film regulation is defined as the overarching frameworks within which censorship and classification decisions are made and justified; film censorship when films are re-edited, cut or banned; and film classification being the age and generic categories used to control access to films. First of all, the chapter outlines the theoretical perspectives which frame the analysis of *The Passion of the Christ*. This is then followed by an engagement with the official and voluntary regulation, censorship and classification of the film. The chapter ends with a discussion of specific aspects of the cultural regulation and censorship of *The Passion of the Christ* within Britain. Within these accounts links are made to self and economic forms of regulation, censorship and classification.

The theoretical approach adopted during this chapter enables the analysis of *The Passion of the Christ* to move beyond a narrow understanding of legal and official forms of film regulation to take into account a wider range of interrelated social, cultural and economic factors. More specifically, it will be advanced that this analysis offers several atypical insights into the regulation,

* Dr Shaun Kimber joined the Media School at Bournemouth University in 2008 as a Senior Lecturer in Media Theory. Before that he spent eight years working at the University of Winchester. He gained his PhD in Sociology from Sheffield University in 2000. His doctorate examined the censorship of film violence in the UK from the perspective of genre film fans. Recent research activities include a monograph examining the controversy surrounding the film *Henry: Portrait of a Serial Killer* (1986) for the forthcoming series 'Controversies'.

censorship and classification of film violence in contemporary Britain. Firstly, *The Passion of the Christ* created a situation where letters of complaint were written to the British Board of Film Classification (BBFC) arguing that this film, classified 18 due to its violent content, should have been given a lower classification despite its strong and sustained violence. Secondly, *The Passion of the Christ* has become an example of a film that has been voluntarily censored to enable the creation of a second alternative version with less violence and a lower classification. Thirdly, the film created a state of affairs where groups traditionally concerned with the negative impact of film violence upon audiences actively promoted the exhibition and consumption of *The Passion of the Christ*, a film which contained extended scenes of strong violence.

The chapter is informed by two interrelated theoretical positions. The first is a revisionist approach to regulation, censorship and classification. Within literature on film censorship a distinction is often drawn between conventional and revisionist approaches (Staiger 2000). A conventional analysis tends to draw upon a narrow definition of film censorship, focusing on official, deliberate and prohibitive forms, what Jansen (1991) calls regulative censorship. This conventional view often recognizes film censorship as a tool of the state and has historically informed liberal anti-censorship and conservative pro-censorship perspectives. This approach has tended to manifest in legal, institutional and policy-orientated studies of British film censorship (see Phelps 1975; Robertson 1989; Mathews 1994). It is suggested that a conventional approach to the analysis of *The Passion of the Christ* would be insufficient because it would fail to take into account the wide range of overlapping unofficial influences that have impacted upon its regulation, censorship and classification in Britain.

Revisionist approaches have shifted their focus to recognize film censorship as a complex, dynamic and relational set of practices and processes, which are productive as well as restrictive (see Bernstein 2000; Hendershot 1998; Lyons 1997; Kuhn 1988; Thompson 1997). The theoretical impetus for this shift is often cited as originating in the writing of Foucault on discourse and power. For example, Jansen (1991) has developed the term constituent censorship to refer to how human communities establish taken-for-granted rules and operations of discourse which function to organize everyday life. Hendershot (1998) believes censorship is a productive process involving complex power relations that not only create cultural meaning but also reveal rather than hide social fears and anxieties. According to Post (1998) this shift in thinking has led to a destabilization of traditional links between liberal anti-censorship and conservative pro-censorship positions. This issue will be picked up in more detail below. Criticisms of the revisionist approach relate to its broadness and its potential to overlook State censorship, making any challenge to its official or unofficial manifestations at best difficult or at worse impossible.

On closer inspection the boundaries outlined here can be challenged. Historically theorists such as Kuhn (1988) have drawn attention not only to the productive nature of film regulation but also the impact of wider influences on BBFC decisions. Furthermore, in line with Post (1998) it is argued that the revisionist understanding of censorship is most effective when it is used to complicate and not reject the conventional definition. It is possible to do this when analysing *The Passion of the Christ* by employing an approach that takes into account the interrelationships between official and unofficial mechanisms of film regulation, censorship and classification within the British context.

The second position to inform this chapter is a film cultures approach. This perspective has been influenced by recent shifts within certain areas of Film Studies which draw their insights from Cultural Studies, Audience Studies, Media Studies, Sociology and Geography (see Harbord 2002; Jancovich 2003; Turner 1999, 2002). This form of analysis seeks to explore film as a social practice and cultural experience. This is achieved by examining the relationships between films and the everyday lives of audiences and takes into account a range of issues including consumption, meaning, pleasure, ritual and identity (Turner 2002). This approach also seeks to locate the analysis of film within its overlapping industrial contexts and processes including production, marketing, distribution, exhibition and regulation (see Harbord 2002; Jancovich 2003; Turner 2002). This interdisciplinary approach foregrounds film as a set of social and industrial practices as well as an aesthetic object within local, national, international and global spaces. It is suggested that a benefit of employing these two theoretical frameworks in the analysis of *The Passion of the Christ* is that it facilitates a paradigmatically different approach to much literature on the film.

The next part of the chapter will examine the official and voluntary regulation, censorship and classification of the violence in *The Passion of the Christ* within the British context. Here official regulation refers to all official, deliberate and prohibitive forms of film regulation that shape classification decisions and which may result in official forms of censorship. Official regulation is constituted by several overlapping layers including state, legal and institutional. Voluntary regulation invokes the myriad of ways in which filmmakers, distributors, marketers and exhibitors regulate and censor themselves often to ward off other forms of regulation, censorship and classification. During this analysis links will also be made to self, cultural, and economic regulation and censorship.

The Passion of the Christ was submitted to the BBFC by Icon Film Distribution limited in 2004 (BBFC 2007). The BBFC passed the film uncut, with an

18 certificate for theatrical release on 18 February (BBFC 2007). In other territories the film was rated differently: 12 in France and Japan, 14 in Chile and Peru, 15 in Ireland and Sweden, R in the USA and was banned in Iran and China (IMDB 2007). These examples illustrate how official classification decisions not only vary from territory to territory according to legal, social, cultural, economic, political and religious differences, but that such decision making is often based upon a complex set of contested power relations between the law, official regulators, film industries and audiences.

The DVD version of *The Passion of the Christ* was classified for release in Britain with an uncut 18 certificate on 8 July 2004 (BBFC 2007). Accompanying the theatrical and video releases was the consumer advice that the film "contains extended scenes of strong violence," suggesting that whilst the BBFC felt the violence was containable within an 18 certificate, it was necessary to offer a warning to consumers (BBFC 2007). This censorial mechanism employed by the BBFC helped to establish a framework within which *The Passion of the Christ* would go on to be distributed, marketed, exhibited and consumed in Britain. For example this advice, if read, could impact upon the viewing experiences of audiences and possibly lead to acts of self-censorship, including choosing to watch or not to watch the film because it contains strong violence. Here self-regulation applies to the complex ways in which audiences make sense of and react to official and unofficial forms of film regulation, censorship and classification within their everyday lives. This example offers some insights into the interrelationship between official, cultural, self and economic film regulation and censorship and will be returned to later.

According to the UK Film Council, *The Passion of the Christ* opened on 12 March 2004 taking £229,426 and by the end of its third weekend had taken a total of £2,784,344 to become number one at the UK box office (UK Film Council, 12–14 March and 26–28 March 2004). During its third weekend *The Passion of the Christ* beat *Dawn of the Dead* (Zack Snyder 2004) into second place and *Starsky & Hutch* (Todd Philips 2004) into third place at the British box office (UK Film Council, 26–28 March 2004). The Film Distributors Association reports that in total the film grossed £11,078,861 making it the fifteenth most successful film in UK cinemas during 2004 (Film Distributors Association 2004). What this shows is that, in the UK, controversy over a film, and especially film violence, can translate into box-office success. This type of economic success can be seen as productive in that it creates, circulates and maintains a range of economic and cultural outcomes including a desire to see the film, thus illustrating an articulation between cultural and economic forms of regulation. Here economic regulation refers to the ways in which the marketplace and culture industries impact upon the censorship and classification of film.

In their 2004 Annual Report the BBFC outlined how they received a number of letters criticizing their decision to award *The Passion of the Christ* an 18 certificate (BBFC 2004). According to the report the letters argued that the film should have received a lower rating due to its important message (BBFC 2004). It is worth noting that all of the trailers for the film had been classified PG, possibly raising the expectations of certain audience segments that the film would be awarded a lower certificate (BBFC 2007). The BBFC defended their decision to award the film an 18 certificate stating that the film broke their guidelines for violence and horror at the 15 category because it dwelt on the infliction of both pain and injury (BBFC 2004). According to the BBFC Guidelines at the 15 level "violence may be strong but may not dwell on the infliction of pain or injury" and that in relation to horror "strong threat and menace are permitted" but "the strongest gory images are unlikely to be acceptable" (2005, 18). Moreover, the BBFC outlined in the 2004 Annual Report that whilst the story of the Passion would be familiar to many audiences the film's focus on the agony of Christ could be extremely distressing to fifteen year olds (BBFC 2004). It is suggested that these letters of complaint, and the BBFC's response to them, illustrate how regulatory power in Britain is contested between a range of interested parties, and how cultural concerns and anxieties over the potential harm that can be caused by film violence are rarely far from the minds of official regulators, due in part to the constraints of the Video Recordings Act (1984).

The Passion—Recut was submitted to the BBFC by Icon Film Distribution Limited in 2005 for a theatrical release (BBFC 2007). The re-edited version of *The Passion of the Christ* was awarded an uncut 15 certificate on 25 February (BBFC 2007). The 2004 BBFC Annual Report stated that the re-edited version had replaced the strongest violence with less violent material. BBC News Online (2005) outlined how Mel Gibson in a press statement suggested that *The Passion of the Christ* had been re-edited into *The Passion—Recut* "to cater to those people that perhaps might not have seen the original because of its intensity or brutality." The Guardian Unlimited (2005) reported that a BBFC spokesperson had told *The Hollywood Reporter* that the filmmakers "have toned down the visual impact of the violence," and that, "We think they have removed a lot of what we call 'the processed violence' from the film. It's still at the high end of '15' but they have made enough alterations." It is suggested that the release of *The Passion—Re-cut* theatrically constitutes a form of voluntary censorship by Mel Gibson and Icon Film Distribution Limited in an attempt to reach new audiences whilst addressing some of the cultural regulatory concerns circulating around violence in the original film. As Gibson suggested, he hoped the re-edited film would attract cinema fans who thought "the intensity of the original film was prohibitive" (Guardian Unlimited 2005).

Accounts of the time differences between *The Passion of the Christ* and *The Passion—Recut* vary between 4 minutes 53 seconds (BBFC 2007) and 6 minutes (BBC News Online 2005). According to Chris Utley (2005) most of the removed footage comes from the two scenes involving the scourging and crucifixion of Jesus. During the scourging scene shots of bodily injury are replaced with shots of Jesus' face, the reactions of the crowd and soldiers and newly inserted shots of Mary's reactions (Utley 2005). In the post-scourging scenes images of the crown of thorns being pressed and beaten into Jesus' head have been removed (Utley 2005). During the crucifixion scene images of the nails being hammered into Jesus' hands and feet, the cross being flipped to secure the nails and then flipped back again and the bird pecking out the unrepentant thief's eye have all been cut and re-edited (Utley 2005). Anthony Breznican (2005) suggests that there has also been some re-editing of the subtitles and sound track, with the language used to describe the crucifixion by the soldiers softened and audio adjustments made to tone down the impact of the violence in some scenes. Whilst it is debatable whether the changes made to *The Passion of the Christ* in creating *The Passion—Recut* have changed the overall message of the film, it does illustrate how the re-editing of scenes of violence can alter the cultural meanings and impact generated by that violence from the point of view of official regulators. Whilst the BBFC awarded *The Passion—Recut* a 15 certificate for theatrical exhibition in Britain, in the US it was awarded a PG13 and in Canada (Quebec) a 13+ further illustrating the cultural and institutional specificity of film regulation (IMDB 2007).

The theatrical release of *The Passion—Re-cut* was accompanied by the same consumer advice as the 18 version, that the film contains "extended scenes of strong violence" (BBFC 2007). As a result, despite revisions to the film's violence it is clear that it is located towards the top end of the 15 classification and as such the same warning as the 18 version was deemed necessary by the BBFC. Building upon what has gone before, it is put forward that this censorial mechanism of keeping the same consumer advice as *The Passion of the Christ* located *The Passion—Recut* within a similar interpretative framework as the original film but without the controversy and hype which may well have impacted upon its lack of commercial success in Britain. This could have resulted in the film not reaching its intended new audiences because it was seen as being too similar to the original. According to the UK Film Council, *The Passion—Recut* opened on 18 March 2005 in 13 cinemas and took just £1,675 (UK Film Council, 18–20 March 2005). There were no more box-office details for the weeks that followed on the UK Film Council website.

On 19 February 2007 the BBFC awarded the *The Passion—Recut* a 15 certificate for DVD release on behalf of Twentieth Century Fox Home

Entertainment (BBFC 2007). *The Passion of the Christ (Director's Edition)* was released in time for Easter 2007. The Director's Edition contains the theatrical 18 Version and Re-Cut 15 Version, four commentaries and a range of special features. It is suggested that the release of *The Passion—Re-cut* at the cinema and then as part of a director's edition DVD exemplifies an attempt on the part of Gibson, Icon Film Distribution Limited and then Twentieth Century Fox Home Entertainment to generate additional revenue by creating additional seasonal opportunities for distribution, exhibition and consumption. This, it is argued, illustrates a further articulation between official, voluntary and economic forms of film regulation and censorship.

The final section of this chapter focuses upon the cultural regulation and censorship of the violence in *The Passion of the Christ* within the British context. Here cultural regulation is seen as operating through shifting discourses relating to taste, decency and taboo, and often manifests in anxieties over film violence and its potential influence and risk. The outcome of this multifaceted form of film regulation is often cultural forms of film censorship linked to specific films, such as controversy, hype, viewer complaints and extended media coverage. During the course of this analysis direct links will be made to self-censorship and indirect links to voluntary censorship and official and economic regulation.

The Passion of the Christ was a high-profile and controversial film which generated a diverse range of responses from an even wider range of audiences. Woods et al. (2004) suggest that *The Passion of the Christ* generated strong reactions because audiences tended to interpret the film through their own faith perspectives. They suggest that advocates of the film tended to focus on the historical and theological accuracy of the film's representation of the suffering of Christ, the opportunity the film offered for a spiritually enriching individual and communal worship experience, and the challenge the film made to the general maligning of faith within popular culture. Critics of the film, according to Woods et al. (2004), tended to foreground the film's historical and theological inaccuracies, Gibson's theological and artistic embellishments, the anti-Semitic elements of the film and the way the film presented violence as glorified spectacle within a Hollywood blockbuster.

It is argued that these audience and critical responses to *The Passion of the Christ* exemplify two key features relating to the interrelationship between cultural regulation and cultural censorship within the British context. First, these censorial responses were framed by and also helped to reinforce macro cultural regulatory discourses relating to the impact and role of popular cultural forms within British culture, which have been built up over many years (see Murdock 2001; Petley 2001). What is being suggested is that British reactions to *The Passion of the Christ* were not formed in isolation; rather they were framed by an enduring set of cultural discourses, which whilst not exclusive to Britain, serve a significantly regulatory function in this country. Second, these responses constitute a set of specific ways of thinking about *The Passion of the Christ* which have established, promoted and maintained a range of meanings, pleasures and anxieties that frame and continue to shape the way audiences experience and make sense of the film. These responses to the film also feed back into macro-cultural concerns about popular cultural forms thus galvanizing the interrelationship between cultural regulation and censorship.

A manifestation of this framing of *The Passion of the Christ* through cultural forms of regulation and censorship is its articulation with self-regulation and self-censorship. According to Hill (1997) self-censorship is central to the viewing process involving complex and context-specific negotiations between personal and social thresholds and the use of physical and mental barriers to test personal boundaries relating to the consumption of film violence. Building upon this work and thinking about *The Passion of the Christ* it is held that self-regulation refers to the dialogue that takes place between personal and social thresholds relating to the consumption of film violence. For example: a need to see the film to find out what all the controversy is about, a wish to avoid the film because of its extended scenes of strong violence, a desire to see the film because it provides an opportunity for a parachurch worship experience or an inclination to not see the film because of its perceived anti-Semitism or historical inaccuracy. Self-censorship relates to the ways in which individual audience members use physical and or mental barriers to help them negotiate their consumption of the violence within *The Passion of the Christ*. For example, the use of hands to cover eyes or ears to block out certain images and sounds during the scourging scene or psychological distancing of oneself from the violence by reflecting upon its constructed nature through the use of prosthetic and digital special effects during the crucifixion. What is being suggested is that the way in which a film is positioned culturally can significantly impact upon how audiences consume, regulate and censor films for themselves.

A key aspect of cultural regulation linked to *The Passion of the Christ* concerns the way in which certain Christian groups in Britain embraced and actively promoted the film despite the fact that it contained graphic violence. This account draws upon evidence gathered from audience research and reception studies within the US context. Whilst King (2004) suggests the reception of *The Passion of the Christ* in the US was distinct to the one it received in other territories, it is held that sufficient overlaps can be seen to warrant its use within this analysis of its reception in Britain. Be this as it may, it is recognized that the groups under discussion are not homogeneous in their views and actions and as such the ideas explored here briefly are inevitably reductionist.

Historically sections of conservative and evangelical Christian groups in Britain have been critical of the use of strong violence within popular cinema. These groups have often decried the levels of sadistic and gratuitous violence employed exploitatively as entertainment within many mainstream films. This criticism is often extended to suggest that sadistic and gratuitous violence not only desensitizes audiences, it can also lead to violence within society. Moreover, these groups often lobby the government, the film industries and the BBFC to place stricter regulatory and censorial limits over the production, distribution and exhibition of violent films. Despite this, some of these faith groups set aside their critique of the sustained and arguably sadistic or masochistic violence contained within *The Passion of the Christ*. King (2004) suggests that for these particular audience segments strong film violence becomes acceptable when it is used to offer insights into historical or theological truths. In such examples the power of film and its potential influences are seen to be harnessed for the good; for example, in this case it has the potential to bring audiences closer to God.

For some members of these faith groups *The Passion of the Christ*'s use of extended scenes of brutal and intense violence were seen as essential in representing the truth of Jesus' suffering and self-sacrifice for the sins of humankind (King 2004; Woods et al. 2004). The use of strong violence in this particular film has also been seen to challenge the sanitization of previous film versions of the life of Jesus (King 2004; Woods et al. 2004). Woods et al. (2004) also found that due to familiarity with the story of the Passion, the faith message of the film and the opportunity the film offered for a parachurch worship experience, conservative Christians did not the view the violence in *The Passion of the Christ* like the violence in other films. As Woods et al. suggest, "Ironically, when asked whether the film was too violent for those under 18, religious conservatives disagreed most strongly… Evidently Christian conservatives are much more accommodating of film violence within a biblical context than in movies in general" (2004, 176). This may also account for some of the letters received by the BBFC after the film was initially classified an 18 and illustrates an articulation between cultural and official forms of censorship.

Building upon the revisionist ideas of Post (1998) outlined earlier, it is argued that this example highlights the destabilization of the traditional alliance between conservative and pro-censorship positions with conservative and evangelical Christian groups protesting against the regulatory controls placed upon *The Passion of the Christ*. Beyond this King (2004) reports how the legitimization of the violence within the film resulted in it becoming viewed as a "must see" for evangelical Christians and the basis upon which they would defend the film against criticisms of its use of excessive and graphic violence.

It is put forward that two things come out of this analysis of conservative and evangelical Christian response to *The Passion of the Christ* which shed light on this particular group's position in relation to the role and legitimacy of film violence within contemporary cinema. First, as King (2004) suggests, conservative and evangelical Christians do not necessarily reject the use of violence in films. Rather they see themselves as engaging with a wider cultural and theological struggle over its appropriate use in cinema. As such these faith groups feel that so long as film violence is used in an appropriate and historically accurate way then it is acceptable to them. Second, members of conservative and evangelical Christian audience segments view their perspective on film violence and its potential influence as being wholly consistent. This is because they would argue that they recognize all film violence as being powerful and potentially influential and as such care is always needed to ensure that it is fittingly used within films (King 2004). Applied to *The Passion on the Christ* this would imply that for this audience segment the strong and sustained use of bloody violence is acceptable due to the theological message and the perceived historical and theological accuracy of the film.

Finally, it is worth making a link between cultural and economic censorship. It is argued that a byproduct of the cultural controversy surrounding *The Passion of the Christ*—Gibson's track record of making "Christian friendly" films (King 2004), the way the film was marketed to Christian audiences, the defence of the film on several fronts by Christian groups, the active promotion of the film by Christian groups and the potential for the ritual seasonal distribution and exhibition of the film—is the financial realization by the film industries that profits could be made out of films which appeal to religious groups. It still remains to be seen whether there will be a major increase in films aimed at Christian audiences within mainstream film-making but 26 March 2007 did see the release of *The Passion of the Christ (Director's Edition)* just in time for Easter!

8 *The Passion* as Media Spectacle

*Oluyinka Esan**

Even prior to its release, Mel Gibson's *The Passion of the Christ* (2004) attracted remarkable media attention and upon release it delivered a record number of audiences worldwide. That this is an "event film" (Austin 2002) is thus undoubted. In this chapter I argue that the film is a media spectacle, reflecting prevalent culture, and demonstrating how media power can be harnessed.

Kellner argues that the techno-culture prevalent today promotes a proliferation of media spectacles. "Culture industries have multiplied media spectacles in novel spaces and sites, and *spectacle itself is becoming one of the organising principles of the economy, polity, society and everyday life*" (Kellner 2003, 1; my emphasis). Indeed, the use of media (public) spectacles is not alien to the church (Cohen 2007). This film thus exemplifies some organizing principles of contemporary times. It demonstrates the need to rely on strategies that deliver greater proportions of "the spectacular" before the attention of audiences can be secured.

Societies in different times and locations have had their spectacles which served a range of purposes. They were opportunities for convergence of the different elements within society and often a space to exhibit the prowess and splendour of the society. Spectacles, constituted as state events, could be focused on sports, military prowess, entertainment and religious ceremonies. These were milestones in the social existence, instructive for social and political relations.

There is a notion that spectacles create a sense of unity though this may be exploited by the dominant forces, the state or other agencies within

*   Dr. Oluyinka Esan is a Senior Lecturer (Media Studies) at the University of Winchester, UK. Her initial fascination with *The Passion* was on account of her Christian faith but she has since returned to it with a scholarly gaze. Her research focus on media audiences and television is reflected in this attention to the construction of a media spectacle. She has also researched and written on Nigerian films otherwise known as *Nollywood*.

society. Spectacles have been used both within the fascist and capitalist cultures:

> The history of spectacle is inextricably tied to the politics of illusion, seduction, pageantry, and exhibition. Voyeurism and fantasy work together through various representations and practices organized within diverse pedagogical sites to render subjects willing to surrender their potential as agents to the state and more recently, the demands of the market. The pedagogical function of the spectacle is to promote consent (though it has also functioned coercively), integrate populations into dominant systems of power, heighten fear, and operate as a mode of social reproduction largely through the educational force of the broader culture. (Giroux 2006, 27–28)

It has been argued that the spectacle dominates the collective consciousness under late capitalism (Debord 1994). This observation is arguably more pertinent as new media technologies facilitate increased access, delivering greater audience attention than ever before. Unlike the size and patterns of crowds constituted around paintings or religious ceremonies in the medieval church for example (Griffiths 2007), mass media are able to deliver much larger and much more diverse audiences. Similarly movies, like television programmes, have affective properties that differ from those of medieval artwork (Chattaway 2004). Besides, these new modes of communication offer a ceaseless stream of spectacles that are usually regarded as benign entertainment when in fact they often conspire to mask the actual (political) significance of the spectacle. Not so with *The Passion*, which became a platform for many thorny discussions (Jacobs 2004; Astell 2006).

Defining the Media Spectacle

Media spectacles demonstrate the increased importance of the media and popular culture in contemporary society. Mindful of the central position of the media in contemporary society, Kellner (2003) adopts a broad view of media spectacles. To him, media spectacles employ a range of highly visual media forms which compel society to be attentive.

There are political spectacles such as the American presidential debates. In order to transcend the clutter within the contemporary mediascape, global corporations now create advertising spectacles. Likewise certain media spectacles are generated by celebrities, music industry, sports and games, fashion, charitable organizations and films. Just about any aspect of life that can be branded and *sold* (including religious messages) is made into media spectacle. This liberal view of what constitutes a media spectacle is informed by the relatively easy access to technology and the prevalent need for information and entertainment.

Dayan and Katz (1992) have a more rigorous frame for defining media events. To them, media events are moments when fixed schedules and routines are altered, to accommodate celebrations or ceremonies. These are more than the marking of festive events, but they are also occasions to flaunt the wealth and prowess. Such media spectacles serve multiple purposes of endorsing particular values, validating particular individuals or groups, maintaining political balance and marking cultural or historical moments. They may be constructed around the rites of passage of significant members of society, such as the funeral of a statesman or public figure. Other examples, like the coronation or wedding of a monarch, suggest that there is justification for the rapt and reverential (at least passionate) attention that they attract. These are preplanned programmes for large (television) audiences and they highlight the importance of media processes in the constructed-ness of media spectacles. Hence media spectacles are "media texts" which are able to commandeer more-than-regular resources for production; they are therefore to be distinguished from other routine output of the media.

Though its focus was on a particular genre within television, this model is instructive, in its recognition of media spectacles as "cultural rituals" that celebrate society's deepest values and indicate its notional centre (Dayan and Katz 1992).

The convergence of audience attention conveys the impression of a society that is united. Although certain scopes of social life are more typical arenas for spectacles, media spectacles can be constructed around any aspect of social life; from acts of nature (2004 Boxing Day Indian Ocean Tsunami; 2005 USA Hurricane Katrina) to human acts—usually but not always those with an elevated status, people who are capable of turning the wheels of the publicity machinery.

Media spectacles are indicators of hierarchies. There must be a justifiable reason before the media spectacle enjoys apparent monopoly within the media space. Producers and audiences will only break out of their normal schedules for the spectacle when the celebration (or condemnation) is warranted. Such participation is a matter of honour, for group or collective identity. Spectacles thus offer a glimpse into the norms and values that are upheld or contested within groups. They also offer a chance for negotiation, therefore not as benign as the usual gloss, pomp and pageantry attending them suggests.

Convergence of audiences around a media spectacle may imply uniformity in their participation. It may even be assumed that audiences are passive spectators or at best ceremonial participants who observe with reverence the protocols imposed by the text. Such assumptions fail to account for the active nature of audiences or the complex nature of texts that accounts for variety in responses. Much of the course of spectacles is difficult to chart as

they are framed within multidiscursive, socially diverse arenas. They are informed by history and dynamic cultures. Fiske (1994) illustrates this with the
metaphor of a sudden eruption of a calm flowing river, visible turbulence
brought on by the usually unseen topography of the river (the material conditions, rocks, eddies, trees that can modify its course, even reverse its flow):

> Currents that had been flowing together can be separated, and one turned on
> the other, producing conflict out of calmness. There are deep, powerful cur-
> rents [in society] carrying meanings of race, gender and sexuality, of class and
> age, these intermix in different proportions and bubble up to the surface as
> discursive "topics"... (Fiske 1994, 7)

Indeed media spectacles are a site of popular engagement inviting audiences
from across social boundaries, and when audiences occupy different positions in relation to the media or the spectacle, media spectacles are nothing
if not sites of struggle, struggles over identity and values.

In the case of sporting spectacles, the virtues of contestation, values of
winning success, honour and money are privileged, especially as regards
(national or group) identity. At times spectacles are used to highlight transgressions, condemn the unacceptable or simply to label what is different.
The notoriety generated when spectacles are constructed around scandals,
deviant or criminal acts, especially when the rich and powerful are involved
(as in the 1995 OJ Simpson murder trial or the incidents of 9/11), attract
large-scale media attention.

It is usual for several features of media spectacles discussed above to be
seen in film. Cinema is highly visual and stylistically compatible for such
narratives. The big screen relies on stars and celebrities, the publicity machinery, fashion, glamour, opulence, sets and stories of epic proportions. For
the purposes of marketing and reception, popular film is "framed by a con-
stellation of institutions, texts and practices" (Austin 2002, 3). It is commer-
cially logical that films should court a range of audiences across different
markets and "taste formations" therefore the industry employs strategies
that encourage audiences to find their sorts of pleasure and meanings within
film. This requires promotional activities through the media or editorial coverage that attracts the highest possible share of the market, as characteristic
of consumerist culture. The practice is more pronounced with "event films."

Event films are a small number of films which have exceptional perfor-
mances in the market. Such films benefit from star presence, major advertising campaigns, large-scale theatrical openings and a dominance of the
distribution and exhibition outlets. They attract a large turn out of *frequent
viewers*, less traditional audiences, and occasional cinema goers. With its
exceptionally creative production strategy, Mel Gibson's *The Passion* falls in
this category even to a greater degree than the likes of *Basic Instinct* (1992),

Batman Returns (1992), *Lethal Weapon 3* (1992) and *Fatal Attraction* (1987). These were films that commanded media and public attention especially as regards their use of sex or violence.

Religion has had a long relationship with the media. Besides the activities of religious leaders (Papal Mass or televangelists), biblical epics also formed part of Hollywood's "Golden Age." These include *The Ten Commandments* (dir. DeMille 1956), a story which, like *The Passion*, is also based on biblical spectacles. Some suggest that this relationship is being conformed by the consumer culture (Miller 2005). Similarly it can be argued that *The Passion* as a media spectacle reflects the times. I shall consider this in the following section.

The Passion as a Spectacle

Box-office figures show that the film attracted record audiences: "the highest grossing religious film in worldwide box office of all time"; "the highest grossing R rated film in the US box office history" (http://www.imdb.com/title/tt0335345/trivia). This success stems from much more than the usual marketing efforts used in the industry.

Though it lacked direct backing of the huge Hollywood marketing structures, the film enjoyed a great deal of publicity. It lacked star presence on screen, but with the stature of Gibson as the director and the controversy shrouding the production it generated extraordinary pre-release publicity. The missionary zeal and the strategy with which Gibson pursued the project were adequate talking points. Gibson's self-confessed pursuit of truth, for example, his decision to employ obscure languages (Latin and Aramaic) and a cast of less familiar performers served to arouse curiosity. The media were quick to establish links and contrasts between this project and Gibson's previous accomplishments. Critics saw traits of different film genres that are almost characteristic of Gibson in this film. In these, his declaration of faith, his involvement with the Catholic Church and the nature of the violence employed stand out. The curiosity appeal served to build up anticipation for this media spectacle.

Though his divinity is often questioned, the prominence of Christ as a world figure is often not in doubt, so a film about him may have become a spectacle on this merit. However, by choosing to focus on the suffering and death of Christ (twelve hours of intensive pain and suffering, topics that had hitherto been glossed over; Johnston 2004) and using such graphic violence, the film is positioned as a more interesting spectacle. The violence was of such magnitude that it was compared with horror and splatter films

(Hammer and Kellner 2005). It was more violent than any of the previously circulated "sanitized" and "palatable" cinematic presentations of Jesus:

> Rather than present still another gentle, blue eyed Jesus, one thought to be consistent with modern sentiment, Gibson portrayed the ancient Jewish "Man of Sorrows," someone who as the movie's epigraph states, "was wounded for our transgressions . . . and with His stripes we are healed" (Isaiah 53:5). (Johnston 2004, 56)

This was a risky strategy that proved to be very successful. If the crucifix is the most easily recognizable icon of the Christian faith, one can argue that the death (and resurrection) of Christ is the most significant event in Christian history. The death of the guiltless—the just for the unjust—is the epitome of love. This is the evidence of God's love, and the kernel of the gospel. It is the ultimate sacrifice that makes possible the reconciliation of deity and humanity, and although it is a spectacle of love, it does not paint a pretty picture. Mel Gibson's *The Passion of the Christ* is remarkable in that it captures and dwells on this incongruity, the very gory details of this event.

Considering techniques that may work in contemporary society, a departure from more oblique postures of previous films was necessary. Improvements in media technology have facilitated the circulation of graphic (violent) images. Sometimes these are factual and necessary (news, documentaries), or fictional and gratuitous (video games, movies). Perhaps audiences are too desensitized to be moved by less gory images. For the Christian message to have a chance, it has to speak the language of the times. This it did with the improved special effects, digitalized imagery, *mise-en-scène*, colour (or absence of it), language, lighting, camera angles, editing, flashbacks and slow motion (Astell 2006; Prince 2006; Chattaway 2004). It was a novel way of presenting the gospel. Against the backdrop of prevalent global religious tensions, particularly in the Middle East, any religious film was likely to hit raw nerves. In this case, the search for truth further compounds the situation as truth claims are set to exacerbate factional tensions within the Church, and between Christians and Jews. Yet the limits of the film's claim to authenticity raise the perennial challenges of artistic representation of Christ (Antonakes 2004). Gibson's discourse stems from Catholicism, the narrative steeped in signifiers which may be obtuse to those outside of this community, such as its flashbacks and veiled references to the struggle that had been since before creation through the recurring figure of the devil incarnate at critical moments. Without acknowledging this wider knowledge, the criticism and charges of anti-Semitism are inevitable. Yet, to some, the film is a presentation of the larger story, where the villains are not Jews, but humanity in its pre-redemptive state.

Holderness (2005) demonstrates the symbolic twinning of the film with the Catholic mass:

> *The Passion of the Christ* is something more than, or at least other than, a film. It is a votive offering, a memorial of Christian redemption, a celebration of the Eucharist. The audience is not invited passively to "gaze" nor even actively to "watch"; but rather voluntarily to participate in a ritual of shared suffering. (Holderness 2005, 395)

The film was released to coincide with Easter, and adopted as the high point of the Easter ritual. Group viewings were organized by churches around the world as an aide for Good Friday reflection. It was thus a cultural event, a tool for evangelism, an exhibition of the core of the Christian faith.

Clearly not every viewer participated in the religious ritual but diverse audiences converged to view this film. The convergence was just an illusion of unity, as media spectacles tend to be. Audiences differed based on their backgrounds, allegiances, aspirations and interpretations of the experience. This reveals the complexity involved in charting audience reception. From all indications, there were three broad categories of viewers for this film: the sceptics, the apathetic and the active believers. They reflect the type of ideological positions that attend media spectacles.

Anecdotal evidence and self reports on a number of websites support this. There are reports of conversion to faith even amongst the cast and viewers. Prince reports that some viewers were willing to suspend disbelief, breaking out of the frame of fiction, adopting the enacted violence as a form of reality. Those least likely to support the use of extreme violence were willing to justify its use on the ontological basis that it gave a more accurate account of the sacrifice made on their behalf.

> The Christian viewers who were most in tune with the film understood its extreme violence was a necessary prerequisite to transcendence. Therefore, the more violent the film could be, the deeper and truer an evocation of the ritual sacrifice it would offer. Thus, its violence, provided it was graphic and not oblique, provided the most direct route to realism that is to the truth of the ritual that was being enacted through violence. (Prince 2006, 13)

This response though not universal marks the distinction and distances between communities and contributed to the construction of the media spectacle. The tensions between the Jewish and Christian communities were glaring throughout this film, and in fact it was banned in certain Islamic countries where the representation of prophets is disallowed.

Of all the facilitators of the spectacle, the democratization of the media is that which perhaps should receive the greatest credit. The alternative media network facilitated by the new media technologies was responsible for the publicity that the film received, even when it lacked the support of the

Hollywood establishment. Easy access to new media has inspired and sustained an activist culture which means that mainstream institutions can be bypassed and ultimately compelled to pay attention. A Google search for "The Passion of the Christ" conducted in December 2007 resulted in 3,200,000 results. Various interest groups had the space in these alternative networks (email chains, websites, weblogs) to share their views and promote the viewing of the film—making it such a celebrated media spectacle. There was, for example, adequate scope for critical scrutiny (Tabor 2004) and outright condemnation (Leupp 2004).

With the increased dependence on mediated experiences that characterize postmodern society, what Debord refers to as the society of spectacle, we should be mindful of the distinctions between reality and what the media offers in our deliberations about media spectacles. This is more the case when we are considering spectacles that are constructed around historical events and the controversies that these generate. Indeed controversy and attendant media publicity add more layers to the spectacle, further blurring the lines between reality and mediated images (hyperreality), between the copy and the original (simulacrum), especially for audiences located far from the event. These will be in the majority when speaking of audiences for media spectacles in contemporary times. The cynicism and doubts about the integrity of the media spectacles will thus persist. So it is with *The Passion of the Christ*, the film that has drawn much flack from within academic and religious communities alike, giving it an aura more of legend than historical event.

Conclusion

In this chapter, I have argued that the magnitude of interest generated by *The Passion* as a spectacle was more than usual for three main reasons: the subject of the film, the creative ingenuity and religious conviction of Mel Gibson, and the techno-culture that framed its production. When these are set against the prevalent socio-political order, the film could not but be a spectacle.

Mel Gibson has presented us with a Christ who is an action hero. He has drawn on his mastery of the industry to command media attention for what is his deep personal conviction. In this is a model on how to harness popular culture for religious ends.

Yet the success of this model is much more than the orchestration of the media can take credit for. *The Passion* demonstrates for us the nature of media spectacles, how they gather momentum beyond the control of the initiator. They also reveal the fault lines in society.

Gibson has been criticized for the lack of historical accuracy and inauthenticity in the representations of the events portrayed. He has also received praise for presenting what is so far the most credible media simulation of the event in spite of the extreme use of violence. I have argued that this creative expression of the event has employed a language that resonates with the audience at this time.

Society's increased capacity for violence is evident in the deluge of images from news or eyewitness accounts of global conflicts, like the war in Iraq, and frightful images of violence amongst children and such citizens' record of violence on social networking sites. I therefore argue that this spectacle has been framed by the context of production.

As suggested earlier, spectacles have their purposes. Even long before the advent of the mass media, societies had deliberate purposes for spectacles. They could be for entertainment, to provide a sense of community, to celebrate the acceptable and esteemed or show up the ridiculous. Often political spectacles are used to demonstrate the power, splendour and dominion of the state (take, for example, the 2002 Golden Jubilee anniversary of Queen Elizabeth II as monarch). *The Passion of the Christ* should be deemed a political, albeit religious, spectacle. In it, the depth of God's love to humanity is demonstrated. Gibson flaunts the otherwise unattainable price of the salvation. This is exhibited on the cross and in the events leading up to that iconic act of sacrifice. The film is the display of triumph – the eventual victory of good over evil, right over wrong, light over darkness. Yet perhaps inadvertently, it also unearths the historical, political, and social relations that precede it. Much of these linger still, and for that reason the media spectacle was further intensified.

Clearly this spectacle has set new standards. Through all it accomplished a new appreciation of the adaptable nature of media audiences and the fluidity in the concept of violence emerges. From responses to *The Passion of the Christ* in certain quarters, audiences showed that thresholds of tolerance for violent images may be extended, only if the viewing of such can be justified. The film has been described as a pastiche of Hollywood, employing a range of generic convention, thus it can be different things to different groups of people. It certainly reflects the relativism of the "society of spectacles."

9   Protest as Reaction, Reaction as Text: The (Con)Textual Logics of *The Last Temptation of Christ* and *The Passion of the Christ*

*Leighton Grist**

In November 1983, four days before shooting had been scheduled to commence, and after nearly eleven months of pre-production, Paramount pulled the plug on director and lapsed Catholic Martin Scorsese's planned adaptation of Nikos Kazantzakis's novel *The Last Temptation*, *The Last Temptation of Christ*. The reasons for the film's cancellation were manifold. The disappointing commercial performance of Scorsese's immediately preceding features, coupled with the move away from big-budget, *auteur*-driven filmmaking in the wake of the box-office disaster that had been *Heaven's Gate* (Michael Cimino, 1980), had made an expensive and lengthy shoot not the most attractive prospect, particularly as it was to be filmed in Israel, far beyond Paramount's direct purview (Christie and Thompson 2003, 95).[1] It became even less attractive when, by the end of pre-production, its budget and shooting schedule had risen from $12 million and 90 days to $16 million and 100 days. However, also contributing to the film's abandonment was the campaign organized against it by the Christian right, which saw Paramount's parent company Gulf+Western receiving 500 letters a day and sustained telephoned complaints. Ultimately Paramount studio head Barry Diller informed Scorsese, "We just don't want to make it. It's not worth the trouble" (Christie and Thompson 2003, 97).[2]

---

*   Leighton Grist is Senior Lecturer in Media and Film Studies at the University of Winchester, where he is programme director for the MA in Film Studies. The writer of numerous articles published in edited collections and in journals, his output has included work on classical and post-classical Hollywood, on genre, and on matters pertaining to film theory, psychoanalysis, and gender. He is in addition the author of *The Films of Martin Scorsese, 1963–77: Authorship and Context* (Basingstoke: Macmillan, 2000), and is presently completing a follow-up volume.

The Last Temptation of Christ was revived as a project upon Scorsese sign-
ing with agent Michael Ovitz and Creative Artists Agency (CAA) on 1 January
1987, with a deal being quickly brokered for a film financed jointly by Universal and theatre chain Cineplex Odeon. While the resuscitation of the
project was testimony to the influence of Ovitz and CAA within Hollywood
at the time, the film became a much-reduced production in terms of both
schedule and money, being shot in Morocco in late 1987 in 58 days and at a
cost of $7 million. Universal took measures to pacify the religious right, only
for their collapse to unleash what Michael Morris has termed "a public outcry
of a magnitude unprecedented in the history of religious films" (1988, 44).[3]
Mobilized through the multiple communication channels available to various
churches, and fuelled by "religious broadcasters who spread the language of
victimization" (Riley 2003, 124), complaint increased almost exponentially in
vehemence and intensity through the summer of 1988, and encompassed
not only, again, letter-writing and telephoning campaigns, which were directed against both Universal and its parent company Music Corporation of
America (MCA), but petitions, television, radio and print media interventions, the threatened boycotting of Universal and other MCA companies'
products and services, an (as it turned out, bogus) attempt to purchase the
film in order that it could be ritually destroyed, and mass protests.[4] Yet if the
last culminated on 11 August when 25,000 people assembled outside
Universal's Los Angeles studio, then the same partook of an anti-Semitic
edge when a gathering led by Reverend R. L. Hymers marched on and burnt
an effigy of MCA's Jewish chairman Lew Wasserman outside Wasserman's
Beverly Hills home. Anti-Semitism was in addition implicit to certain pronouncements made by more mainstream figures such as Donald Wildmon,
Jerry Falwell and Pat Robertson (Lyons 1997, 165; Riley 2003, 77–79). Because of the campaign against the film, Universal advanced the release of
The Last Temptation of Christ from 23 September to 12 August—hence the
sizeable protest the preceding day. With the refusal of United Artists Theaters to screen the film having been another factor in its previous cancellation by Paramount, the significance of the involvement of Cineplex Odeon
in its production was underscored when numerous theatre chains declined
to screen the film.[5] Mass protests continued upon the film's release, although the feared—and even promised—violence was restricted to localized skirmishes and vandalism, at least in the USA. In both France and
Kazantzakis's homeland, Greece, the film's release was met with more serious violence.[6] Its release in the USA further saw a move towards increased
political lobbying against it and a number of unsuccessful legal challenges,
one of which nevertheless reached the Supreme Court. Despite everything,
The Last Temptation of Christ finally took about $12 million at the box office
($8 million domestic, $4 million foreign), a not negligible return given also its

budget and its being what Scorsese has described as "an 'art movie' according to the American definition" (Christie and Thompson 2003, 124). However, in the film's effective theatrical exclusion within the USA from all but major cities, and the national attention granted its opinions and actions, the Christian right had no less demonstrated its economic and cultural clout.

Such was further, if contrastingly, demonstrated with respect to *The Passion of the Christ*. Released in 2004, and carrying a negative cost of $25 million, the film was very much a project personal to practising, traditionalist Catholic Mel Gibson, who not only co-produced, co-scripted and directed the film for his company Icon, but financed the project with an estimated $40–50 million of his own money. Moreover, while the film was distributed in the USA by independent company Newmarket Films, it was distributed in certain other territories—including the UK and Australia—by Icon itself. With the film having been shot in Italy, on location at Matera and at Cinecittà, it would seem correspondingly to have been made and released in apparent avoidance of Hollywood. This is similarly implied by its promotion and marketing. In contrast to common Hollywood routine, there were no press junkets, and only a limited television advertising campaign. Emphasis was instead placed on screening the film to church groups, a process often inclusive of related discussion sessions and/or personal appearances by Gibson. *The Passion of the Christ* thus wooed, and was accepted by, a demographic section that has historically been hostile towards Hollywood, and that had protested against *The Last Temptation of Christ*. More especially, the film—irrespective of Gibson's traditionalist Catholicism, and its being based in part upon nineteenth-century Catholic mystic Anne Catherine Emmerich's contentious account of Christ's crucifixion, *The Dolorous Passion of Our Lord Jesus Christ*—was ardently embraced by the Protestant evangelical right, whose support was not inconsequential to the film taking $370 million domestically, making it at the time the ninth-highest grossing film at the American box office.[7] In addition to churches using and disseminating materials provided by Icon,[8] congregations were bussed to view the film, websites set up to promote it, viewing and repeat viewing encouraged and undertaken as almost an act of faith, entire theatres bought out, and even, with the film perceived as having substantial outreach potential, tickets given to non-believers—tactics that found less extensive reflection outside the USA, with the film garnering another $241 million worldwide.

Ironically, however, the tacitly validating anti-Hollywood credentials of *The Passion of the Christ* would seem, on closer inspection, to be more apparent than actual. Apart from the film being effectively financed through Gibson's earnings as a Hollywood actor and Academy Award-winning director, both its star, Jim Caviezel, and many of its key production personnel were established Hollywood professionals. The film's director of photography was Caleb Deschanel, its editor was John Wright and its score was composed by John Debney. All three have extensive Hollywood credits. One might likewise query whether the film's peculiar promotion was not as much predicated upon economic pragmatism as ideological commitment. The film's prints and advertising budget has been quoted as being $10 million: not inconsiderable, but comparatively small by contemporary Hollywood standards. The promotional approach adopted for *The Passion of the Christ* has also subsequently been followed by Hollywood with respect to other "Christian-friendly" films, including *The Chronicles of Narnia: The Lion, the Witch and the Wardrobe* (Andrew Armstrong 2005). A yet more pressing irony is manifest textually in the stylistic indebtedness of the lauded *The Passion of the Christ* to the reviled *The Last Temptation of Christ*. Like its predecessor, *The Passion of the Christ* presents, for example, a location-founded emphasis on an ostensible historical realism with respect to costume, setting, and customs; elliptical, *nouvelle vague*-derivative editing; and the employment on its soundtrack of a *melangé* of ethnic musics, although this is in *The Passion of the Christ* increasingly subsumed by Debney's melodramatically insistent orchestral arrangements.[9]

Indeed, the films also display significant differences, stylistically and otherwise. Take their respective aspect ratios and choice of languages. The decision to shoot *The Last Temptation of Christ* in the normative 1:1.85 aspect ratio was made by Scorsese expressly to preclude the spectacle conventionally associated with Christ films. This is complemented by the film's dialogue consisting predominantly of colloquial American English, which, while deriving from Kazantzakis's use of demotic Greek in his novel *The Last Temptation*, and possibly or initially incongruous, can be regarded as seeking to facilitate intellectual engagement with what is, comparatively, a verbally discursive film text (Christie and Thompson 2003, 126–27). By contrast, not only is the use of the 'Scope 2:2.35 aspect ratio for *The Passion of the Christ* consistent with a film in which the visual outweighs the verbal, spectacle overwhelms a comparatively sparse narrative, but the use of "authentic," subtitled Aramaic, Latin and Hebrew tends, while being seemingly historically accurate, less further to naturalize the film's period realism than to heighten its authority as a putative promulgation of biblical truth.[10]

Moreover, if these differences can in themselves be regarded as being symptomatic of the films' not unfamiliar ideological characterization as respectively liberal and conservative, then as much is underscored by their divergent representations of the figure of Christ. Opening with words from Kazantzakis's "Prologue" to his novel concerning the "dual substance of Christ," "the yearning, so human, so superhuman, of man to attain God," the Christ of *The Last Temptation of Christ* (Willem Dafoe) can be seen to foreground— blasphemously, for the Christian right—Christ as human, as a man who gradually and with difficulty comes to acknowledge and accept his divinity. There is, correspondingly, an emphasis, from Kazantzakis via scriptwriter Paul Schrader, on the "Nietzschean" aspect of the character's battle (Jackson 2004, 137–39). This is not to deny the intimation of the predestined and the supernatural within the text, but throughout the focus is mainly upon Christ's "human" struggle, failings, fears and doubts. The Christ of *The Passion of the Christ* (Caviezel) is shown suffering little from such. Reciprocally, there is, and Christ is represented as having, no doubt as to his godhead: asked directly by Jewish High Priest Caiphas (Mattia Sbragia) whether he is "the Messiah," the "son of the living God," Christ replies, unequivocally, "I AM"—a response that is, for good measure, translated in the subtitles in upper case. True, the film opens with a troubled Christ at Gethsemane, where he despairingly asks God to "let this chalice pass from me," but thereafter he tends stoically, although painfully, to undergo his inflicted agonies.[11]

The issue of pain returns us to that of violence. Certainly, violence is far from absent from *The Last Temptation of Christ*—as witness the scenes of Christ being beaten and scourged, as well as that of his crucifixion—but the stress throughout is predominantly upon the figure's psychical torment and anguish. In *The Passion of the Christ* the psychical is, however, almost entirely elided before the physical, with the film—which veteran film critic Roger Ebert at the time described as "the most violent" that he had "ever seen" (2004)—being almost unremitting in its graphic representation of the variously vicious, vindictive and/or institutionally endorsed violence inflicted upon its central character. Essentially, the spectacle that the film purveys is that of violence given and received. Moreover, with Christ, the early Gethsemane scene excepted, represented as unquestionably divine, as both knowing and accepting of his fate, with the promise of resurrection tacit, such violence would appear to have no clear, much less pressing, narrative purpose. The suggestion is rather that of a sustained, brutal assault on the spectator. Further, the film's violence is unsettling not just in its set-piece scenes of violence—Christ's scourging, for instance, or his crucifixion—but in its often seemingly offhand, casual near-omnipresence. Consider Christ's treatment following his arrest and during and following his questioning by the Sanhedrin, which sees him, in addition to being dangled from a bridge by his chains, repeatedly lashed, punched, otherwise struck, spat at and roughly manhandled—all of which prompts Pontius Pilate (Hristo Naumov Shopov), upon Christ being brought before him, to ask, "Do you always punish your prisoners before they're judged?"

Switching perspective, one might propose that the violence contextually implicit to and threatened but largely repressed during the protests against *The Last Temptation of Christ* can be regarded to return textually in *The Passion of the Christ* in the form of its explicit and untrammelled representation.

It does so, moreover, with anti-Semitism intact. As has been much rehearsed, not only are the Sanhedrin represented as physically unattractive ("like a pack of sneering stage Shylocks with bulbous noses and eyes heavy-lidded with cruelty"; James 2004, 17) and as predominantly malevolent, but their representation contrasts—as his complaint about Christ's treatment might imply—with that of a sympathetic Pilate who is, historical evidence to the contrary, resistant to Christ's crucifixion, and only forced into sanctioning it by hysterical Jewish demand. According to philosopher Philo of Alexandria, Pilate was "a man of a very inflexible disposition, and very merciless," a figure infamous for "his cruelty, and his continual murders of people untried and uncondemned, and his never ending, and gratuitous, and most grievous inhumanity" (Crossan 2006, 65). Further, Pilate's blame before that of the Jews, and specifically Caiphas, is excused by Christ himself, who declares—unanswerably—that "it is he who delivered me to you who has the greater sin." The charge that the film is guilty of restating the accusation of deicide that has historically formed the ground for anti-Semitism would correspondingly appear to be far from invalid.[12]

This besides needs to be considered in relation to the enthusiastic, even zealous, approbation of *The Passion of the Christ* by not only the Christian right but the broader Christian community. Regarded from outside this cluster, it is an approbation that appears masochistically perverse. More exactly, given the testimonies of renewed guilt, of assumed, sinful culpability for Christ's crucifixion that have attended the same, the implication is that of Sigmund Freud's conceptualization of moral masochism.[13] That is, a perversion in which the ego "seeks punishment" from "the super-ego or from the parental powers outside" (Freud 1924, 424): further to which, as the super-ego, the internalized agency of conscience, of the individual's ideological determination, is for Freud "a substitute for a longing for the father," so "it contains the germ from which all religions have evolved" (1923, 376). More exactly still, one can adduce Theodor Reik's Christian variant of moral masochism, regarding which the masochist accepts "misery, humiliation, disgrace" on a faith in "what is to come afterward," a condition that Reik proposes need not be "limited to the individual" but can encompass larger social and religious groupings (1949, 363–64). In turn, if Reik's model of Christian moral masochism is predicated upon the identification with Christ that is foundational to Christianity, and embodied institutionally in his ritual incorporation that is the Eucharist (Freud 1913, 216–17), then this is complemented by the identification with Christ as the sympathetic, unjustly punished victim that is offered filmically by *The Passion of the Christ*.[14] It is, moreover, an identification proffered exactly in terms of Christ's self-sacrificial acceptance of suffering in the name of humankind's sins, of his being, in the words of John 1:29, "the Lamb of God, which taketh away the sin of the world." That *The Passion of the Christ* was released in the USA on 25 February, Ash Wednesday 2004 becomes thus noteworthy not just with respect to its subject matter but as tacitly placing the film as a means of Lenten self-abnegation, although in this commercial considerations once more cannot be discounted.

Freud in addition contends that masochism is indivisible from sadism, that "masochism is actually sadism turned round upon the subject's own ego" (1915, 124). This arguably illustrates why, in the case of *The Passion of the Christ*, that which is intensely but masochistically embraced by its Christian advocates can be conversely regarded, by those that refuse that spectatorial position, to be simply, vengefully sadistic. Consider, for instance, certain mainstream critical responses to the film. Thus for David Denby, *The Passion of the Christ* "is a sickening death trip, a grimly unilluminating procession of treachery, beatings, blood, and agony" (2004), while David Ansen opined that it "plays like the Gospel according to the Marquis de Sade" (2004). Correspondingly indicative is the punitive nastiness that is apparent in the representation of certain of the film's characters and incidents. Witness, again, the negative representation of the Sanhedrin, or of Jews in general, who in the main are shown as little more than a heedless, easily-manipulated rabble, or, especially, the incident during the crucifixion when the "bad thief" Gesmas (Francesco Cabras), upon his laughing mockingly at Christ's assuring the "good thief" Dismas (Sergio Rubini) that he will join Christ "in paradise," promptly—and vindictively—has his eye pecked at by a raven. Similar malevolence is implicit to the representation of Judas Iscariot (Luca Lionello), who is in *The Passion of the Christ* a craven wretch, eventually driven to hanging himself by possibly satanic, possibly guilt-induced tormenting children. By contrast, that the Judas of *The Last Temptation of Christ* (Harvey Keitel) is the strongest of the disciples, a former Zealot who, at Christ's bidding, and despite himself, betrays Christ so that Christ may fulfil his purpose, becoming, as Pam Cook puts it, "the loving agent of his master's death" (1988, 288), brings us back not only to the differences in terms of representation between *The Passion of the Christ* and *The Last Temptation of Christ*, but, inescapably, to the films' divergent ideological perspectives.

This likewise urges consideration of what was at stake in the films being respectively protested and championed by the religious right. If the initial cancellation of *The Last Temptation of Christ* in 1983 can, other contingencies notwithstanding, be regarded as being symptomatic of the reciprocal strength of the political and the Christian right in the USA in the early 1980s, then the extensiveness and virulence of the protests against the film in 1988 can be seen as a reactive asserting of continuing cultural pertinence in the face mutually of the unravelling of the decade's conservative preponderance—this irrespective of the election that year to the Presidency of George Bush Sr—and of the sex scandals involving televangelists Jimmy Swaggart and Jim

Bakker that had sullied the Christian right's moral and social reputation. In short, the religious right's campaign against *The Last Temptation of Christ* in 1988 was, in Charles Lyons's words, "not just a protest against cinematic transgression but a struggle for the survival of their coalition and for its members' 'vision' for America" (1997, 24–25). The film and its protestation were, accordingly, as Schrader has noted, part of a larger contest for "cultural hegemony."[15] It is a contest from which by 2004 the political and the Christian right would have appeared to have emerged triumphant, with the box-office success of *The Passion of the Christ* being seemingly consistent with an historical and political context that the same year saw the re-election as President, on the back of a substantial Christian vote, of George W. Bush. However, it should be remembered that it was an election that many had expected George W. Bush to lose, and that it took place within—and George W. Bush subsequently presided over—a USA more polarized politically than at any time since the Vietnam War. We might hence ponder why *The Passion of the Christ* need be so insistently relentless in, depending on perspective, its inculcation of masochistic guilt or infliction of sadistic requital, or why its supporters needed to have been so ardent in its lauding. Again, the implication is of a lack of surety rather than otherwise, of a text and its praising that do insist too much.

The relation of the Christian right to the films at hand in addition resonates with connotations that are ideologically both more specific and of broader import. Compounding for the religious right the blasphemous humanizing of Christ in *The Last Temptation of Christ* is the temptation of the title: Christ's fantasy when on the cross of his being saved to have an ordinary—although polygamous—life as a husband and father. It is also a fantasy that is revealed to be the work of Satan and that Christ must reject in order to fulfil his goal. Concordantly, as the film's humanizing of Christ can be seen to be undermining of the hierarchical presuppositions that are central equally to the political and to the religious right, so the last temptation, as it extends Christ's humanization, renders the family, the social unit that each places as social end and ideal, as insufficient, tacitly demonic and obstructive of (self-)transcendence. Hierarchy is, by contrast, unsurprisingly, given the film's approval by the Christian right, in *The Passion of the Christ* firmly upheld. Apart from the indisputable divinity of Christ, consider the film's representation of the Romans. This splits between that of a positively represented, noble higher class—not only Pilate, but the centurion Abenader (Fabio Sartor), or Pilate's wife, Claudia Procles (Claudia Gerini), who is "already instinctively Christian" (James 2004, 17), and who gives some linen to Mary (Maïa Morgenstern) and Magdalen (Monica Belluci) to mop up Christ's blood after his scourging—and a lower-class soldiery who are represented, again, punitively, as near-pantomimic in their inanity and cruelty.[16] Moreover, if that in the protests against *The Last Temptation of Christ* some sought to uphold their dominance but most thus merely confirmed their complicity in their own subordination once more evokes moral masochism, then it almost unavoidably calls to mind Karl Marx's oft-noted words concerning religion as "the *opium* of the people"—"the sigh of the oppressed creature, the heart of a heartless world and the soul of soulless conditions" (1844, 244). Further, in the play of masochism and sadism, the concern with hierarchy, as well as the establishment of a distinct division between an in- and an out-group, between the elect and the damned, that are variously informing both of *The Passion of the Christ* and of the contrasting responses of the Christian community to it and to *The Last Temptation of Christ* there is implied a parallel with the framework of fascist propagation outlined via Freud by Theodor W. Adorno and Max Horkheimer (1982). While this links suggestively with the historical indivisibility of the political and the religious right, the latter's hostility towards *The Last Temptation of Christ* is, in turn, perhaps clarified by the film being, though not a Marxist text, approachable in terms of Marx's related contention regarding religion, that it "is only the illusory sun which revolves around man as long as he does not revolve around himself" (1844, 244).[17]

There thus remains another irony with respect to the production of *The Passion of the Christ*. The choice of Matera meant that the film was in part shot at the same location as that used for *The Gospel According to St Matthew*, a film that, directed by Pier Paulo Pasolini, and released in 1964, has been seen to lend the Christ story a Marxist inflection.

Part Four

In Sport

10 The Religious Significance of Violence in Football

Rina Arya*

> I suppose I can't think of any musical equivalent to the feeling I felt when Allen Kennedy scored in the Parc des Princes. I can't think of anything to match that musically. I actually thought, if I die now, I won't care, you know, nothing could ever be as good as this again. I always say, rather flippantly, but it's not a million miles from the truth, that football supplies many of the requirements that other people seek and find in religion, with the difference that you can actually see the truth of it being demonstrated on the pitch every Saturday afternoon, and that's enormously gratifying.
>
> (*When Saturday Comes* magazine, 1987; in Finn 1994, 105–106).

The above emotive response was recalled by the late music disc jockey John Peel with reference to the match between Liverpool and AS Roma in the 1984 European Champions Cup Final in Paris. The goal scored by Allen Kennedy was the pivotal moment in the match and secured the win for Liverpool. The hyperbolic language that Peel used to express his state of elation is by no means unusual and is comparable with the sentiments expressed by so many football fans, who directly (as in the example above) or indirectly discuss the transformative effects that the game has on their lives.

In this essay I want to investigate the transformative power that football has on the lives of so many people and the significance that violence has in this relationship. In his commentary Peel astutely remarked that football does indeed supply many of the requirements that people seek and find in religion and that this is continually affirmed on (at least) a weekly basis. Religion can be defined as a "set of beliefs, symbols and practices (for example rituals) which is based on the idea of the sacred, and which unites believers into a socio-religious community" (Scott and Marshall 2005, 560).

Before the "death of God" was acknowledged as a cultural shift of thinking in the West the idea of the sacred was intertwined with the theistic belief

* Rina Arya is a Senior Lecturer in Critical and Contextual Studies at the University of Chester. She has published in the areas of theology and the arts and critical theory.

in God/gods. The "death of God" confirmed the untenability of belief in the Christian God (the transcendent guarantor) but it did not eliminate the sacred. The sacred was rather dislocated from its ecclesiastical/theistic (and transcendent) context and was relocated in social and collective expressions of transgression and violence (in immanence). My thesis is as follows: in the cultural climate of the "death of God" the sacred can be experienced in the collective expressions of transgression in football which transport the crowd from the state of ordinariness, which in theological terms is described as the profane, to an experience of the sacred. This has important sociological functions since, as many sociologists of religion would claim, the sacred dimensions of reality are essential for the formation and renewal of social bonds (see Mellor and Shilling 1997).

Beginning with an analysis of the relationship between religion and football I will then move on to to deal more specifically with the recovery of the sacred through violence and the relationship that violence has to the ritual.

In the last twenty years the sociology of sport has been a growing field in academia. With centres such as the "Leicester School," which has been subsequently renamed the Sir Norman Chester Centre for Football Research, the discipline of sport studies, led by Eric Dunning, is examined as a focus of sociological enquiry. Whilst drawing upon the expository studies of the aforesaid it is my intention to provide an interdisciplinary interpretation that combines methodologies from theology, sociology and anthropology.

The History of Football and Religion

Religion is a crucial factor in the history of the game. Steven Wagg documents the active participation of religious figures in the initial stages of club formation: "In the case of association football the game was evangelised principally by employers and priests: many of the biggest and best known English clubs began life in the last century either as works teams or as church sides" (cited in Eyre 1997, 4).

Eyre observes how in the instances where football clubs grew out of church or parish associations, there has often been retained an explicit link between team and denomination, and singles out Glasgow as a city which has a longstanding history of sectarian violence between Rangers (which has its origins in Protestantism) and Celtic (which is Catholic; Eyre 1997, 5). This pattern continues for generations: many families have their chosen team which serves to reinforce a group identity. Eyre, quoting McGuire, states that, "where a religion is particularistic or exclusivist, the potential for expressed conflict is greater" (Eyre 1997, 6). Football has a sociological function

and can unite or divide groups of people across religious, ethnic, geographical and economic lines. For the purposes of the essay I am less interested in
the particular dynamics that may exist between football teams and religious
denominations or sects and am more concerned with the behavioural and
perceived identity changes (of fans) that occur throughout the duration of
the match (and in many cases for an extended while afterwards). It is during
these transformative changes that I believe we can speak of the elementary
forms of religious behaviour and can discern the effects of the sacred. In
other words, whilst the external aspects of institutionalized religion such as
the specific team allegiances are hugely topical in demographic discussions
in football what I believe is fundamental to the ascription of the descriptor,
"religious," is the behavioural tendencies vis-à-vis "the idea of the holy" or
the "numinous" (Otto 1958, xvii, 6).

Returning to the point made above regarding the historical instances of
unity and division, this propensity is seen in the framework of religion. Mark
C. Taylor observes how the etymology of the term "religion" inextricably
links it to the Latin stem "leig," which means "to bind" (Taylor 1998, 8). The
need for binding presupposes a sense of fragmentation and a teleology of
wholeness. Hence religion (*religare*) can be construed as a rebinding of the
fragments that have fallen apart. Within the Christian narrative this fragmentation is witnessed on the broken body of Christ in the Crucifixion, which is
made whole—is salved—in the resurrection. This instance of *sparagmos* is
by no means unique to Christianity and is represented in other traditions,
such as the myth of the Bacchus in Greek mythology and the myth of Kali in
the Hindu tradition. The fragmentation caused in religion can be attributed
to the expression of the sacred. Religion and more specifically the ritualistic
practices contained within it operate as the mechanism or process which
divides the sacred from the profane. Many sociologists, theologians and cultural theorists who investigate the morphology of the sacred, such as Durkheim,
Otto, Eliade and Callois, discuss the sacred in relation to the profane, where
the two are presented as dichotomous. Eliade describes how they represent
two modes of being, where the experience of the sacred is opposite to the
profane (Eliade 1959, 10, 14). The effervescent, contagious and "special"
nature of the sacred, its status of being "set apart and forbidden" (Durkheim
1995, xlvi), means that it needs to be separated from the profane, and within
religious, sociological and anthropological discourse, the ritual functions to
mediate between the two. Assuming the distinction between the two, Caillois
emphasized the need for the ritual to protect the contagious nature of the
sacred whilst also conveying the interdependence of their experiences.

> On the one hand, the contagiousness of the sacred causes it to spread instan-
> taneously to the profane, and thus to risk destroying and dissipating itself

uselessly. On the other hand, the profane always needs the sacred, is always pressed to possess it avidly, and thus to risk degrading the sacred or being annihilated by it. Their reciprocal relationships, therefore, have to be strictly regulated. (Caillois 2001, 8)

The ritual is in place to protect the community from the fragmentary and dislocating effects of the sacred. Within the context of the football match I argue that the violence that erupts between rival groups of fans, for example, articulates the transgression of the taboo. The norms of social order have been violated and chaos ensues. What results is the experience of the sacred. The specific moment I am focusing on is the lapse of the ritual function, that is, the moment the ritual falls apart and the profanity of the everyday is transformed into a qualitatively different order, which is invariably referred to as the "wholly other" (Otto 1958, xviii).

The History of Violence in Football

In the above discussion I referred to the violence that erupts during a football match without clarifying what constitutes violence. The term "violence" is used equivocally by the media in discussions of football fans, and debates about the boundaries of violent conduct remain open-ended. Violence can be construed as a whole spectrum of behaviour and action, which ranges from slight altercation in its mild sense to a full-blown uncontrollable battle in its more extreme manifestation, which may result in severe injury or even death. Indeed in the last decade within the football context the term has become inclusive of non-physical, namely verbal, offences. The violence I am referring to here is that which results when boundaries are transgressed. This could denote, for example, the physical boundary of the body, the geographical boundary of territory, or the social boundary of law and propriety. Violence is demonstrated in the illicit crossing of these markers. The term given to denote these extreme expressions of violence is "hooliganism," which as a term emerged in the late 1890s and literally meant gangs of rowdy youths (Scott and Marshall 2005, 275).

Football hooliganism is commonly identified as a social phenomenon, forms of which have been a frequent accompaniment of association football since the 1870s (Dunning, Murphy and Williams 1988, 1). By the late 1970s and early 1980s the football hooligan had become a dominant character of British political and social discourse (Brick 2000, 166). Whilst it would be erroneous to deny the seriousness of the pervasive sense of violence within football, a few points should be considered. Firstly, there is a degree of uncertainty and ambiguity as to what is regarded as permissible. Giulianotti, Bonney and

Hepworth raise some of these questions in their own research: "Why is it that particular social practices are designated 'football hooliganism'? Which social groups are identified as 'football hooligans,' and by whom? Where are the clear demarcations or grey areas between particular modes of fan behaviour, in terms of fanaticism, 'hooliganism' or generally expressive support?" (Giulianotti, Bonney and Hepworth 1994, 2). Frank Furedi states how, in the current legislation on football and fandom, "a look or gesture may now be interpreted as a routine sign…of harassment" (quoted in Brick 2000, 166). There is a tendency within the media and (national and local) press to exaggerate and fabricate. Incidents relaying hooliganism are often given disproportionate coverage. This in turn may have the effect of inducing a moral panic in the general public especially when conspiracies allude to the possible affiliations between hooliganism and the ideologies of far-right groups (Dunning, Murphy and Williams 1988, 8–9). Whilst football-related violence may seem to indicate a growth or escalation in incidents, this has to be interpreted within the context of more sophisticated strategies of monitoring, reportage and the management of violence by the police and other authorities (the implementation of the Taylor report, which was set up in 1990 to investigate the Hillsborough disaster a year earlier, was significant in football history and a catalyst for change). Finally, it must be noted that hooliganism cannot be localized to football alone, since it can be observed in a number of other sport and non-sport-related contexts. The Football Spectators Act 1989 stipulates that an offence committed up to one hour after a match comes within the remit of its clauses. To what degree of certitude, then, can a violent incident be regarded as "football-related" if it occurs after that time limit?

The above points serve to acknowledge the various ambiguities and complexities within the developing awareness of the social problem of hooliganism. However, this should not discredit the claim that hooliganism is notoriously persistent within the game of football (Dunning, Murphy and Williams 1988, 4).

The Need for Violence

Sociologists have identified a correlation between sport and leisure activities and the release of tensions. Dunning and Rojek explain how in sport everyday rules are relaxed and enable us to "vent the passions which are subdued in everyday life…it is for this reason that sport and leisure activity is often associated with behaviour that is rougher and more aggressive than in other areas of social life" (Dunning and Rojek 1992, xii). In his influential study,

Violence and the Sacred (1972), René Girard discusses the accumulation of violence in the social sphere and the subsequent need to vent it through various channels. In his anthropological perspective, violence is a necessary aspect of communal life.

In the introduction I quoted John Peel's emotionally motivated response to football and commented on the prevalence of religious overtones, which peppers the language of fans and approaches that they take when they discuss their allegiances. This meta-religious discourse is conveyed when discussing resources within the game. Fans often regard their team as being sacred, or set apart, and the accompanying vestigial attributes as being equally sanctified, such as the notion of the stadium as hallowed ground. This feeling of reverence extends to the status of players who are glorified if they are playing well or on occasion defiled (if they are letting the side down). The duality of enhancement/debasement matches the fluctuating status of Christ in the Bible, who was both sanctified and reviled (through kenotic acts which emptied the Godhead into lowly forms, such as *The Suffering Servant* in Isaiah 53:4-12). The highly emotive attitude expressed by fans towards their team and its aspects can manifest itself in terms of violence towards rival or competing teams especially with regard to territorial boundaries. In his chapter, "Conflict," Bruce Lincoln discusses how communities and institutions that define themselves in terms of religion have a tendency to frame their conflicts in claims to territory (Lincoln 1998, 66). This is indeed the case in football culture. Fans often "define their cause as moral and holy and define the goods they desire in similar terms: sacred land…sacred symbols" (Lincoln 1998, 66). Within this emotionally charged context the presence of violence seems inevitable as a way for fans to stake out territory and to safeguard the sanctity and special status of their team.

Within the history of football, violence has prevailed. In *The Roots of Football Hooliganism* (1988), Dunning, Murphy and Williams explain the presence of contemporary attitudes of football hooliganism by tracing it back to "the cultural conditions and circumstances which reproduce in young working-class males an interest in a publicly expressed masculine style" (Dunning, Murphy and Williams 1988, back cover). They address a number of issues which I feel are significant in the discussion of violence—namely, the processes of "bourgeoisification" and "internationalization" (Dunning, Murphy and Williams 1988, 74–75). The status of the game has changed radically over the years for social, economic and political reasons. Its origins as a working-class sport have been widely documented. What has altered considerably over the years has been the target audience, which has widened to accommodate people from other social strata, minority ethnics, women and families. One of the most significant changes has been the commodification of the sport. It has been transformed from its humble origins to become the centre of lucrative transactions between stakeholders, sponsors and managers. This has inevitably extended its identity from the local to the global, particularly in the more "celebrated" teams, such as Manchester United, which, arguably, can be described as exhibiting a brand identity. The influx of economic and cultural capital has impacted on the fan base, which is aptly described by the term "bourgeoisification." From a commercial perspective football has demonstrated a high level of success. However, the current climate on "internationalization" (which is evidenced in the constitution of the team, including the nationalities of team players and managers) can have negative ramifications. Players are bought and sold in this global market which may affect the stability of alliances with their team since they are conceived of as economic pawns. This disrupts the sanctified status of the team as "chosen." The furore following the takeover of Manchester United by the American sports tycoon Malcolm Glazer in May 2005 is a case in point. Fans felt embittered by what appeared to be a deal based solely on economic advancement (there have been speculations that Glazer and his family were seeking to expand the club's brand name in the United States and Asia), which they felt was in contradistinction to their allegiances to their team. There was concern that, amongst other things, ticket prices would soar and in protest a shareholders' association was formed to buy club shares and try to protect it from Glazer's clutches. This is one of a growing number of instances where a conflict of interests arises: the economic commercialism of corporate identity on the one hand against the deep-rooted loyalty exemplified by the fan base on the other. With the changing face of football, violence emerges as a way of realigning the more traditional aims and objectives, such as reclaiming the status of working-class male identity. Violence is a way of reinforcing the sanctified values of football. Violence often results in the transgression of boundaries of law and order but transgression also serves to reinforce these boundaries. The growing commercialization also reveals a paradox. Many clubs and teams need the financial backing of businesses and other profit-oriented organizations. However, by accepting financial support they seek to compromise the priceless and unquantifiable value of their team.

Mimetic or "Staged" Violence

A recurrent theme that underpins sociological enquiry into the field of football is that of mimetic or "staged" violence. This is the notion that many of the outbreaks of violence that occur do not start off as being about "real" violence. In other words, much of what initially may appear to be potentially destructive scenarios are often releases of machismo tensions or bravado. They are mimetic or "staged" tensions which are fuelled by "artificially induced fears and imaginary dangers" (Dunning and Rojek 1992, xii). Dunning and Rojek draw comparisons between the spectatorship of football and the processes of viewing at the cinema and discuss how the conflicts that are acted out in both contexts are conceived of as "play." We do not expect these conflicts to continue after the match/film has ended. They are regulated. The "suspension of disbelief" enables spectators to be drawn in, which contributes to the interactivity and even intimacy. The catalogue of emotions and the level of physiological awareness has the effect of raising adrenalin levels, which contribute to the catharsis, or release of tension, that we feel after the performance is over. In "The Quest for Excitement in Leisure" Elias and Dunning outline the pattern of rise and fall observed in a number of mimetic events: "the gradual working up of tension-excitement reaching…a protracted climax…of near frenzy, which then slowly resolves itself. A gradual rising of tensions leading, through a climax, to a form of tension-resolution" (Elias and Dunning 1986, 83). However, there are occasions when the heightened tensions do not dissipate and escalate into uncontrollable forms of violence, which I shall refer to as the "real presence" of violence. Ironically, it is often social-control policies which are designed to curb crowd control and mob violence, which actually serve to aggravate the situation by exacerbating the levels of violence thereby causing the transition from "mimetic" violence to "real" violence (Rojek 1992, 23). During this outbreak of "real" violence what happens is that the function of the ritual, which keeps tension under control and the outbreak of violence in abeyance, falls apart. When this happens the levels of violence escalate to an insurmountable degree causing destruction and even death in more extreme instances. This is the "real presence" of violence. I have used the phrase "real presence" to indicate that we are witnessing something that is beyond staging and make-believe, which coheres with its theological meaning as the actual (body of Christ) rather than the figurative. However, it must be emphasized that the intended effect is not to minimize the sociological importance of mimetic violence. Indeed, "the mimetic sphere, through creating imaginary and staged settings, forms a distinct and integral part of social reality. It is no less real than any other part of social life" (Maguire 1992, 106).

The "Real Presence" of Violence

Unlike the "mimetic" violence which is contained within a ritualistic framework, what happens here is that the violence can no longer be contained.

These two states are qualitatively different and can be described within the terms of the profane and the sacred, where the former represents the "staged" violence and the latter is an expression of the "real presence" of violence. Durkheim's interpretation of the sacred in his seminal text, *The Elementary Forms of Religious Life* (1912), can be used to support this reading of violence. Since the sacred is not a substantive it is useful to see it in the context in which it is focused, that of the ritual. During the ritual, identity alters from being an individual experience to becoming a collective experience. This passage from the individual to the collective is effected through the process of transgression. Durkheim expands on the aspect of change that occurs, which is transformed through the ritual doing. What happens is that the individuals within the group experience a heightening of sensations, "they experience themselves as grander than at ordinary times; they do things they would not do at other times; they feel, and at that moment really are, joined with each other and with the totemic being. They come to experience themselves as sharing one and the same essence—with the totemic animal, with representation, and with each other" (Durkheim 1995, xli). This heightening of sensations, which occurs throughout the ritual and transforms the group from being individuated and apart from one another to partaking of a fervour which binds them communally, conveys the switch from the profane to the sacred (which can be paralleled to comparable terms from Tönnies's discourse: from *Gesellschaft* to *Gemeinschaft*). Durkheim explains the forces that transform the group from being comprised of an identity of individuals into a collective sense of identity, which imparts a feeling of totality, where the whole is greater than the sum of its parts. This is effected through "collective effervescence" (Durkheim 1995, xli). Mapping these changes onto my analysis of the violence in football, what happens during hooliganism is that a transformation occurs from individual identity to collective identity, where the collective is greater than the sum of its parts. Chaos ensues as individuals become subsumed in the violence which has no bounds.

The connections between violence, the sacred and communal identity are made explicit in Girard's *Violence and the Sacred*. Girard's central argument focuses on the proximity of violence and the sacred. He states how, "I have used the phrase 'violence *and* the sacred'; I might as well have said 'violence *or* the sacred.' For the operations of violence and the sacred are ultimately the same process" (Girard 1977, 258). In his anthropological outlook violence is omnipresent and omnipotent and "if held in check" too long "will overflow its bounds." Failure to acknowledge violence as an active presence is detrimental to social stability. To quote:

> Although men cannot live in the midst of violence, neither can they survive
> very long by ignoring its existence or by deluding themselves into the belief

that violence, despite the ritual prohibitions attendant on it, can somehow be put to work as the mere tool or servant of mankind. (Girard 1977, 268)

He uses the analogy of a vessel on an ocean to describe the effects the violence has on community, where the vessel represents community and the ocean the tumultuous nature of the sacred. Consider the following description:

> Each community sees itself as a lonely vessel adrift in a fast [sic] ocean whose seas are sometimes calm and friendly, sometimes rough and menacing. The first requirement for staying afloat is to obey the rules of navigation dictated by the ocean itself. But the most diligent attention to these rules is no guarantee of permanent safety. The ship is far from watertight; ceaselessly, insidiously, it takes in water. Only a constant repetition of rites seems to keep it from sinking. (Girard 1977, 267)

The ritual functions to release the violence that builds up in the community. The escalation of the staged violence described earlier as "real" violence can be viewed as being of social and anthropological importance because during the overflow of violence the function of the ritual, which mediates between the sacred and the profane, falls apart. But paradoxically this has the effect of reinforcing the importance of the ritual function—to recapitulate, transgression is a way of breaking and yet reaffirming the law.

Girard echoes many of Durkheim's ideas about the social/anthropological bases of human sociality. In Durkheim's formulation of the *Homo Duplex* we experience the duality of human nature, which is both aware of the individual as well as the need for the social. Girard explores the omnipresence and omnipotence of violence which requires release through communal outlets.

Another point that warrants emphasis is the dualistic notion of the sacred. It was largely through the work of Durkheim's followers, namely Mauss, Hubert and Hertz, as well as the pioneering work of the College of Sociology (1937–1939), that we see a difference between formulations of the duality of the sacred, which Hertz identified as the "right" and the "left" sacred (in *Death and the Right Hand*, 1909) and Girard as the "beneficent" and the "maleficent" (Girard 1977, 257). Michael Taussig describes how negation is built into the word "sacred," in its meaning of accursed as well as holy, impure as well as pure (Taussig 1998, 349). The "right" sacred focuses on the more positive effects of the sacred: "those which preserve and lengthen life, which are conducive to health, social pre-eminence…those powers which are exercised in harmony with nature," whilst the "left" sacred focuses on "the powers of death and destruction, the sources of illness, disorder, epidemics, and crimes, everything that enfeebles, diminishes, corrupts, and decays" (Caillois 2001, 42–43). In *Violence and the Sacred* Girard promulgates the anthropological necessity of both aspects of the sacred. We need the more destructive effects of the sacred in order to perpetuate the generative side of life. Applying this to the football match and the escalating violence that ensues, one can argue that we are witnessing the anthropological necessity of the release of violence and the "mimetic" structure of violence is the first stage of outletting. The interaction of police/others does not serve to dampen the spirits and instead fuels the violence. During this phase, which I have described as the "real presence," the violence becomes all-consuming, serving to destroy everything with which it comes into contact. Here we are witnessing the phenomenon of football hooliganism and in terms of the above discussion the "left" sacred. Durkheim explains how, "the contagion is not a kind of secondary process by which sacredness propagates, once acquired, but is instead the very process by which sacredness is acquired" (Durkheim 1995, 328). From the first stage of mimetic violence to the second phase of the "real presence" of violence we experience something which is different not simply in degree but also in kind. In the mimetic stage violence is vented under controlled conditions. This is not transgressive. In the second phase we move beyond a rational understanding of violence to an irrational response which exceeds all boundaries and takes us to the experience of excess, or what Bataille would term *dépense*. In *The Accursed Share* (*La part maudite*, 1949) Bataille demonstrates the centrality of this idea of excess which in his terms denotes a shift from the "restricted economy" of the profane to a "general economy," which is where we experience the virulence of the sacred. In mimetic violence we experience the precarious relationship that exists between transgression and the taboo, but without the latter being broken. However, the "real presence" of violence entails a shattering of limits and a feeling of the loss of self through collective representation. This state resembles the Bakhtinian notion of the carnivalesque, "in which people can lose their individuality and cognitive control insofar as they choose to 'open' certain aspects of their sensuality to flux, interaction and absorption" (Mellor and Shilling 1997, 174).

It is only in the experience of *dépense* that we experience the sacred through the slippage of the ritual function. Therefore, it is only in instances of football hooliganism, where we see the extremes of violence, that we can speak of the sacred. In the post-Christian culture of the "death of God" one of the manifestations or expressions of the sacred is in the violent transgressions experienced in sport. Indeed the claim that football is the new religion in the twenty-first century is not merely media hyperbole. In this new religion we experience the sacred in instances of the greatest profanity and transgression.

Conclusion

The main findings in my paper are as follows: firstly, it is only in the "real presence" and not in the mimetic instances of violence that we can discuss the experience of the sacred. Superficially, we see aspects of religious behaviour in the chanting of the fans and the glorification of their heroes but it is only in the ritualistic mediations between the profane and the sacred that we can discuss what Durkheim identified as the elementary forms of religious behaviour. In the "collective effervescence" that results, we experience the transition from the profane to the sacred and then from the sacred to the profane. In the game we see the irrational bases of sociality which Durkheim claims underpin religion. Football-as-religion is situated on the knife-edge of creativity (the "right" sacred) and destruction (the "left" sacred) and we can interpret the cycle of violence and destruction in terms of appropriation. With the increasing commercialization and commodification of the sport, turbulence and violence is often the mechanism by which fans reassert control and identity. The affiliations that many fans have towards their teams are often construed in terms that are highly emotive and encompass notions of personal ancestry, history and hopes for the future (Eyre 1997, 6). Football, like religion, may function as a vehicle through which family values are passed down. Worpole argues that in secular life people often form ties with their local community which contributes to their emotional sense of belonging. Pledging loyalty towards the local team is often the way in which communities reinforce their identities. Violence operates as the means by which the local is asserted within the context of the global. Elias presents a convincing case when he discusses Le Bon's theories of mob violence in relation to football spectator violence. His argument is that the motivations are largely the same. The crowds riot because they are bereft of something. In Le Bon, *The Crowd* (1896) the factor of deprivation was bread; in this case of football, Elias argues, the rioters are deprived of meaning (existentially speaking). Being from the less affluent areas of town and with fewer possibilities of change, the football ground is an arena in which working-class males can use their masculinity as a weapon of attack, to avenge what they perceive as their less privileged status in society (Elias and Dunning 1986, 57). Thus they attempt to reclaim power and autonomy through violent means. This is yet another example which explains violence in sociological terms.

Secondly, football culture draws from the material symbols of Christianity both in specific images used and also in its use of a number of concepts that are religious. Examples include the notion of the saviour or the "chosen" one, the sacred, hallowed ground, the Day of Judgement, to name but a few. The match itself is a series of quasi-religious rituals from the quiet moments of contemplation to the exuberant transcendental heights of victory. However, beyond the explicit parallels, what is deeply religious about football is the experience of the numinous that it generates in its followers. In *The Idea of the Holy* (1917) Rudolf Otto discusses the two-part nature of the idea of the holy, that is, the rational factor and the non-rational aspect. The rational part can be quantified, conceptualized and articulated in positive terms. It includes the beliefs, practices and rituals that are handed down from generation to generation. Although these components give the religion structure and meaning, the ingredient that makes a religion *religious* is the quality of the numinous (the non-rational; Otto 1958, xvii). This is analogous to the feeling of the sacred experienced during the collective effervescence of the football match. The focus of this chapter has been on the numinous experience and the concomitant feelings of violence. It is the propensity to the sacred which is experienced during a match that encourages football to be conceived of as a religion.

Thirdly, and finally, in contemporary culture the sacred is experienced in the profane, and this is demonstrated in the example of football. Let me unpack this. Earlier I discussed the tendency to view the sacred and the profane in terms of a dichotomy: the sacred is what the profane is not and vice versa. In this post-Christian "death of God" climate the situation is very different. In the example of football culture I have established how it is precisely in the acknowledgement of the profanity and violation of the profane that the sacred is recovered. This is seen in football hooliganism, where the profane understanding of the sanctity of law and order is violated and we see instances of escalating violence, moving towards disaster and destruction. I also mentioned the detrimental impact that the commercialization and commodification of the sport can have on the psyche of the fans. Many of these practices can be viewed as sacrilegious, where the sanctity of the ontological reality of football-as-religion is defiled and the sport is conceived of in economic or business terms. In such cases violence is used as a means of reasserting identity and of re-establishing territorial boundaries. In football culture the sacred is experienced by metaphorically entering into the profane. In Girardian terms this can be seen as a way of realigning violence with the sacred.

11 Cultivated Outrage: World Wrestling Entertainment and the Religious Excess of Violence

Hugh S. Pyper*

Any British reader old enough to have been watching television in the 1960s and 70s will know that 4.00 on a Saturday afternoon was the witching hour for the discussion of wrestling. Millions of Britons were faced with the choice between watching Rugby League on BBC or Kent Walton and ITV wrestling. Nostalgic reminiscences of the epic battles of Big Daddy and Giant Haystacks, Jackie Pallo and Catweazle are close to the surface in the memories of a surprising number of older Britons.

Say one name to them, however, and there may be an interesting reaction: Mick McManus. He was the dirtiest fighter of the lot, for whose blood elderly ladies would scream. The level of hysteria that a traditionally repressed British audience could generate in response to McManus's constant use of his trademark straight-finger jab on the blind side of the referee was quite astonishing—and troubling.[1]

My thesis in this paper is that what Mick McManus was deliberately cultivating was the power of outrage and that this is one important secret in the otherwise baffling success of professional wrestling. ITV wrestling may be a relatively innocuous example of this, but I want to argue that the same mechanism is behind the phenomenal global reach of Vince McMahon's great commercial empire, World Wrestling Entertainment (WWE), with its shows now watched regularly by 60 million viewers in 90 countries.

Furthermore, I want to show that the WWE consciously uses religious imagery in its cultivation of outrage, and also explicitly connects its output to American foreign policy and the war on terror. It is an established fact in

* Hugh Pyper is Professor of Biblical Studies at the University of Sheffield. After an earlier career as a science teacher, he turned to biblical studies and has written widely on the appropriation of biblical texts in popular culture as well as in scientific writing, literature and music. His interest in wrestling goes back to wet Saturday afternoons in Edinburgh in the late 1960s.

research in this area that the viewing figures for wrestling are cyclical, with a clear correlation between the number of viewers and the level of concern about American national security and foreign policy (see Sammond 2005, 61). The WWE is peculiarly self-conscious about the manipulation of the dynamics of outrage but the same rhetorical and theatrical devices are at work in the way that violence is encouraged, condoned and justified in American foreign policy. The WWE is parasitic on wider political discourse but for that reason can provide a fascinating if worrying glimpse into the workings of that wider mechanism.

In particular, the use of religious imagery and narratives in the cultivation of outrage in professional sports entertainment not only exemplifies the power of religious imagery in this context, but also feeds off and in some ways feeds into the real rather than fantastic world of violence in contemporary political and religious events.

Outraged Innocence

First, then, let us look more closely at the dynamic of "outrage." It is a strange term. It describes an emotional condition—"I am outraged"—but also an event—"an outrage"—which I can commit. It carries with itself the sense of excess, a place "beyond rage" and thus of a limit transgressed. When limits are transgressed, we enter the realm of the religious.

The excess of outrage and its religious consequences can be seen in the biblical law which is designed to curb outrages, the *lex talionis*, the eye for an eye. "An eye for an eye" is often presented as if it was a simple statement of justice restored because a balance is regained. In fact, that is precisely what it is not. Both victim and perpetrator end up with one eye, which may look fair, but an essential element is left unaddressed.

The point is that what has happened is not just the loss of a body part but that the victim was innocent. He is not only physically injured but has had his innocence violated. The victim is not just injured, but outraged. The perpetrator, on the other hand, has his eye removed as a just punishment for an unprovoked attack. He may well be distressed by this, but he is unlikely to be outraged if he admits his guilt and no one who accepts the operation of the biblical law is likely to feel outrage on his behalf. A true restoration of the equivalence between victim and perpetrator would therefore demand either that the victim's innocence is restored to him or that the perpetrator has his innocence violated in turn.

The problem is that innocence, like virginity, is hard to restore. Removing the perpetrator's eye will not give the victim back his innocence. Neither will it necessarily make the perpetrator himself feel that he in turn has been the subject of an outrage. He would have the option of reacting like the good thief at the crucifixion who is able to accept his fate as a just punishment and is rewarded with a place in paradise. For the balance to be truly restored, the perpetrator must feel the same sense of outrage as the victim. The catch, however, and the reason why retribution spins so easily out of control, is that the only thing that will satisfy the victim that justice has been done and the moral balance has been restored is for the perpetrator to be convinced that justice has *not* been done to him and so that his moral world is out of balance.

The popular expression of this feeling is the clichéd refrain, "Hanging is too good for him." It is not enough that a murderer should die—after all, we all do that, good and bad alike—but he must experience the sense of anguish and betrayal that his victim and his victim's relatives have undergone.

So, paradoxically, the victim can only experience the punishment as fair if the perpetrator is convinced that it is unfair and that innocence has suffered. The easiest way of ensuring this, sad to say, is to wreak revenge on someone or something that the perpetrator holds dear and that cannot be held responsible for the original transgression. By targeting the perpetrator's loved ones, or his children, maybe he can be made to feel the anguish of innocence betrayed which the victim and his loved ones have felt. This is one of the complex reasons why the rape of civilian women becomes a tempting tactic of inflicting outrage on a hated enemy population.

Another and effective way to achieve the same end is to attack and deface inanimate objects and symbolic structures that the enemy hold dear and which in fact represent justice for them. By attacking these objects, they are provoked to outrage along the lines of, "I may have hurt you, but what did my flag, or my cherished sacred place, ever do to you?" There is a simple if horrid logic in the targeting of churches or mosques in reprisal attacks, or the escalation of the so-called Baedeker bombings in WW2 as Germany and Britain began deliberately to target historical monuments and cities precious to each other's cultural identity rather than industrial or military sites.

Any such discourse of innocence, justice and transgression is trespassing into religious language. The *lex talionis* sets out to exclude the excess of outrage which it seems to enforce. The question is: Where does the excess of injured innocence go and how is it discharged? The biblical answer is simple: " 'Vengeance is mine,' says the Lord, 'I will repay' " (Rom. 12:19).[2] God becomes the instrument for the restoring of order without the escalation of outrage of the innocent.

In the Hebrew Scriptures, this is not because he bears the outrage as the innocent victim, but because he has the resources only available to a god to outrage the innocence of those who are in worldly terms utterly corrupt and bereft of innocence. So, for instance, it is God who arranges for the massacre of the innocent firstborn children of the Egyptians in retribution for Pharaoh's oppressive regime. Innocence pays the price in a way that exonerates the Israelites from blame. God is thus the point of discharge for the excess that is generated by outrage.

Put another way, we could say that the need for such a point of discharge is one element in the need for a god. Religion feeds on and thus keeps in check the impulse of outrage by providing an outlet for the excess of injured innocence. Yet, given a situation where different religious systems are involved in a conflict, it becomes a potent source of potential outrages in itself. Many things are forgivable, but the deliberate desecration of a sacred symbol or space can be guaranteed to cause outrage in the enemy, and is therefore a tempting option for those who feel themselves the victims of outrageous injustice. An attack on the God who is the guarantor of justice is a particularly outrageous act.

Behind this spiral of excess is also an apocalyptic hope that outrage can be carried to such a degree as to dismay and disarm one's opponent. In biblical terms, this is one interpretation of the strange episode where the king of Moab sacrifices his firstborn son on the walls of his besieged city in the sight of the army of Israel (2 Kings 3:27). A "great wrath" comes upon Israel and they retire from the city. This seems an odd reaction, but may reflect the sort of despair that, for instance, the seemingly meaningless atrocities of the Lord's Resistance Army in Uganda can induce in the local population. A desperate act of outrage may overwhelm the enemy's emotional and spiritual resources for resistance.

As we have seen, it falls to God's role at times to inflict such a final outrage on Israel's enemies, or on Israel itself when it is rebellious. One sense at least of the word God is that which guarantees the balance of justice by absorbing and redistributing the excess of violence and the violation of innocence that is generated by the sense of outrage and which otherwise generates an endless cycle of attrition. On the other hand, that possibility of endless generation of outrage is exactly what the producers of popular spectacle would like to tap into.

WWE and the Spectacle of Excess

It is as an arena for generating and discharging that sense of excess that the world of wrestling is so intriguing and from which it derives much of its popular fascination. Nothing written on wrestling to my knowledge surpasses in insight Roland Barthes's classic essay in his collection *Mythologies*, which in English is entitled "The World of Wrestling" (Sammond 2005, 23–32).[3] Although Barthes is writing in 1952, long before the grand spectacle of the WWE, he is clear that the essence of wrestling is what he calls the "spectacle of excess." He even asserts that it has a "grandiloquence which must have been that of ancient theatres" (Sammond 2005, 24).

The theatricality is something he stresses, and which is stressed continually by those who defend professional wrestling against its detractors. Whoever complains, the argument goes, that Macduff always wins the fight against Macbeth at the end of Shakespeare's play? Barthes points out that the wrestler's main task is not to win, but to go through the expected motion of wrestling, what he calls "immediate pantomime." It shares with theatre the display of archetypal passions with the advantage that these are immediate and, mostly, non-verbal, although that latter observation needs to be further nuanced.

The great spectacle, Barthes tells us, is of "Suffering, Defeat and Justice" (Sammond 2005, 26–27). He quite rightly points out that wrestling is not sadistic; it is not about the infliction of suffering, but the intelligibility of suffering. The key point is justice, counterintuitive as this may seem in what to outsiders may seem at first a rule-less contest, and then a continuing series of transgression of what rules there are. This is to make a fundamental mistake. Law is the foundation of the spectacle. To quote Barthes again, "Justice is … the embodiment of a possible transgression; it is from the fact that there is a Law that the spectacle of the passions derives its value" (Sammond 2005, 29).

Barthes goes on to make the point that it is not the breach of official rules mediated by the referee that matters. What really riles the public is the cheat who claims the support of the rules to save his own skin, diving for the ropes to break a hold that his skill will not let him break, but who is quite prepared to punch and gouge behind the referee's back. We may go beyond Barthes's analysis here and see the referee as the embodiment of the blindness of official justice, while the audience become the outraged witnesses of an effectively condoned breach of the rules. This is a crucial dimension to the transaction in that it puts the crowd in the position of the arbiter of justice and yet denies it any power of redressing the balance. The crowd's own sense of justice is betrayed and yet it is unable to achieve redress. This is a collective outrage. To become truly caught up in the spectacle, the crowd must feel that its own standards and expectations are under threat.

This leads them to endorse the summary justice meted out by the victim, even—or, rather, especially—if that involves him in breaching the rules in his turn to return the outrage. "For a wrestling fan," writes Barthes, "nothing is finer than the revengeful fury of a betrayed fighter who throws himself vehemently not on a successful opponent but the smarting image of foul play" (Sammond 2005, 29).

The transgression of rules can become the justification for revenge. Manifest unfairness at the end of a given bout provides the cliff-hanger that can sustain storylines across several weeks of WWE output. When a favourite wrestler is beaten unfairly, the crowd is on tenterhooks to see retribution enacted, maybe not this time, but in a rematch. The opponent must not only be beaten but humiliated. As Lee Benaka puts it, "The spectators feel immensely powerless and can only protest and wait, like Job, for justice to be served and evil to be banished, usually in the next pay-per-view WWF extravaganza. In the depths of despair, the fan is forced to hope that the cosmic order of the wrestling world will be restored through the ritual of the grudge match and wait for their idols to right evils" (1990, ch. 10).

The physical action in the ring is only part of the spectacle. Equally important is the wrestler's ability "on the mike," his confidence and inventiveness with language in trading insults and verbal humiliation with his opponents. A surprisingly large proportion of any WWE broadcast is taken up with wrestlers issuing challenges to each other and responding to the verbal provocation of their opponents. If, however, the wrestler can not only insult his opponent but can outrage the crowd, then that is all to the good. The skilful wrestler or his writers then find the "hook" which will lead the crowd to feel that their own innocence has been outraged and the excess punishment meted out by the wrestler is all the more satisfying.

Moreover, the WWE has gone further than most of its competitors in going behind the scenes of the wrestling, showing supposedly candid shots of wrestlers confronting each other in the locker room to give further back stories to the actual bout. Complex storylines involving various acts of disrespect not only to the wrestlers, but to their girlfriends and families, are played out in what has been called "masculine melodrama" or "soap-opera for men" (see Sammond 2005, 33–66). The audience knows that the wrestlers in the ring in front of them are not just there to fight for a title, but to settle scores. Outrages have already occurred before anyone sets foot into the public arena and so the escalation of violence in the search for revenge is something that the crowd expects and can condone.

Barthes's insights are interestingly borne out by a piece of research published in the prestigious letter pages of Nature entitled "Empathic neural responses are modulated by the perceived fairness of others" (Singer et al. 2006). The researchers found, admittedly in a rather small sample, that there is a clear difference in the chemical reactions in male and female brains to the sight of a rule-breaker getting his comeuppance. Men show a lack of empathetic response to pain if they witness a social transgressor being punished and an increased activity in reward related areas, expressed as a desire for revenge. They only show empathy to what they perceive as a fair player. Women, on the other hand, show no such differentiation.

If true, this pleasure in the spectacle of the perceived villain being punished has a deep biological root, and we need not be at all surprised that it seems to have an almost universal cultural appeal. Barthes's final summary may seem exaggerated to those resistant to the call of wrestling. "What is portrayed by wrestling is … an understanding of things; it is the euphoria of men raised for a while above the constitutive ambiguity of everyday situations and placed before the panoramic view of a univocal Nature, in which signs at last correspond to causes, without obstacle, without evasion, without contradiction." The religious implication is spelled out by him: "no-one can doubt that wrestling holds that power of transmutation which is common to the Spectacle and to Religious Worship" (Sammond 2005, 31–32).

WWE and the Gulf Wars

Even in Barthes's day, he was aware of a distinctive element in the American version of wrestling in its appeal to patriotism and political events as a way of communicating the moral status of the ring participants and creating heroes and villains. What is particularly interesting here is the way in which political and religious elements are used and fused, as a disturbing mirror of political discourse in the US. There is a strange dynamic here as the WWE seeks to boost its ratings by buying into what it conceives of as popular stereotypes. The "real world" provides the narrative framework for the wrestling event. At the same time, politicians use the same rhetorical tropes to influence public opinion in the real world, mythologizing it in terms of the confrontation between heroic representatives of good and evil.[4]

From the point of view of the WWE, a great deal of effort in building storylines can be saved by latching onto figures whose back history of conflict can be taken for granted by the audience. The sense of communal frustration and the inchoate awareness that the excess of outrage has not yet been discharged is available for the wrestlers and commentators to play on.

At times, this is quite blatant. During the First Gulf War, the undying feud between the Iron Sheik and the blue-eyed blond American icon Hulk Hogan was a great set piece. What has happened in relation to the Second Gulf War has been rather intriguing. In itself, it epitomizes the politics of outrage. To fly civilian airliners into the iconic buildings of the World Trade Centre was as clear an attempt to outrage American public opinion as could be imagined. It was justified by Al Qaeda as its response to the perceived outrage of American assistance to Israel and its other interventions in the Arab world.

The US response was equally explicit in its invocation of the dynamics of outrage. The much-touted phrase "shock and awe" used in describing American reprisals reveals that military action was unequivocally aimed at evoking an emotional response from America's enemies. As the originators of the strategy, Harlan K. Ullman and James P. Wade, define it under its more formal title of the doctrine of rapid dominance, it is designed to "so overload an adversary's perceptions and understanding of events that the enemy would be incapable of resistance at the tactical and strategic level," thereby inducing a state of helplessness and lack of will (Ullman et al. 1996, section 25).[5] Although the word was not used, the programmatic use of outrage is clear.

From the point of view of the WWE and its writers, however, there was a complication in that the response to the outrage of 9/11 was not at first focused on the people of Iraq in political rhetoric. The war was a war against terror and a war to liberate the Iraqis from the murderous tyranny of Saddam. In contrast to the situation in the first Gulf War where the Iraqis could be portrayed as the aggressors, playing out this new conflict by introducing an Iraqi wrestler as a villain was actually not in the spirit of American foreign policy. Fortunately, an obvious villain was at hand.

The real source of outrage, or at least the place where it could most easily be discharged, was France, which refused to join the coalition against Iraq. Here was a readymade story of betrayal and refusal to respect the rules that could provide a framework for a series of bouts. Within weeks of beginning of the Gulf War, "La Résistance" had appeared on the scene—two handsome but insufferably arrogant and superior French wrestlers, who repeatedly had their asses whupped good and proper by good down-home American boys.

One of these wrestlers, René Duprée, was then given his own character. In a typical scene, accompanied by Fifi the poodle, he brought a full French dinner into the ring together with a model of the Eiffel Tower in order to educate the audience he taunted as barbarians and to insult American womanhood. This was too much for crowd favourite John Cena, whose gimmick is white street rap, who unceremoniously dumped the whole lot including the wrestler out of the ring.[6] Duprée's transgression of the bounds of redneck American masculinity and his arrogant disrespect for the American way of life, not to mention the Iraq war mean that cultural and sexual definitions of outrage are brought together in a match between the crude but honest, in-your-face street energy of the New World and the decadence of the old.

As time went on, however, the political mood changed. American soldiers died in Iraq at the hands of the people who, so the public rhetoric had it, should have been grateful to be rescued by them. This ingratitude added insult to injury. The WWE came up with an ingenious take on this mounting tension by bringing in the character of Mohammed Hassan, an

Arab-American wrestler—a real Iraqi was still, perhaps, a step too far. Hassan was "played" by an Italian-Jordanian wrestler brought up in the US, Mark Copani. Hassan entered the ring wearing a stereotypical Arab head-dress to the strains of Arabic music reminiscent of the call of the muezzin, accompanied by his stereotypically swarthy sidekick who encouraged him from ringside with loud expostulations in Arabic (or so it was represented; it was actually Farsi) and was always ready to deal a treacherous blow to Hassan's opponent on the blind side of the referee.

As an example of how this played out, we can take the bout between Muhammad Hassan and Gerry "The King" Lawler in Puerto Rico in which we see the principle of outrage exemplified, with a distinct nod towards the religious dimension of the conflict.[7] The crowd is first shown a flashback scene from a debate between Hassan and Daivari and two veteran commentators of the WWE, Jim Ross and Jerry Lawler, where the two young Arab-Americans launch a vicious attack on the older men. This is clearly a more serious breach of the conventions than an attack on one of the other wrestlers as these are not combatants but "innocent" bystanders. This then cuts to an interview with Hassan in which he accuses the WWE of showing only part of the tape, an action which he relates to the general bias of the media's treatment of Arab-Americans. He protests that Lawler's taunt that the two Arab-Americans should "go home" has been cut. In his view, the two commentators "got what they deserved." In an intriguing twist which exemplifies the way in which political and racial tensions are grist to the WWE writers' mill, he then expresses his pleasure that he heard he had the chance to fight in Puerto Rico. If anyone should understand the Arab-American, it is the Puerto Rican audience, he says. To the accompaniment of increasing jeers from the crowd, he points out that Puerto Rico is not a state and its inhabitants are all second-class citizens. He then goes on to express his disappointment that he and Daivari have been treated with prejudice even in Puerto Rico and ends by saying that if the Puerto Rican people want to make an enemy of him, they are welcome.

The WWE is obviously playing with something powerful but dangerous here which was to backfire on them. In a later match, Hassan was seen "praying" and surrounded by five men in stereotypical terrorist outfits in his defeat of another iconic figure, the Undertaker. This recorded footage was shown on the UPN television channel just hours after the London bombings of 7 July 2006. The media attention this drew prompted UPN to pressure WWE to drop the character and Muhammad Hassan was removed by being reportedly severely injured by the Undertaker in a return match. Mark Copani has subsequently left the WWE.

Vince McMahon and the Clash with God

The WWE is always vulnerable to the intrusion of reality on its storylines, all the more so because it itself blurs the boundaries between fiction and fact. Nowhere is this more fascinatingly the case than in the career of the multi-millionaire boss of the WWE, Vincent McMahon. One of McMahon's innovations was to sell the WWE as "sports entertainment" rather than as legitimate sport. Here he played with the sacred notion of "kayfabe," a term used by fans and insiders to describe the maintenance of the illusion that the fights are genuine and not staged. I have discussed elsewhere the peculiar way in which McMahon occupies a structural position in the WWE which is formally remarkably similar to that of Yahweh in the biblical story (Pyper 2006). In both stories, the boss behind the scenes who is the ultimate arbitrator and decides which characters survive and what stories are played out is himself implicated in the story, thus complicating the position of the one who represents absolute justice outside the story.

For those who might think this analogy far-fetched, I can do no better than to refer to a storyline in the WWE which I would not have dared to invent. In the story McMahon, determined to ruin the career of a confessedly Christian wrestler, Shawn Michaels, announces that he is proclaiming a new religion, McMahonism, where he, and Shane, his "only begotten son" (*sic*)—his son in real life and an executive director of the family firm—are the sole authorities within his world, the world of the WWE wrestling ring. He challenges Shawn Michaels to a tag team match: McMahon father and son versus Shawn Michaels and—God. The match took place on 30 April 2006 at *Backlash 2006*, held in Lexington, Kentucky.

The DVD of this episode reveals Mr McMahon pretending to turn water into wine and attempting to lay healing hands on a pneumatic young lady's chest. We are treated to the spectacle of McMahon and son in the ring taunting God for being too chicken to show up, at which point there is a flash of (stage) lightning, a burst of thunder, and a mysterious light begins to move towards the ring as McMahon eggs God on.

What is fascinating here is the way in which outrage can go too far. The crowd just cannot quite get behind this scenario and seems puzzled as to what reaction is expected. What is this strange boundary that can be overstepped where pantomimic outrage becomes a real disquiet? There is a camp quality to this discourse of excess, but perhaps what happens here is that a real foundational symbol within the social system is coming too near to being threatened.

A similar moment when the boundaries are transgressed is to be seen in footage of the wrestler Raven, an antihero in the rival wrestling company of the 1990s, ECW (Extreme Championship Wrestling). As its title indicates, ECW was characterized by a level of violence and dare-devil moves and stunts that was designed to push the boundaries of the genre. Even its fans, however, reacted negatively to an episode where Raven lashed his opponent to a wooden cross in the ring. The crowd went silent and Raven had to appear after the commercial break and apologize for the excess.[8]

The Reality of Outrage: The Case of Chris Benoit

Truth, however, has a well-known way of not only being stranger but more brutal than fiction. It is instructive to see how the WWE management deals with unplanned and genuine horror and outrage which breaks into its world of cultivated outrage. It is also sobering for those who affect an ironic distance in dealing with the world of wrestling. The cartoon violence can come home to roost.

This became clear when the news broke that the well-respected Canadian wrestler Chris Benoit had been found dead. Sadly, it is not uncommon for one of the stars of the WWE to die. The constant punishment that their bodies receive which often leads to a spiral of drug-taking to relieve pain and then to counter the depressive effects of painkillers, the pressure to achieve and maintain an almost inhuman level of physical development, the availability of alcohol, the contrasts between in-ring adulation and the difficulty of making and maintaining close relationships in a career that involves constant travelling; all these conspire to shorten the lives of professional wrestlers. Firm statistics are difficult to unearth, but professional wrestlers are reportedly 20 times more likely to die before the age of 45 than professional footballers. Since 1997, some 65 out of around 1000 professional wrestlers in the US have died before the age of 50.[9]

In November 2005, Eddie Guerrero, an immensely popular Latino wrestler who had a well-documented history of battles with addiction, died of a heart attack aged only 38. His death was marked by a series of memorial programmes and televised testimonials from his colleagues. The crowd still chants his name as his nephew and his fellow Latino wrestlers dedicate their fights to him, pointing heavenward as they do so in the WWE's own version of a rite of collective mourning and memory.

The breaking news that Benoit had died on 25 July 2007, aged 40, thus prompted the WWE management to run a testimonial programme to him. He had, after all, won many championships and was widely considered to be one of the best technical wrestlers of his generation. In addition, he had never been involved in any particularly outrageous stories outside the ring and to many fans he represented an older set of values where skill and courage in the ring were the point of the display.

Unsettling news followed, however. Benoit had been found dead with his wife and his seven-year-old son. Rumours soon began that they had been the victims of a murder plot. Some internet fans even speculated whether the whole story was a piece of kayfabe. By a coincidence of timing, the WWE was running at that time a story where Mr McMahon had just been seen to be blown up in a car and was presumed dead. This was one story very few fans bought, but it may have contributed to an atmosphere of uncertainty about the Benoit case.

Subsequent police announcements, however, revealed the shocking scenario that Benoit had killed his wife and son before hanging himself. It also appeared that the murders had been spread over a weekend, with his wife dying on the Friday, his son on the Saturday, and Benoit himself on the Sunday. In a bizarre detail, he had laid a Bible by the body of each of his victims.

The WWE response was swift. Completely disregarding the storyline of his own death, Vince McMahon made a short special announcement which was notable for its rhetoric of finality. He made it clear that not only this incident, but Benoit himself, would have no further mention on the WWE. All merchandise with Benoit's name was quietly removed from the WWE outlets, and matches which included him have been edited out of its back catalogue of videos.

At the same time, the WWE issued a statement attempting to scotch the growing rumours that Benoit's actions had been a product of what is known as "roid rage": the ungovernable fits of extreme and violent anger that are a side-effect of the abuse of steroids. The argument they used was that the murders showed signs of premeditation as they were spread out over a whole weekend. The detail of the placing of the Bibles was also invoked as a proof that this was a considered action. This is the final statement on the matter WWE issued. It is not difficult to see that the main concern here is not so much Benoit's reputation but to reassert the WWE's claim that it has cleaned up its act on drugs in the wake of a number of narrow brushes with the law on steroid abuse in the 1990s.

The fans reacted with confusion, as evidenced by discussions on the numerous websites devoted to the heroes of the WWE. How were they now to approach the memory of someone they had admired for his physical prowess and his aggression (Benoit's nickname was "the rabid wolverine") when he had transgressed one of the few absolute taboos of the moral universe of the WWE, child murder?[10] Here, if anywhere, innocence had been outraged.

Indeed, it was known to fans that Benoit's son suffered from a congenital disease (Fragile X Syndrome), compounding his vulnerability, and that his great joy in life was to watch his father wrestle.[11] There are scenes, now very difficult to watch, of the frail little boy kissing his bloodied father at ringside after matches. A final awful irony was in the rumour that forensic evidence suggested the child had died as the result of Benoit applying his signature finishing move, the "Crippler Cross-face." Fan websites oscillated between absolute denunciations of Benoit as a monster and the desire to honour his achievements without being seen to condone his actions, which were most often put down to some kind of mental instability.

The case is still under review and the whole matter is genuinely distressing. Any glib comment would be distasteful. Still, it is telling that, faced with a real situation which genuinely seemed to rupture the taboos that the WWE lives by flouting, its corporate response is an imposed silence. It needs the taboos to be maintained if it is to retain the possibility of flirting with breaking those taboos. Benoit's actions not only reveal the tastelessness of the whole structure but also put it at risk. The outrageous world of the WWE depends on deep religiously sanctioned boundaries to be in place before it can take the risks of flouting them in the special place of the arena and the alternative reality of kayfabe.

The detail of the Bible beside each body is also uncanny. By most accounts, Benoit was not particularly religious. Several of his fellow wrestlers, however, testified that he was shattered by the death of his friend Eddie Guerrero who was well known to be a regular Bible reader and to have a strong Christian faith which he would share with his friends. An article by Cordell Waldron on the blog "Iconic Books" raises the question in an entry on the murders as to what the symbolism of placing of a Bible beside the victim might be, but also and perhaps more importantly, how the media construe this gesture (Waldron 2007). Most often, it is interpreted as a kind of consolation to the victims. A leading Canadian forensic psychologist interprets this as part of a wider syndrome in murder-suicides. These are typically carried out by a psychotically depressed father in the belief that the whole family would be better off dead.

However, the blogger goes on to ask how the media would have interpreted a Qur'an placed in a similar way and how CDs of heavy metal music are also interpreted when found at the scene of a murder or suicide. Does the gesture suggest that there is a biblical justification for the act, or that the book itself is somehow implicated in the motivation of the killer? These questions cannot be answered in this case, but the point is well made. The Bible itself, in one reading, lives off the dynamic of outrage and outrage can spill out of its pages, so to speak.

Uncontainable Outrage

What this awful case reveals is how the WWE depends on a complex negotiation between the "real," the "believable" and the "fake," a set of categories where the boundaries are constantly shifting. The breaching of the rules
about physical violence or the sexual innuendo of the shows is allowable as
long as it can be contained in the ring. However, it gains its energy by leach-
ing off elements that are outside the ring. The strange category of kayfabe is
vulnerable both to fakery and reality.

It also depends on a certain sort of religious and political semi-literacy in
its audience. As a "guilty pleasure," it provides a locus for excess which can
only be enjoyed as such because there are constant reminders of the boundaries which are being exceeded. Some of these boundaries are provided by
what might be called guilty Christianity. When explicitly Christian figures are
invoked in the ring, they are usually seen as killjoys. No nice churchgoing
boy or girl ought to be attending a WWE show or admitting that they watch
it, but after all, it is "only" entertainment. The fact that religious leaders may
denounce the pernicious effects of the WWE on adults and especially children only increases the guilty pleasure of transgression. Once again, the
WWE has to play a dangerous game of keeping the outrage of conservative
religious figures at a sufficient level to appear shocking without provoking a
major moral or legislative backlash.

In the ring, Vince McMahon is a strange sort of fallen God, a source of
sovereign power. Outside the ring, he is a businessman at the mercy of
shareholders, financial markets, the legal requirements of the state, the pay-
ing public and the wider public opinion of those who do not pay for his
product.[12] He makes his living by provoking outrage, but an outrage too far
can spill out of the ring and damage his credibility not just with viewers but
with commercial sponsors. Religion, and specifically biblically-based Christianity, is one of the most powerful and easily worked arenas of outrage but,
for that very reason, carries a dangerous potential to disrupt the fantasy and
to exact its own kind of revenge. The dynamics of the cycle of outrage
demand that it constantly risks imploding.

What is true of the WWE, however, is, as we have seen, true of the Bible
itself. The instability of the WWE is parasitic on, but also a *mise en abyme* of,
the dynamics of divine sovereignty and the claim to biblical authority. The
Bible's fantasies of violence and revenge are contained by the social structures both of the church and of the legal systems of society. As Kierkegaard
points out in his *Fear and Trembling*, the same pastor who is preaching the
sacrifice of Abraham would be the first to denounce a member of his congre-
gation who claimed divine or biblical justification for the attempted murder

of his son (Kierkegaard 1985, 58–59). The dynamics of outrage can be contained by being enacted in the privileged space of the wrestling ring or within the pages of the Bible, but this process can be reversed. The contained and choreographic violence of the ring, or the Bible, can be devastating when it spills out into real life.[13] With this in mind, every DVD of a WWE event begins with a series of clips of real accidents and injuries sustained by the wrestlers and the stark message, "Please. Don't try this at home." Could a case be made that every copy of the Bible should contain the same warning?

Notes

Chapter 1

1. An earlier version of this article appeared as "Posting Images on the Web: The Creative Viewer and Non-Violent Resistance against Terrorism," *Material Religion* 2.2: 146–73. See this article for examples of the images posted.
2. For a useful annotated bibliography see Campbell 2003, 363–68.
3. See, for example, Bunt 2004 and Brasher 2001.
4. See Turkle 1995. Turkle's work has been both developed and criticized. See for example Dawson and Cowan 2004 and Hoover et al. 2004.
5. See, for example, Campbell 2005; Rheingold 1993 and 2000; and Wellman 1999.
6. See especially Cowan's discussion on "Online Community: Illusion or the Illusion of Reality?" (2005: 54–58).
7. Durkheim 2001 [1912], 18.
8. See Morgan 2005.
9. See, for example, Bourdieu 1992.
10. I am grateful to Alfie Dennan for his time and assistance, including an extended interview in Camden Town, London, 25 October 2005.
11. Jolyon Mitchell, personal interview with Alfie Dennan, Camden Town, London, 25 October 2005.
12. See Bellah 1970, especially 172–86. For a critical analysis of the term "civil religion," see Demerath 2003, 348–58.
13. I have fused Edward Bailey's definitions found in *Implicit Religion* (1998, 22–25).
14. Jolyon Mitchell, personal interview with Alfie Dennan, Camden Town, London, 25 October 2005.
15. http://www.notinthenameofpeace.com/?p=55 is now no longer available on the Web.

Chapter 2

1. For the superhero as an archetype see *The Myth of the American Superhero* (Lawrence and Jewett 2002).
2. The interaction between comic books and the Bible is not new. In an "alternative history" set in a misogynistic Victorian England, Wonder Woman herself is forced to act in a theatrical production of "Susannah Battles the Elders," "Eve Conquers the Snake" and "Lady Samson and the Temple" (Messner Loebs, et al. 1997). It has become increasingly common to re-imagine the Bible in comic

book form such as in *The Lion Graphic Bible* (Maddox and Anderson 1998). Biblical scholars are beginning to analyse this interaction, although rarely as a means of developing new understandings of biblical characters. The online *SBL Forum* from the Society of Biblical Literature includes examples (www.sbl-site.org).

3. Carey Moore's commentary on Judith is the most comprehensive available to date. Also see Otzen (2002), Craven (1983) and Enslin and Zeitlin (1972). For a Judith bibliography see Craven (2003).

4. As of November 2007.

5. Particularly Artemis (i.e. Vol.2, Iss.97, 1996) and Donna Troy (i.e. Vol.3, Iss.1, 2005).

6. A note on comic referencing: I am using one possible classification. The issue number is stated on the front page of the comic book but the volume is date dependent. This prevents confusion between numerically identical issues.

7. Due to the complexities of retroactive continuity there are multiple creation stories for most comic book characters. Ares does appear in Volume 1—and is just as much of a villain as he is in Volume 2. He tries to ensure that the Allied Forces in World War II are defeated, sets up a home on Mars (subduing the Martians in the process) and attempts to overthrow the Gods of his original home, Olympus.

8. On the subject of irony in the Book of Judith see Moore (1985, 78–85).

9. This is one of the most notorious events in American comic book history, dividing fans and alienating much of the female readership because of the sheer violent, unnecessary brutality of the story. That the rape itself was a piece of retroactive continuity means that the after affects of the rape on Sue were never seen—only the rape itself (in flashback).

10. All traces of the Roman were later removed.

11. There are many moments in the narrative where Wonder Woman could be understood as a female Christ. At one point she is near death when Poseidon takes her into the ocean and gives her new life (just like John the Baptist). When she is "reborn" (the actual word used) she appears a long way above the water so the sky is her background and she is completely bathed in a yellow and red light and she is, of course, in the crucifixion pose (Vol.2, Iss.7, 1987).

12. Cf. Artemisia Gentileschi's "Judith Beheading Holofernes," Theophile Bigot's "Judith and Holofernes," Caravaggio's "Judith Beheading Holofernes." For discussion on depictions of Judith in art and culture see Bal (1994), Stocker (1998) and Stone (1992).

13. Although God is far less present in the Book of Judith than any of Wonder Woman's Olympian Gods.

14. An interesting point about this bondage was raised by Greg Garrett who suggests that this is a simplistic and conservative application of the Akedah (binding of Isaac, Genesis 22:1-10; Garrett 2006).

15. For discussions of Judith in relation to Freud's castration theory see Stocker (1998) and Bal (1994, 7).

16. The most recent writer of *Wonder Woman*, Gail Simone, is the creator of the now infamous phrase "Women in Refrigerators" (WiR) referring to the seemingly inevitable killing, maiming and depowerment of female comic book

superheroes. It developed from her website of the same name, detailing these events (www.unheardtaunts.com/wir/index.html).

17. "Profile: Lynndie England," *BBC News*. http://news.bbc.co.uk/1/hi/world/americas/4490795.stm

18. In April 2004 reports of rape, murder, torture and abuse of Iraqi prisoners at the hands of US soldiers at Abu Ghraib prison were made graphically public. These were in the form of photographs showing soldiers posing with prisoners forced into degrading and humiliating positions. Photographs also depicted soldiers in the process of beating prisoners and taunting them with dogs. Prior to public awareness of these actions the Taguba Report was commissioned to investigate allegations of abuse (January 2004). The report, which was leaked to the public in May 2004, concluded that between August 2003 and February 2004 several US soldiers breached international law and senior leaders failed to prevent detainee abuse (Article 15-6 2004).

19. For discussions of Wonder Woman's virginity, see Salek (2003).

Chapter 5

1. For an analysis utilizing a different reading of "apocalypse" see Stone 2001.

2. See, for example, the literature that has been generated by the *Matrix* trilogy of films, e.g. Flannery-Dailey and Wagner 2001; Lawrence 2004; Baker 2006.

3. This is, of course, a long-standing motif in both science fiction and horror, traceable back at least to Mary Shelley's *Frankenstein* (1818). Within the genre of science fiction, the idea that science and (particularly nuclear) technology can backfire and bring with it unintended and negative consequences is found in a range of classic films, such as *Them* (1954), where atomic testing produces a species of killer ants, *The Day the Earth Caught Fire* (1961), where simultaneous nuclear bomb tests by Russia and the USA knock the earth out of its orbit towards the sun. It is also a major theme in *Godzilla (Gojira)* and its sequels (see Noriega 1987; Napier 1993).

4. This shift is perhaps expressed in no better example than in *12 Monkeys*, which is based on the 1962 Chris Marker film, *La Jetée*. In Marker's film, humanity is wiped out by nuclear weapons, while in *12 Monkeys*, as we have seen, the medium of destruction has shifted to a supervirus.

5. Quoted on the Director and Writer's commentary on the *28 Days Later* DVD.

6. Of course, this would entail the belief that the events described in the prophecies were then prevented from occurring by agents from the future.

7. This draws parallels with older, Cold War-era films, which according to Broderick, were often "highly reactionary" in nature: "While some films have explored (albeit fleetingly) post-holocaust life as a site for ideological contestation, the cinematic renderings of long-term post-nuclear survival appear highly reactionary, and seemingly advocate reinforcing the symbolic order of the status quo via the maintenance of conservative social regimes of patriarchal law (and lore). In so doing, they articulate a desire for (if not celebrate) the fantasy of nuclear Armageddon as the anticipated war which will annihilate the oppressive

burdens of (post)modern life and usher in the nostalgically yearned-for less complex existence of agrarian toil and social harmony through ascetic spiritual endeavours" (Broderick 1993b, n.p.).

8. This "Noah's Ark" theme is also found in *The Day the Earth Caught Fire*, although in this film the "Ark" (if not "New Jerusalem") is situated on another planet (see Sontag 1967, 215).

9. To give an example from another genre of film, the narrative of the film *Titanic* is as much about the tragedy of Jack Dawson and Rose DeWitt Bukater, as it is about the loss of an ocean liner.

10. Several of the films I have discussed feature the motif of the hero or heroine sacrificing themselves for others and/or in order to avert the cataclysm. In *Deep Impact*, for example, the two lead characters sacrifice themselves for others; the Messiah crew crashing their spacecraft into a large chunk of the meteor to destroy it (the first batch of warheads having split it in two) and Jenny Lerner giving up her place in the "Noah's Ark" caves for a mother and her child. Like the Messiah's Crew, Bruce Willis's character in *Armageddon* (Harry Stamper) also sacrifices himself to stay behind to manually detonate the warhead while the rest of his crew escape the meteor. Jericho Cane also, as discussed above, throws himself on St Michael's sword in order to thwart Satan in *End of Days*. Finally, at the climax of *Independence Day* the character played by Randy Quaid (Russell Casse) pilots his plane into an alien's craft beam weapon generator in order to prevent it from being fired.

11. Indeed, to return to an earlier point, it is interesting to note that in two of the films in particular (*The Day After Tomorrow* and *The Core*), the hero(es) and heroines are scientists of some form or other.

12. Indeed, Schwarzenegger's character and Willis's in *12 Monkeys* are both noteworthy for being radically different, and significantly more vulnerable from the traditional action hero roles that both of them are typically associated with. As the writer of *End of Days*, Andrew Marlowe has noted in respect to Schwarzenegger's character, "We always see Arnold as the action hero, larger-than-life character. I wanted to take that and bring it down more to a human level, show him a little bit more down and out, and take him on more of a character journey in the middle of an action movie" (quoted on the "Writer and Director's Commentary" DVD feature to *End of Days*).

This point is echoed by the film's director, Peter Hyams, who observes that in this role Schwarzenegger "plays probably the most vulnerable character he's ever played, and the most accessible and touchable character" (ibid.). Similarly, Terry Gilliam has described how part of his decision to cast Bruce Willis in *12 Monkeys* was an attempt to put "him into situations and [ask] of him things I don't think he's ever done before or that people haven't seen him do." In particular, Gilliam was interested in attempting to tone down the image that Willis had been associated with through his *Die Hard* films, and create a much more vulnerable character than audiences would, until that point, associate with him. Indeed, the finale of *12 Monkeys* was the first time that an audience would have ever seen Willis die on screen (he would subsequently do so again in *Armageddon* three years later; in Lafrance n.d.; see also Fulton and Pepe 1998).

Chapter 6

1. Although very transient, some of the discussion forums and websites featuring guided questions still exist. These include denominational sites (e.g. Presbyterian Church, USA via their guide for viewers at http://www.pcusa.org/today/media/passion/index.htm), non-denominational religious sites such as Christianity Today (http://www.christianitytoday.com/ct/movies/reviews/2004/passionofthechrist.html?start=3#talk), and "The Premiere International Fan Site," which cultivated support for the film on its website (http://www.passion-movie.com/ with a forum available at http://fansofthepassionofthechrist.yuku.com/). Such forums, as well as blogs, encouraged a personal commentary on the film, as well as offering "answers" to questions about the meaning/interpretation of the film.
2. Allen lays a series of charges against the film and its subject matter, including that the Gospels are not historically accurate, the film erroneously constructs period detail, and the text has an anti-Semitic tone, partially explained by Gibson's application of Anne Catherine Emmerich's *The Dolorous Passion of Our Lord Jesus Christ*.
3. Prince notes that the cinematography "emulates the look of old masters" but that "its blood spurts, prosthetic wounds, and slow-motion inserts, places the violence in a cinematic vernacular" (2006, 19). This is true enough, but the overarching representation of Jesus is contextualized by previous depictions in other media.
4. It is significant to point out too that those spectators not familiar with Catholic ideology will not have the same devotional relationship to the suffering either, and will most likely feel the assault most keenly in terms of the counterfactual. In addition, the scarcity of recognizable images may clarify why the photography book accompanying the film (Gibson, Duncan and Antonello 2004) includes only four stills of the beating (and three of witnesses), yet the scene is so central.
5. See Allen (2005, 179–82) for detailed discussion of the scene's inspiration, and Prince (2006, 15–17) for historical accuracy.
6. The timing is based upon the original British DVD version (Icon Home Entertainment 2004); the running time for the film will be longer by approximately 4 per cent due to the differing number of frames per second.
7. Although traditionally attributed to St. Bonaventure, more recent scholarship has suggested John de Caulibus.
8. Enders (2006, 191) inserts her own secondary aspect of realism, that of the use of unfamiliar languages to connote the historically "real."

Chapter 9

1. Originally budgeted at $12 million, *Heaven's Gate* eventually cost $36 million, and its ignominious box-office performance ($1.5 million domestic) contributed to the end of United Artists' tenure as a separate Hollywood financier-distributor. With respect to Scorsese's preceding features, *Raging Bull* (1980) cost $17 million,

but returned just $10 million domestically, while *The King of Comedy* (1983) cost $20 million, but returned just $1.2 million domestically.

2. For more on the initial, aborted attempt to make *The Last Temptation of Christ*, see Christie and Thompson (2003, 116–22), Jenkins (1988), and Kelly (1992, 161–80).

3. Universal hired Tim Penland of Christian Marketing to work as a liaison with Christian groups, but he resigned in June 1988 upon reading an early, subsequently changed draft of Paul Schrader's script for *The Last Temptation of Christ* that had been obtained by and distributed within the Christian community. Another flashpoint was the postponement by Universal because of post-production delays of a screening of a rough cut of the film for religious leaders scheduled for the same month, this despite the studio rescheduling the screening for 12 July.

4. For detailed accounts of the campaign waged against *The Last Temptation of Christ*, see Lyons (1997, 160–75) and Riley (2003, 18–28).

5. Among the theatre chains that at least initially refused to screen *The Last Temptation of Christ* were General Cinema, Loews Theaters, Edwards Cinemas, Carmike Cinemas, Mann Theaters and, as before, United Artists Theaters.

6. For more on the protests that met the film's release in the USA and the trouble that accompanied its release in Greece, see Riley (2003, 28–29 and 31); for more on the violence that resulted upon the film's release in France, see Lyons (1997, 221 n. 71). Kazantzakis's novel when published in 1951 had itself been the cause of controversy in Greece, and had nearly seen him excommunicated from the Greek Orthodox Church.

7. Recorded by Romantic novelist and poet Clemens Brentano, Emmerich's description of events was first published in 1833.

8. Paula Fredriksen notes that Outreach, the company hired by Icon, produced "promotional materials—door hangers, banners, signs, posters, study guides, and other such spin-off tchotchkes—in flood-tide quantities," not to mention "250,000 movie-related DVDs" that were mailed "out to ministers throughout the country" (2006, 95).

9. For both a further consideration of the similarities apparent regarding *The Last Temptation of Christ* and *The Passion of the Christ* and a discussion of the films' relation that differs significantly from that which is presented by this paper, see Middleton (2004).

10. Gibson has been insistent regarding the "truthfulness" of *The Passion of the Christ*, declaring that the film represents Christ's Passion "just the way it happened. It's like traveling back in time and watching the events unfold exactly as they occurred.... We've done the research. I'm telling the story as the Bible tells it" (Levine 2004, 138). However, apart from this dissimulating the film's relation to non-biblical sources such as Emmerich, the epistemological status of the truth presented by the Bible has been long contested. The authenticity of the use of language in *The Passion of the Christ* has similarly been challenged. Apart from the Latin spoken being ecclesiastical Latin and not the Latin that would have been spoken by Romans in 33AD, the absence of the then regionally common Greek has been queried, as has been whether, as in the film, Pontius Pilate would have been able to speak Aramaic or Christ Latin.

11. Peter T. Chattaway besides observes that the "Gethsemane episode" is "one of a handful from the gospels in which Jesus expresses emotions and desires that lend themselves to a more human and subjective interpretation" (2004, 123).

12. As suggested, consideration of *The Passion of the Christ* in terms of anti-Semitism is extensive. See, to cite just some articles from three edited collections on the film, Perry and Schweitzer (2004), Ariel (2004), Wartenberg (2004), Kurtz (2004) and Rubenstein (2006). Emmerich's account of Christ's crucifixion has also been regarded to be anti-Semitic, and the book is the source both of Christ being dangled from the bridge and of Pilate's complaint about Christ's treatment.

13. Regarding the Christian audience's renewed assumption of guilt upon viewing *The Passion of the Christ*, in their survey of responses to the film Robert H. Woods, Michael C. Jindra and Jason D. Baker note that 72 per cent of Christian respondents "agreed or strongly agreed with the statement, 'After seeing this movie I felt more convicted about my personal sins'" (2004, 170). The article in addition cites individual testimonies (Woods, Jindra and Baker 2004, 171). The perversity of the Christian community's embrace of *The Passion of the Christ* is all the more pointed given, as numerous critics have remarked, its usual animus towards film violence.

14. Further to the spectator's invited identification with Christ, see Chattaway's discussion of the film's use of point-of-view shots and flashbacks (2004, 129–30).

15. Schrader's comment was made in the British television documentary *The Passion: Films, Faith & Fury* (Channel 4, 1 April 2006).

16. The provision of linen by Claudia Procles and the mopping up of Christ's blood by Mary and Magdalen are more elements that derive from Emmerich's *The Dolorous Passion of Our Lord Jesus Christ*.

17. Moreover, in "Group Psychology and the Analysis of the Ego," the writing upon which Adorno and Horkheimer found their argument regarding fascist propagation, Freud explicitly indicts religion, noting that "every religion is … a religion of love for all those whom it embraces; while cruelty and intolerance towards those who do not belong to it are natural to every religion" (1921, 128).

Chapter 11

1. For those interested, McManus can be seen in action on the DVD *The Best of ITV Wrestling* (ITV Sport, 2005).

2. See also Lev. 19:18, Deut. 32:35-36; Prov. 20:22, 24:29; 1 Cor. 6:6-8.

3. This appeared originally as "Le monde o? l'on catche" (Barthes 1970 [1957]: 13–24).

4. See here Mondak (1989) and Spark (1995). Henry Jenkins III charts the WWF response to the first Gulf War in Sammond (2005, 60–63).

5. Interestingly, although this rhetoric was widely used in the period around the attack on Afghanistan and Iraq, Ullman was a vocal critic of the Iraq campaign, claiming that it did not meet the requirements envisioned in the doctrine.

6. A series of their encounters is recapitulated on the DVD *Judgment Day 2004*.
7. DVD (*New Year's Revolution 2005*, 9 January 2005, Puerto Rico).
8. This incident, which took place in Philadelphia on 26 October 1996, is discussed on the DVD *The Rise and Fall of ECW*. ECW was a victim of its own success in some respects. The gruesome violence its fans expected was too much for the mainstream media backers to support and this was one contributing factor to its collapse as a separate franchise.
9. See http://www.npr.org/templates/story/story.php?storyId=13829386. The main source for this information is credited as an article by David Meltzer in *Wrestling Observer Newsletter*, 16 July 2007.
10. Even here there are uncomfortable episodes in the WWE's past. Vince's own sometimes ferocious battles against his own children, albeit as adults, skirt near this dangerous area. Even more disturbing is a recurrent storyline where a child is brought into the ring as two wrestlers dispute his paternity. Just before his death, Eddie Guerrero was involved in such a scenario with Rey Misterio, where the real-life nine-year-old son of Misterio was brought into the ring as Eddie threatened to reveal that he was in fact the boy's father. In real life, the two wrestlers were close family friends. The fact, however, that the WWE is willing to exploit the emotional power of seeing a child allegedly exposed to the devastating news that his father is not his real father, and then watch him fight with his oldest friend to prove the point, yet again plays off the crowd's moral repugnance at innocence being imperilled.
11. This medical diagnosis is not confirmed in all reports, but it has certainly been current in discussion.
12. For an informative but hardly dispassionate examination of the history of McMahon's business empire and the rise of the WWE, see Assael and Mooneyham (2004).
13. A recent research report in *Psychological Science*, for instance, found that if the participants were read scriptural texts which gave divine sanction to violence, they were statistically more likely to behave aggressively in further tests. The effect was strongest on believers, but not confined to them (Bushman et al. 2007).

Bibliography

Adorno, Theodor W., and Max Horkheimer. 1982/2001. "Freudian Theory and the Pattern of Fascist Propaganda." In *The Culture Industry*, ed. J. M. Bernstein, 132–57. London: Routledge.

Allen, Nicholas P. L. 2005. "Gibson's *Passion*: Flogging a Dead Horse?" *Journal of Literary Studies* 21 (1 & 2): 164–92.

Ansen, David. 2004. "So What's the Good News?" *Newsweek*, 1 March. http://www.msnbc.msn.com/id/4338528.

Antonakes, Michael. 2004. "Nikos Kazantzakis and Christ as a Hero." *Journal of Modern Greek Studies* 22: 95–105.

Apostolos-Cappadona, Diane. 2004. "On Seeing *The Passion*: Is There a Painting in this Film? Or is this Film a Painting?" In *Re-viewing the Passion: Mel Gibson's Film and its Critics*, ed. S. Brent Plate, 97–108. New York and Basingstoke: Palgrave Macmillan.

Appleby, R. Scott. 2000. *The Ambivalence of the Sacred: Religion, Violence and Reconciliation*. Maryland: Rowman & Littlefield.

Ariel, Yaakov. 2004. "*The Passion of the Christ* and the Passion of the Jews: Mel Gibson's Film in the Light of Jewish-Christian Relations." In *Re-viewing the Passion: Mel Gibson's Film and its Critics*, ed. S. Brent Plate, 21–41. New York and Basingstoke: Palgrave Macmillan.

Article 15-16. 2004. "Article 15-6 Investigation of the 800th Military Police Brigade." *Federation of American Scientists*. http://www.fas.org/irp/agency/dod/taguba.pdf

Assael, Shaun, and Mike Mooneyham. 2004. *Sex, Lies and Headlocks: The Real Story of Vince McMahon and World Wrestling Entertainment*. New York: Three Rivers Press.

Astell, Ann W. 2006. "New Perspectives on Mel Gibson's *The Passion of the Christ*: Review Essay." *An Interdisciplinary Journal of Jewish Studies* 25(1): 152–61.

Atkins, Susan, with Bob Slosser. 1978. *Child of Satan, Child of God*. London: Hodder and Stoughton.

Austin, Thomas. 2002. *Hollywood, Hype and Audiences: Selling and Watching Popular Films in the 1990s*. Manchester: Manchester University Press.

Bailey, Edward. 1998. *Implicit Religion: An Introduction*. London: Middlesex University Press.

Bailey, John, and Stephen Pizzello. 2004. "A Savior's Pain." *American Cinematographer*. 85(3): 48–61. http://www.theasc.com/magazine/mar04/cover/index.html.

Baker, Geoff. 2006. "Portraying the Quest for Buddhist Wisdom?: A Comparative Study of *The Matrix* and *Crouching Tiger, Hidden Dragon*." *Journal of Religion and Film* 10(1). http://www.unomaha.edu/jrf/vol10no1/BakerQuest.htm.

Bal, Mieke. 1994. "Head-Hunting: 'Judith' on the Cutting Edge of Knowledge." *Journal for the Study of the Old Testament* 63: 3–34.

Barthes, Roland. 1970 [1957]. *Mythologies*. Paris: Editions du Seuil.

Brasher, Brenda E. 2001. *Give me that Online Religion.* San Francisco, CA: Jossey-Bass.

Bataille, Georges, trans. Robert Hurley. 1991 [1976] *The Accursed Share. Volume II: The History of Eroticism; Volume III: Sovereignty.* New York: Zone Books.

— trans. Robert Hurley. 1992 [1973] *Theory of Religion.* New York: Zone Books.

Bauldrillard, Jean, trans. Chris Turner. 1995. *The Illusion of the End.* Cambridge: Polity Press.

Baylor Institute for Studies of Religion. 2006. *American Piety in the 21st Century: New Insights to the Depth and Complexity of Religion in the US.* http://www.baylor.edu/content/services/document.php/33304.pdf

BBC News Online. 2005. "Passion Re-cut for Easter Showings." http://news.bbc.co.uk/1/hi/entertainment/film/4305495.stm

BBFC. "BBFC Annual Report 2004." British Board of Film Classification. http://www.bbfc.co.uk/downloads/index.php

— "BBFC Guidelines 2005." British Board of Film Classification. http://www.bbfc.co.uk/downloads/index.php.

— 2007. "The Passion of the Christ." British Board of Film Classification. http://www.bbfc.co.uk/website/Classified.nsf/c2fb077ba3f9b33980256b4f002da32c/d3e1ecb136cc552f80256e3f003194fc?OpenDocument

Bellah, Robert. 1970. *Beyond Belief: Essays on Religion in a Post-Traditional World.* New York: Harper and Row.

Benaka, Lee. 1990. "Of Mats and Men: Rituals and Religious Imagery in Professional Wrestling." Unpublished Senior Thesis, Columbia College, Chicago. http://deathvalleydriver.com/Benaka/thesis(chap10).html (accessed 9 June 2010).

Bendle, Mervyn. 2005. "The Apocalyptic Imagination and Popular Culture." *Journal of Religion and Popular Culture* XI. http://www.usask.ca/relst/jrpc/art11-apocalypticimagination.html

Berger, Peter L. 1990 [1967]. *The Sacred Canopy: Elements of a Sociological Theory of Religion.* New York: Anchor Books.

Bernstein, Matthew, ed. 2000. *Controlling Hollywood: Censorship and Regulation in the Studio Era.* London: Athlone.

Beveridge, William. 1704. *A Sermon Preach'd Before the House of Peers, in the Abbey-Church of Westminster on Sunday, November 5th 1704. Being the Anniversary Thanksgiving for the Happy Deliverance from the Gunpowder-Treason Plot.* London: J. Leake for Walter Kettilby.

Binski, Paul. 1996. *Medieval Death: Ritual and Representation.* New York: Cornell University Press.

Bonaventure, Saint, Cardinal. 1961. *Meditations on the Life of Christ: An Illustrated Manuscript of the Fourteenth Century.* Ed. Isa Ragusa and Rosalie B. Green. Trans. Isa Ragusa. Princeton: Princeton University Press.

Bourdieu, P. 1992. *Practical Reason: On the Theory of Action.* Cambridge: Polity.

Brereton, Thomas. 1715. *Esther, or Faith Triumphant: A Sacred Tragedy.* London: Printed for J. Tonson.

Breznican, Anthony. 2005. "The Passion Re-cut goes easier on the gore." *USA Today.* http://www.usatoday.com/life/ movies/news/2005-03-10-passion-main_x.htm.

Brick, C. 2000. "Taking Offence: Modern Moralities and the Perception of the Football Fan." In *The Future of Football: Challenges for the Twenty-First Century*, ed. J. Garland, Dominic Malcolm and Michael Rowe. London: Frank Cass & Co.

Brin, David. 1998. "The Postman: The Movie. An Impression by the Author of the Original Novel." http://davidbrin.com/postmanmoviearticle.html

Broderick, Mick. 1993a. "Heroic Apocalypse: Mad Max, Mythology and the Millennium." In *Crisis Cinema: The Apocalyptic Idea in Postmodern Narrative Film*, ed. Christopher Sharrett, 251–72. Washington, DC: Maisonneuve Press.

— 1993b. "Surviving Armageddon: Beyond the Imagination of Disaster." *Science Fiction Studies* 20, part 3. http://www.depauw.edu/sfs/backissues/61/broderick61art.htm

Bruce, Steve. 2002. *God is Dead: Secularization in the West*. Oxford: Blackwell.

Bugliosi, Vincent, with Curt Gentry. 1974. *Helter Skelter: The True Story of the Manson Murders*. New York: W.W. Norton.

Bunt, Gary R. 2000. *Virtually Islamic: Computer-mediated Communication and Cyber Islamic Environments*. Cardiff: University of Wales.

— 2003. *Islam in the Digital Age: E-Jihad, Online Fatwas and Cyber Islamic Environments*. London: Pluto Press.

— 2004. "'Rip. Burn. Pray': Islamic Expression Online." In *Religion Online: Finding Faith on the Internet*, ed. Lorne L. Dawson and Douglas E. Cowan, 123–34. New York and London: Routledge.

Bunzl, Martin. 2004. "Counterfactual History: A User's Guide." *The American Historical Review* 109(3): 845–58. http://www.historycooperative.org/journals/ahr/109.3/bunzl.html.

Bushman, Brad L., Robert D. Ridge, Enny Das, Conlin W. Key, and Gregory L. Busath. 2007. "When God Sanctions Killing: Effects of Scriptural Violence on Aggression." *Psychological Science* 18: 204–207.

Caillois, Roger, trans. Meyer Barash. 2001 [1939]. *Man and the Sacred*. Urbana and Chicago: University of Illnois Press.

Campbell, H. 2003. "New Media and Religion." In *Mediating Religion: Conversations in Media, Religion and Culture*, ed. Jolyon Mitchell and Sophia Marriage, 213–28. London and New York: Continuum.

— 2005. *Exploring Religious Community Online: We are One in the Network*. New York: Peter Lang.

Carr, E. H. 1964. *What is History?* Harmondsworth: Penguin.

Carruthers, Jo. 2008. *Esther through the Centuries*. Oxford: Blackwell.

Chattaway, Peter T. 2004. "Come and See: How Movies Encourage Us to Look at (and with) Jesus." In *Re-viewing the Passion: Mel Gibson's Film and its Critics*, ed. S. Brent Plate, 121–33. New York and Basingstoke: Palgrave Macmillan.

Christie, Ian, and David Thompson, eds. 2003. *Scorsese on Scorsese*. London: Faber and Faber.

Clark, J. C. D. 1997. "British America—What if there had been no American Revolution?" In Ferguson 1997a, 125–74.

Clark, James M. 1950. *The Dance of Death in the Middle Ages and the Renaissance*. Glasgow: Glasgow University Publications.

Cohen, Jeremy. 2007. *Christ Killers: The Jews and the Passion; From Bible to the Big Screen*. Oxford: Oxford University Press.

Cook, Pam. 1988. "*The Last Temptation of Christ.*" *Monthly Film Bulletin* 55(657): 287–88.

Cowan, Douglas E. 2005. *Cyberhenge: Modern Pagans on the Internet.* New York: Routledge.

Cowley, Robert, ed. 1998. *What If: The World's Foremost Military Historians Imagine What Might Have Been.* New York: Putnam's.

Craven, Toni. 1983. *Artistry and Faith in the Book of Judith.* Chico, CA: Scholars Press.

— 2003. "The Book of Judith in the Context of Twentieth-Century Studies of the Apocryphal/Deuterocanonical Books." *Currents in Biblical Research* 1(2): 187–229.

Crick, Bernard. 2006. "When is it 'laudable' or 'lawful' to kill a tyrant?" *THES* (9 June). http://www.timeshighereducation.co.uk/

Crossan, John Dominic. 1991. *The Historical Jesus: The Life of a Mediterranean Jewish Peasant.* San Francisco: HarperSanFrancisco.

— 2006. "Jewish Crowd and Roman Governor." In *Mel Gibson's Bible: Religion, Popular Culture, and* The Passion of the Christ," ed. Timothy K. Beal and Tod Linafelt, 59–67. Chicago: University of Chicago Press.

Daniels, Les. 2000. *Wonder Woman: The Life and Times of the Amazon Princess.* San Francisco, CA: Chronicle Books. Art direction and design by Chip Kidd.

Dawson, Lorne L. 2004. "Religion and the Quest for Virtual Community." In *Religion Online: Finding Faith on the Internet*, ed. Lorne L. Dawson and Douglas E. Cowan. New York and London: Routledge.

Dawson, Lorne L., and Douglas E. Cowan. 2004. *Religion Online: Finding Faith on the Internet.* New York and London: Routledge.

Dayan, Daniel, and Elihu Katz. 1992. *Media Events: The Live Broadcasting History.* Cambridge, MA: Harvard University Press.

Debord, Guy. 1994. *The Society of the Spectacle.* New York: Zone Books.

Delicata, Nadia. 2009. "Religion and Violence: The Paradox of a Human Tragedy." *Religious Studies Review* 35(1): 13–22.

Demerath, N. J. 2003. "Civil Society and Civil Religion as Mutually Dependent." In *Handbook of the Sociology of Religion*, ed. Michele Dillon. Cambridge: Cambridge University Press.

Denby, David. 2004. "Nailed: Mel Gibson's 'The Passion of the Christ'." *The New Yorker*, 1 March. http://www.newyorker.com/critics/cinema/articles/040301crci_cinema.

Denzey, Nicola. 2004. "Biblical Allusions, Biblical Illusions: Hollywood Blockbusters and Scripture." *Journal of Religion and Film* 8(1). http://www.unomaha.edu.jrf/2004Symposium/Denzey.htm.

Doherty, Earl. 2001. *Challenging the Verdict: A Cross-examination of Lee Strobel's 'The Case for Christ'.* Ottawa: Age of Reason.

Dunant, Sarah, and Roy Porter, eds. 1996. *The Age of Anxiety.* London: Virago Books.

Dunn, James D. G. 2003. *Jesus Remembered.* Grand Rapids, MI; Cambridge: Eerdmans.

Dunning, Eric, Patrick Murphy and John Williams. 1988. *The Roots of Football Hooliganism: An Historical and Sociological Study.* London: Routledge.

Dunning, Eric, and Chris Rojek, eds. 1992. *Sport and Leisure in the Civilizing Process*. Hampshire and London: Macmillan Press.

Durkheim, Emile. 1961. *The Elementary Forms of Religious Life*. New York: Collier Books.

Durkheim, Emile, trans. Carol Cosman. 2001 [1912]. *The Elementary Forms of Religious Life*. New York: The Free Press.

Dwyer, Simon, ed. 1995. "I Am the Beast: The Trial Testimony of Charles Manson, November 19th 1970, A Transcript." *Rapid Eye*. London: Creation Books, 214–23.

Ebert, Roger. 2004. "The Passion of the Christ." *Chicago Sun-Times*, 24 February. http://rogerebert.suntimes.com/apps/pbcs.dll/article?AID=/20040224/REVIEWS/402240301/1023.

Edgar, Spc.L.B. 2005. "Court sentences England to 3 years." *Army News Service*, 28 September 2005.

Eliade, Mircea, trans. W. R. Trask. 1959. *The Sacred and the Profane: The Nature of Religion*. New York: Harcourt, Brace & World.

Elias, Norbert, and Eric Dunning. 1986. *Quest for Excitement: Sport and Leisure in the Civilizing Process*. Oxford: Blackwell.

Enders, Jody. 2006. "Seeing is Not Believing." In *Mel Gibson's Bible,* ed. Timothy K. Beal and Tod Linafelt, 187–93. Chicago; London: University of Chicago Press.

Enslin, Morton S., and Solomon Zeitlin. 1972. *The Book of Judith: Greek Text with an English Translation, Commentary, and Critical Notes* (Jewish Apocryphal Literature, vol. 7). Leiden: E.J. Brill.

Etherden, Matthew. 2005. "'The Day The Earth Stood Still': 1950's Sci-Fi, Religion and the Alien Messiah." *Journal of Religion and Film* 9. http://www.unomaha.edu/jrf/Vol9No2/EtherdenEarthStill.htm

Evans-Kasastamatis, Joyce. 1999. *Celluloid Mushroom Clouds: Hollywood and the Atomic Bomb*. Jackson, TN: Westview Press.

Eyre, Anne. 1997. *Football and Religious Experience: Sociological Reflections*. Lampeter: Religious Experience Research Centre.

Federal Bureau of Investigation. 2002 [1999]. "Project Megiddo," in *Millennial Violence: Past Present and Future*, ed. Jeffrey Kaplan, 27–52. London: Frank Cass.

Felski, Rita. 1999–2000. "The Invention of Everyday Life." *New Formations* 39: 15–31.

Felton, David, and David Dalton. 1970a. "The Most Dangerous Man in the World." *Rolling Stone* 61 (25 June): 27–29.

— 1970b. "The Book of Manson." *Rolling Stone* 61 (25 June): 31–33.

— 1970c. "In the Land of the Mindless." *Rolling Stone* 61 (25 June): 34–40.

Ferguson, Niall, ed. 1997a. *Virtual History: Alternatives and Counterfactuals.* London: Picador.

Ferguson, Niall. 1997b. "Introduction—Virtual History: Towards a 'Chaotic' Theory of the Past." In Ferguson 1997a, 1–90.

Finn, G. P. T. 1994. "Football Violence: A Societal Psychological Perspective." In *Football, Violence and Social Identity*, ed. Richard Giulianotti, Norman Bonney and Mike Hepworth, 90–127. London: Routledge.

Fiske, John. 1994. *Media Matters: Everyday Culture and Political Change*. Minneapolis: University of Minnesota Press.

Flannery-Dailey, Frances. 2000. "Bruce Willis as the Messiah: Human Effort, Salvation and Apocalypticism in *Twelve Monkeys*." *Journal of Religion and Film* 4(1). http://www.unomaha.edu/jrf/Messiah.htm

Flannery-Dailey, Frances, and Rachel Wagner, R. 2001. "Wake Up! Gnosticism and Buddhism in *The Matrix*." *Journal of Religion and Film* 5(2). http://www.unomaha.edu/jrf/gnostic.htm

Forbes, B. D., and J. H. Mahan, eds. 2005. *Religion and Popular Culture in America*. Berkeley: University of California Press.

Fredriksen, Paula. 2006. "No Pain, No Gain?" In *Mel Gibson's Bible: Religion, Popular Culture, and* The Passion of the Christ," ed. Timothy K. Beal and Tod Linafelt, 91–98. Chicago: University of Chicago Press.

Freud, Sigmund. 1913/1990. "Totem and Taboo: Some Points of Agreement between the Mental Lives of Savages and Neurotics," trans. James Strachey. In *The Origins of Religion*, ed. Albert Dickson, 43–224. Harmondsworth: Penguin.

— 1915/1991. "Instincts and their Vicissitudes," trans. James Strachey. In *On Metapsychology: The Theory of Psychoanalysis*, ed. Angela Richards, 105–38. Harmondsworth: Penguin.

— 1921/1991. "Group Psychology and the Analysis of the Ego," trans. James Strachey. In *Civilization, Society and Religion*, ed. Albert Dickson, 91–178. Harmondsworth: Penguin.

— 1923/1991. "The Ego and the Id," trans. James Strachey. In *On Meta-psychology: The Theory of Psychoanalysis*, ed. Angela Richards, 339–407. Harmondsworth: Penguin.

— 1924/1991. "The Economic Problem of Masochism," trans. James Strachey. In *On Metapsychology: The Theory of Psychoanalysis*, ed. Angela Richards, 409–26. Harmondsworth: Penguin.

— 1963. "Medusa's Head." In *Sexuality and the Psychology of Love*, ed. Philip Rieff, 212–13. New York: Collier.

Fukuyama, Francis. 1993. *The End of History and the Last Man*. Harmondsworth: Penguin Books.

Fulton, Keith, and Louis Pepe. 1998. *The Hamster Factor, and Other Tales about the Making of 12 Monkeys* (included as an extra on DVD release of *12 Monkeys*).

Garrett, Greg. 2006. "Comics and the Bible: Reinterpretation and Mythic Understanding." *SBL Forum*, 21 December 2006 to 28 January 2007. http://www.sbl-site.org/Article.aspx?ArticleId=613.

Giannetti, Louis. 2005. *Understanding Movies*. New Jersey: Pearson Prentice Hall.

Gibson, Mel. 2004. "Foreword." In *The Passion: Photography of the Movie* The Passion of the Christ, n.pag. Wheaton, IL: Tyndale House.

Gibson, Mel, Ken Duncan, and Philippe Antonello. 2004. *The Passion: Photography of the Movie* The Passion of the Christ. Wheaton, IL: Tyndale House.

Gilmore, John, and Ron Kenner. 1971. *The Garbage People*. Los Angeles: Omega Press.

Girard, René, trans. Patrick Gregory. 1977 [1972] *Violence and the Sacred*. Maryland: John Hopkins University Press.

Giroux, Henry. 2006. *Beyond the Spectacle of Terrorism: Global Uncertainty and the Challenge of New Media*. London: Paradigm Publishers.

Giulianotti, R., N. Bonney, and M. Hepworth. 1994. "Introduction." In *Football, Violence and Social Identity*, ed. Richard Giulianotti, Norman Bonney and Mike Hepworth, 1–8. London: Routledge.

Gorightly, Adam. 2001. *The Shadow Over Santa Susana: Black Magic, Mind Control and the 'Manson Family' Mythos*. San Jose and New York: Writers Club Press.

Greenfield, Bob. 1970. "Sharon Tate had one question." *Rolling Stone* 61 (25 June): 16.

Gribben, Crawford. 2006. "After *Left Behind*—The Paradox of Evangelical Pessimism." In *Expecting the End: Millennialism in Social and Historical Context*, ed. Kenneth G. C. Newport and Crawford Gribben, 113–30. Baylor, TX: Baylor University Press.

Griffiths, Alison. 2007. "The Revered Gaze: The Medieval Imaginary of Mel Gibson's *The Passion of the Christ*." *Cinema Journal* 46(2): 3–39.

Grossfeld, Bernard, ed. and trans. 1991. *The Two Targums of Esther*. The Aramaic Bible, 18. Edinburgh: T & T Clark.

Guardian Unlimited. 2005. "Gibson re-edits Passion for Easter audience." http://www.guardian.co.uk/film/2005/mar/01/news

Hammer, Rhonda, and Douglas Kellner. 2005. "Critical Reflections on Mel Gibson's *The Passion of the Christ*." http://www.gseis.ucla.edu/faculty/kellner/essays/gibsonspassion.pdf.

Harbord, Janet. 2002. *Film Cultures*. London: Sage.

Helland, Christopher. 2002. "Surfing for Salvation." *Religion* 32(4): 293–302.

— 2004. "Popular Religion and the World Wide Web." In *Religion Online: Finding Faith on the Internet*, ed. Lorne L. Dawson and Douglas E. Cowan, 23–35. New York and London: Routledge.

Hendershot, Heather. 1998. *Saturday Morning Censors: Television Regulation before the V-chip*: London: Duke University Press.

Heyricke, Richard. 1646. *Queen Esther Resolves: Or A Princely Pattern of Heaven-born Resolution, For all the Lovers of God and their Country: Opened in a Sermon preached before the Honourable House of Commons, at the Monethly Fast, May 27, 1646*. London: F. Macock.

Hill, Annette. 1997. *Shocking Entertainment: Viewer Responses to Violent Movies*. Luton: John Libbey Media.

Holderness, Graham. 2005. "'Animated Icon': Narrative and Liturgy in 'The Passion of the Christ'." *Literature & Theology* 19(4): 384–401.

Hollywood, Amy. 2004. "Kill Jesus." *Harvard Divinity Bulletin* 32(3). http://www.hds.harvard.edu/news/bulletin/articles/hollywood_passion.html.

Hoover, S. H., L. S. Clark, and D. Alters, with J. Champ and L. Hood. 2004. *Media, Home, and Family*. New York: Routledge.

Icon Productions. 2004. *The Passion of the Christ—A Mel Gibson Film—Official Movie Website*. http://www.thepassionofchrist.com/v2/index.html

IMDB. 2007. "The Passion of the Christ." *Internet Movie Database*. http://www.imdb.com/title/tt0335345/

Jackson, Kevin, ed. 2004. *Schrader on Schrader & Other Writings*. London: Faber and Faber.

Jacob, Phillip E. 1955. "Religious Freedom—a Good Security Risk?" *Annals of American Academy of Political and Social Science*: 41–50.

Jacobs, Steven Leonard. 2004. "Can There Be Jewish-Christian Dialogue after *The Passion?*" In *Re-viewing the Passion: Mel Gibson's Film and its Critics*, ed. S. Brent Plate, 43–52. New York and Basingstoke: Palgrave Macmillan.

James, Nick. 2004. "Hell in Jerusalem." *Sight and Sound* 14(4): 14–18.

Jancovich, Mark. 2003. *The Place of the Audience: Cultural Geographies of Film Consumption.* London: British Film Institute Publishing.

Jansen, Sue C. 1991. *Censorship: The Knot that Binds Power and Knowledge.* Oxford: Oxford University Press.

Jenkins, Steve. 1988. "From the Pit of Hell." *Monthly Film Bulletin* 55(659): 352–53.

Johnston, Robert K. 2004. "The Passion as a Dynamic Icon: A Theological Reflection." In *Re-viewing the Passion: Mel Gibson's Film and its Critics*, ed. S. Brent Plate, 55–70. New York and Basingstoke: Palgrave Macmillan.

Karpman, Stephen B. 1968. "Fairy Tales and Script Drama Analysis." *Transactional Analysis Bulletin* 7(26): 39–43.

Keen, David. 2007. "One Down—But There's Always One More to Go." *THES* (31 January). http://www.timeshighereducation.co.uk/

Kellner, Douglas. 2003 *Media Spectacle.* London; New York: Routledge.

Kelly, Mary Pat. 1992. *Martin Scorsese: A Journey.* London: Secker & Warburg.

Kerekes, David, and Mikita Brottman. 2002. "The Cuckoo Clocks of Hell—An Interview with Roger Watkins." *Headpress 23 Funhouse* (June): 88–138.

Kerekes, David, and David Slater. 1994. *Killing for Culture: An Illustrated History of Death Film from Mondo to Snuff.* London: Creation Books.

Kierkegaard, Søren. 1985. *Fear and Trembling.* London: Penguin.

King, Greg. 2000. *Sharon Tate and the Manson Murders.* Edinburgh and London: Mainstream Publishing.

King, Neale. 2004. "Truth at Last: Evangelical Communities Embrace *The Passion of the Christ.*" In *Re-viewing the Passion: Mel Gibson's Film and its Critics*, ed. S. Brent Plate, 151–62. New York and Basingstoke: Palgrave Macmillan.

Kirkpatrick, Stewart. 2004. "Lazy Guide to Net Culture: Doing a Lynndie." *Scotsman*, 25 August. http://news.scotsman.com/lazyguidetonetculture/Lazy-Guide-to-Net-Culture.2558294.jp

Koslovic, Anton Karl. 2002. "Superman as Christ Figure: The American Pop Culture Movie Messiah." *Journal of Religion and Film* 6(1). http://www.unomaha.edu/jrf/superman.htm

Kuhn, Annette. 1988. *Cinema, Censorship and Sexuality, 1909–1925.* London: Routledge.

Kurtz, Paul. 2004. "*The Passion* as a Political Weapon: Anti-Semitism and Gibson's Use of the Gospels." In *Mel Gibson's* Passion *and Philosophy: The Cross, the Questions, the Controversy*, ed. Jorge J. E. Gracia, 90–100. Chicago: Open Court.

Lachman, Gary Valentine. 2001. *Turn Off Your Mind: The Mystic Sixties and the Dark Side of the Age of Aquarius.* London: Sidgwick & Jackson.

Lafrance, J. D. n.d. "Twelve Monkeys: Dangerous Visions'." http://www.smart.co.uk/dreams/monkvive.htm

Lawrence, John Shelton, and Robert Jewett. 2002. *The Myth of the American Superhero.* Grand Rapids, MI: Eerdmans.

Lawrence, Matt. 2004. *Like a Splinter in your Mind: The Philosophy behind the Matrix Trilogy.* Oxford: Blackwell.

Lawson, George. 1804. *Discourses on the Whole Book of Esther.* Edinburgh: J. Pillans & Sons M'Crie.

Leary, Timothy, Ralph Metzner and Richard Alpert. 1964. *The Psychedelic Experience: A Manual Based on the Tibetan Book of the Dead.* New Hyde Park, NY: University Books.

Le Bon, G. *The Crowd: A Study of the Popular Mind.* London: T Fisher Unwin.

Lefebvre, Henri. 1971. *Everyday Life in the Modern World.* London: Allen Lane.

Leupp, Gary. 2004. "On Viewing 'The Passion of the Christ': An Unmoving Movie." CounterPunch *Out of Bounds* magazine, 20–21 March. http://www.counterpunch.org/leupp03202004.html

Lev, Peter. 2003. *History of the American Cinema Volume 7: 1950–1959.* Berkeley; Los Angeles; London: University of California Press.

Levine, Amy-Jill. 1992. "Sacrifice and Salvation: Otherness and Domestication in the Book of Judith." In *'No One Spoke Ill of Her': Essays on Judith,* ed. James C. VanderKam, 17–30. Atlanta, GA: Scholars Press.

— 2004. "Mel Gibson, the Scribes, and the Pharisees." In *Re-viewing the Passion: Mel Gibson's Film and its Critics,* ed. S. Brent Plate, 137–49. New York and Basingstoke: Palgrave Macmillan.

Lewis, David. 1979. "Possible Worlds." In *The Possible and the Actual—Readings in the Metaphysics of Modality,* ed. Michael J. Loux, 182–89. Ithaca; London: Cornell University Press.

Lifton, Robert J. 2003. "American Apocalypse." *The Nation* (22 December). http://www.thenation.com/doc/20031222/lifton

Lincoln, Bruce. 1998. "Conflict." In *Critical Terms for Religious Studies,* ed. Mark C. Taylor, 55–69. Chicago and London: University of Chicago Press.

Lyons, Charles. 1997. *The New Censors: Movies and the Culture Wars.* Philadelphia: Temple University Press.

MacDonald, Ian. 1997. *Revolution in the Head: The Beatles' Records and the Sixties.* London: Fourth Estate.

Maguire, J. 1992. "Towards a Sociological Theory of Sport and the Emotions: A Process-Sociological Perspective." In *Sport and Leisure in the Civilizing Process,* ed. Eric Dunning and Chris Rojek, 96–120. Hampshire and London: Macmillan Press.

Manson, Charles. 1986. *Manson in his Own Words as Told to Nuel Emmons.* New York: Grove Press.

Marx, Karl. 1844/1975. "Contribution to the Critique of Hegel's Philosophy of Right. Introduction," trans. Gregor Benton. In *Early Writings,* 243–57. Harmondsworth: Penguin.

Mathews, Tom D. 1994. *Censored.* London: Chatto & Windus.

Mayer, John. 1647. *Many Commentaries in One: Upon Joshuah, 1 and 2 Samuel, Ezra, Judges, 1 and 2 Kings, Nehemiah, Ruth, 1 and 2 Chronicles, Esther.* London.

M'Crie, Thomas. 1838. *Lectures on the Book of Esther.* Edinburgh: William Blackwood & Sons; London: Thomas Cadell.

McCrillis, Neal R. 2002. "Atomic Anxiety in Cold War Britain: Science, Sin and Uncertainty in Nuclear Monster Films." In *Screening Scripture: Intertextual Connections between Scripture and Film,* ed. George Aichele and Richard Walsh, 42–57. Harrisburg, PA: Trinity Press International.

McKelvey, Tara. n.d. "A Soldier's Tale: Lynndie England." *Marie Claire*. http://www.marieclaire.com/world/news/lynndie-england-1

McLaren, Paul. 2002. "George Bush, Apocalypse Sometime Soon, and the American Imperium." *Cultural Studies Critical Methodologies* 2(3): 327–33.

McLuhan, Marshall. 1964. *Understanding Media: The Extensions of Man*. New York: McGraw-Hill.

Meier, John P. 1991. *A Marginal Jew: Rethinking the Historical Jesus: The Roots of the Problem and the Person*, vol. 1. Anchor Bible Reference Library. New York and London: Doubleday.

Mellor, Philip A., and Chris Shilling. 1997. *Re-forming the Body: Religion, Community and Modernity*. London: Sage.

Middleton, Darren J. N. 2004. "Celluloid Synoptics: Viewing the Gospels of Marty and Mel Together." In *Re-viewing the Passion: Mel Gibson's Film and its Critics*, ed. S. Brent Plate, 71–81. New York and Basingstoke: Palgrave Macmillan.

Miller, Vincent. 2005. *Consuming Religion: Christian Faith and Practice in a Consumer Culture*. New York and London: Continuum.

Mondak, Jeffery J. 1989. "The Politics of Professional Wrestling." *Journal of Popular Culture* 23: 139–50.

Moore, Carey A. 1985. *Judith*. New York: Doubleday.

Morgan, David. 2004. "Catholic Piety and *The Passion of the Christ*." In *Re-viewing the Passion: Mel Gibson's Film and its Critics*, ed. S. Brent Plate, 85–96. New York and Basingstoke: Palgrave Macmillan.

— 2005. *The Sacred Gaze: Religious Visual Culture in Theory and Practice*. Berkeley, CA: University of California Press.

Morris, Michael. 1988. "Of God and Man." *American Film* 14(1): 44–49.

Murdock, Graham. 2001. "Reservoirs of Dogma: An Archaeology of Popular Anxieties." In *Ill Effects: The Media/Violence Debate*, ed. M. Barker and J. Petley, 150–69. London: Sage.

Nadel, Alan. 1993. "God's Law and the Wide Screen: *The Ten Commandments* as Cold War 'Epic'." *PMLA* 108: 415–30.

Napier, Susan J. 1993. "Panic Sites: The Japanese Imagination of Disaster from *Godzilla* to *Akira*." *Journal of Japanese Studies* 19(2): 327–51.

National Science Board. 2004. *Science and Engineering Indicators 2004*. 2 vols. Arlington, VA: National Science Foundation.

Neff, David, and Jane Johnson Struck. 2004. "Dude, that was graphic." *Christianity Today*. http://www.christianitytoday.com/ct/movies/interviews/2004/melgibson.html

Nelson, Bill. 1991. *Tex Watson: The Man, the Madness, the Manipulation*. Anaheim, CA: Pen Power Publications.

Nielsen, Donald A. 1984. "Charles Manson's Family of Love—A Case Study of Anomism, Puerilism and Transmoral Consciousness in Civilizational Perspective." *Sociological Analysis* 45(4): 315–37.

— 2005. *Horrible Workers: Max Stirner, Arthur Rimbaud, Robert Johnson, and the Charles Manson Circle: Studies in Moral Experience and Cultural Expression*. Lanham, MD and Oxford: Lexington Books.

Noriega, Chon. 1987. "Godzilla and the Japanese Nightmare: When Them! Is U.S." *Cinema Journal* 27(1): 63–77.

O'Leary, Stephen D. 1994. *Arguing the Apocalypse: A Theory of Millennial Rhetoric.* Oxford: Oxford University Press.

— 2000. "Apocalypticism in American Popular Culture: From the Dawn of the Nuclear Age to the End of the American Century." In *The Encyclopaedia of Apocalypticism, Volume 3: Apocalypticism in the Modern Period and Contemporary Age,* ed. Stephen J. Stein, 392–426. London: Continuum.

Oropeza, B. J. 2005. "Introduction: Superhero Myth and the Restoration of Paradise." In *The Gospel According to Superheroes: Religion and Popular Culture,* ed. B. J. Oropeza, 1–24. New York: Peter Lang.

Orr, D. Alan. 2002. *Treason and the State: Law, Politics and Ideology in the English Civil War.* Cambridge: Cambridge University Press.

Ostwalt, Conrad. 1998. "Visions of the End: Secular Apocalypse in Recent Hollywood Film." *Journal of Religion and Film* 2(1). http://avalon.unomaha.edu/jrf/OstwaltC.htm

— 2000. "*Armageddon* at the Millennial Dawn." *Journal of Religion and Film* 4(1). http://www.unomaha.edu/jrf/armagedd.htm

— 2003. *Secular Steeples: Popular Culture and the Religious Imagination.* London: Trinity Press International.

Otto, Rudolf, trans. John W. Harvey. 1958 [1917]. *The Idea of the Holy. An Inquiry into the Non-rational Factor in the Idea of the Divine and its Relation to the Rational.* Oxford: Oxford University Press.

Otzen, Benedikt. 2002. *Tobit and Judith.* Sheffield: Continuum.

Ovey, Michael. 2006. "Victim Chic? The Rhetoric of Victimhood." *Cambridge Papers,* 15.1 (March). http://www.jubilee-centre.org/online_documents/

Partridge, Christopher. 2004. *The Re-Enchantment of the West: Volume 1. Alternative Spiritualities, Sacralization, Popular Culture and Occulture.* London: T&T Clark.

— 2005. *The Re-Enchantment of the West: Volume II. Alternative Spiritualities, Sacralization, Popular Culture and Occulture.* London: T&T Clark.

Perry, Marvin, and Frederick M. Schweitzer. 2004. "The Medieval Passion Play Revisited." In *Re-viewing the Passion: Mel Gibson's Film and its Critics,* ed. S. Brent Plate, 3–19. New York and Basingstoke: Palgrave Macmillan.

Petley, Julian. 2001. "Us and Them." In *Ill Effects: The Media/Violence Debate,* ed. M. Barker and J. Petley, 170–85. London: Sage.

Phelps, Guy. 1975. *Film Censorship.* Lindon: Gollancz.

Post, Robert C., ed. 1998. *Censorship and Silencing: Practices of Cultural Regulation.* Los Angeles: Getty Research Institute for the History of Art and the Humanities.

Prince, Stephen. 2006. "Beholding Blood Sacrifice in *The Passion of the Christ*— How Real is Movie Violence?" *Film Quarterly* 59(4): 11–22.

Pyper, Hugh S. 2006. "Wrestling the Bible." *SBL Forum.* http://www.sbl-site.org/Article.aspx?ArticleId=569.

Reik, Theodor. 1949/2002. *Love and Lust: On the Psychoanalysis of Romantic and Sexual Emotions.* New Brunswick: Transaction.

Rheingold, Howard. 1993. *The Virtual Community: Homesteading on the Electronic Frontier.* Reading, MA: Addison-Wesley. See also his revised edition: 2000. *The Virtual Community.* Cambridge, MA: MIT Press.

Rickard, John. 1999. "'The Spectacle of Excess': The Emergence of Modern Professional Wrestling in the United States and Australia." *Journal of Popular Culture* 33: 129–37.

Riley, Robin. 2003. *Film, Faith, and Cultural Conflict: The Case of Martin Scorsese's* The Last Temptation of Christ. Westport: Praeger.

Roberts, Andrew. 1997. "Hitler's England—What if Germany had Invaded Britain in May 1940?" In Ferguson 1997a, 281–320.

Robertson, James C. 1989. *The Hidden Cinema: British Film Censorship in Action.* London: Routledge.

Robinson, Lillian. 2004. *Wonder Women: Feminisms and Superheroes.* New York and London: Routledge.

Roitman, Adolfo D. 1992. "Achior in the Book of Judith: His Role and Significance." In *'No One Spoke Ill of Her': Essays on Judith,* ed. James C. VanderKam, 31–45. Atlanta, GA: Scholars Press.

Rojek, C. 1992. "The Field of Play in Sport and Leisure Studies." In *Sport and Leisure in the Civilizing Process,* ed. Eric Dunning and Chris Rojek, 1–35. Hampshire and London: Macmillan Press.

Rubenstein, Richard L. 2006. "Mel Gibson's Passion." In *Mel Gibson's Bible: Religion, Popular Culture, and* The Passion of the Christ," ed. Timothy K. Beal and Tod Linafelt, 109–19. Chicago: University of Chicago Press.

Salek, Rebecca. 2003. "Oh, the Wonder of her Virginity: Wonder Woman, Sex, an Island Fulla Maybe-Lesbians, And What the Heck is a Virgin, Anyway?" *Sequential Tart*. February 2003, http://www.sequentialtart.com/archive/feb03/art_0203_4.shtml.

Sammond, Nicholas, ed. 2005. *Steel Chair to the Head: The Pleasure and Pain of Professional Wrestling.* Durham: Duke University Press.

Sanders, Ed. 1972. *The Family: The Story of Charles Manson's Dune Buggy Attack Battalion.* London: Rupert Hart-Davis.

— 1990. *The Family: The Manson Group and its Aftermath.* Revised and updated edn. New York: Signet Books.

Sanders, E. P. 1985. *Jesus and Judaism.* London: SCM.

— 1993. *The Historical Figure of Jesus.* London: Allen Lane.

Schiller, Gertrud. 1972. *Iconography of Christian Art*, vol. 2, trans. Janet Seligman. London: Lund Humphries.

Schiller, Lawrence. 1970. *The Killing of Sharon Tate: Exclusive Story by Susan Atkins, Confessed Participant in the Murder.* New York: Signet Books.

Scott, John, and Gordon Marshall, eds. 2005. *Oxford Dictionary of Sociology.* New York: Oxford University Press.

Self, Will. 1998. "Introduction." In *Revelation, Authorised King James Version*, vii–xiv. Edinburgh: Canongate.

Shapiro, Jerome F. 2002. *Atomic Bomb Cinema: The Apocalyptic Imagination in Film.* London: Routledge.

Singer, T., B. Seymour, J. P. O'Doherty, K. E. Stephan, R. J. Dolan, and S. D. Firth. 2006. "Empathic Neural Responses are Modulated by the Perceived Fairness of Others." *Nature* (18 January 2006).

Smith, David E. M. D., and Alan J. Rose. 1970. "The Group Marriage Commune: A Case Study." *Journal of Psychedelic Drugs* 3(1) (September): 115–19.

Smith, David E. M. D., and John Luce. 1971. *Love Needs Care: A History of San Francisco's Haight-Ashbury Free Medical Clinic and its Pioneer Role in Treating Drug Abuse Problems*. Boston and Toronto: Little Brown.

Sobel, Robert. 1997. *For Want of a Nail: If Burgoyne Had Won at Saratoga*. London: Greenhill.

Sontag, Susan. 1967. "The Imagination of Disaster." In *Against Interpretation and Other Essays*. London: Eyre and Spottiswoode.

Spark, Alasdair. 1995. "Wrestling with America: Media, National Images, and the Global Village." *Journal of Popular Culture* 29: 83–98.

Staiger, Janet. 2000. *Perverse Spectators: The Practices of Film Reception*. London; New York University Press.

Stocker, Margarita. 1998. *Judith, Sexual Warrior: Women and Power in Western Culture*. New Haven: Yale University Press.

Stone, Jon R. 2001. "A Fire in the Sky: 'Apocalyptic' Themes on the Silver Screen." In *God in the Details: American Religion in Popular Culture*, ed. Eric M. Mazur and Kate McCarthy, 65–82. London: Routledge.

Stone, Nira. 1992. "Judith and Holofernes: Some Observations on the Development of the Scene in Art." In *'No One Spoke Ill of Her': Essays on Judith*, ed. James C. VanderKam, 73–93. Atlanta, GA: Scholars Press.

Strobel, Lee. 1998. *The Case for Christ: A Journalist's Personal Investigation of the Evidence for Jesus*. Grand Rapids, MI: Zondervan.

Symington, Alexander, M. 1878. *The Story of Esther the Queen: A Popular Exposition*. London: Religious Tract Society.

Tabor, James. 2004. "Personal Reflections on My Viewing of Mel Gibson's 'The Passion of the Christ'." http://www.religiousstudies.uncc.edu/jdtabor/passion.html.

Taussig, Michael. 1998. "Transgression." In *Critical Terms for Religious Studies*, ed. Mark C. Taylor, 349–64. Chicago and London: University of Chicago.

Taylor, Mark C. 1998. "Introduction." In *Critical Terms for Religious Studies*, ed. Mark C. Taylor, 1–20. Chicago and London: University of Chicago.

Thompson, Kenneth, ed. 1997. *Media and Cultural Regulation*. London: Sage in association with the Open University.

Film Distributors Association. 2004. "Top 100 Film in UK Cinemas 2004." http://www.launchingfilms.com/databank/factsandfigures.php?name=Top+100+films+in+UK+cinemas#2004

Tottenham, Edward. 1848. *A Sermon Preached in Laura Chapel, Bath, on Sunday Evening, November 5th, 1848*. London: Hatchard and Sons; Bath: M. A. Pocock.

Turkle, Sherry. 1995. *Life on the Screen: Identity in the Age of the Internet*. New York: Simon & Schuster.

Turner, Graeme. 1999. *Film as Social Practice*. 3rd edn. London: Routledge.

Turner, Graeme, ed. 2002. *The Film Cultures Reader*. London; Routledge.

UK Film Council. "UK Box Office Statistics Archive—March 12th–14th 2004." http://www.ukfilmcouncil.org.uk/cinemagoing/archive/?p=D4A1572507bd8194B4sTl1EE985E&skip=156.

— "UK Box Office Statistics Archive—March 26th–28th 2004." http://www.ukfilmcouncil.org.uk/cinemagoing/archive/?p=D4A15725081501AEF5jSy120FC83&skip=156.

— "UK Box Office Statistics Archive—March 18th–20th 2005." http://www.ukfilmcouncil.org.uk/cinemagoing/archive/?p=D4A1577807e311D746RpHm6AFDC6&skip=104.

Ullman, Harlan K., James P. Wade, L.A. Edney and National Defense University Institute for National Strategic Studies. 1996. *Shock and Awe: Achieving Rapid Domination.* Washington: National Defense University Press.

Urban, Hugh B. 2006. "America, Left Behind: Bush, the Neoconservatives, and Evangelical Christian Fiction." *Journal of Religion and Society* 8. http://moses.creighton.edu/JRS/pdf/2006-2.pdf.

Utley, Chris. 2005. "The Passion Recut." Hollywood Jesus.Com. http://www.hollywoodjesus.com/coments/chris/2005/03/passion-recut.html.

Walliss, John. 2004. *Apocalyptic Trajectories: Millenarianism and Violence in the Contemporary World.* Bern: Peter Lang.

Walsh, Richard. 2002. "On Finding a Non-American Revelation: End of Days and the Book of Revelation." In *Screening Scripture: Intertextual Connections between Scripture and Film,* ed. George Aichele and Richard Walsh, 1–23. Harrisburg, PA: Trinity Press International.

Wartenberg, Thomas E. 2004. "*Passions of the Christ*: Do Jews and Christians See the Same Film?" In *Mel Gibson's* Passion *and Philosophy: The Cross, the Questions, the Controversy,* ed. Jorge J. E. Gracia, 79–89. Chicago: Open Court.

Watkins, Paul, with Guillermo Soledad. 1979. *My Life with Charles Manson.* New York: Bantam Books.

Watson, Tex, with Chaplain Ray Hoekstra. 1978. *Will You Die For Me?* Old Tappan, NJ: Fleming H. Revell.

Wellcome Trust, The. 2000. *Science and the Public: A Review of Science Communication and Public Attitudes to Science in Britain.* London: Wellcome Trust.

Wellman, Barry, ed. 1999. *Networks in the Global Village.* Boulder, CO: Westview Press.

Wellman, Barry, and Bernie Hogan. 2004. "The Immanent Internet." In *Netting Citizens: Exploring Citizenship in the Internet Age,* ed. Johnston R. McKay, 54–80. Edinburgh: St Andrew Press.

Wheatley, Dennis. 1971. *The Devil and All His Works.* London: Hutchinson.

Willis, Brett. 2004. "Movie Review—*The Passion of the Christ. Christian Spotlight.*" http://www.christiananswers.net/spotlight/movies/2004/thepassionofthechrist.html

Winkler, Allan M. 1999. *Life under a Cloud: American Anxiety about the Bomb.* Champaign, IL: University of Illinois Press.

Wojcik, Daniel. 1997. *The End of the World as We Know It: Faith, Fatalism, and Apocalypse in America.* New York: New York University Press.

Woods, Robert H., Michael C. Jindra, and Jason D. Baker. 2004. "The Audience Responds to *The Passion of the Christ.*" In *Re-viewing the Passion: Mel Gibson's Film and its Critics,* ed. S. Brent Plate, 163–80. New York and Basingstoke: Palgrave Macmillan.

Wright, Melanie J. 2007. *Religion and Film: An Introduction.* London: IB Tauris.

Zaehner, R. 1974. *The Savage God.* London: Collins.

Comics

Andreyko, Mark, Javier Pina and Robin Riggs. February–May 2007. *Manhunter* 26–30.

Heinberg, Allan, Terry Dodson and Rachel Dodson. June 2006. *Wonder Woman* 1.

Luke, Eric, Matthew Clark and Tom Simmons. December 1999. *Wonder Woman* 151.

Maddox, Mike, and Jeff Anderson. 1998. *The Lion Graphic Bible*. Oxford: Lion Publishing.

Marston, William Moulton (under the pen name Charles Moulton) and Harry Peter. December 1941. Wonder Woman. Insert in *All-Star Comics* 8. New York: All American Comics.

— (under the pen name Charles Moulton) and Harry Peter. August 1942. Wonder Woman. In *All-Star Comics* 12. New York: All American Comics.

— (under the pen name Charles Moulton) and Harry Peter. Summer 1942. *Wonder Woman Vol.1, Iss.1*. New York: All American Comics.

Messner Loebs, William, Phil Winsdale and Patricia Mulvihill. 1997. *Amazonia: A Tale of the Wonder Woman*.

Messner Loebs, William and Mike Deodato. May 1995. *Wonder Woman* 97.

Perez, George, and Cynthia Martin. September–December 1991. *War of the Gods 1–4*.

Potter, Greg, George Perez, Bruce Patterson and Len Wein. February–August 1987. *Wonder Woman* Vol.2, Iss.1–7.

Rucka, Greg, Rags Morales and Mark Propst. September 2005. *Wonder Woman 219: Sacrifice 4 of 4*.

Rucka, Greg, David Lopez and BIT. October 2005. *Wonder Woman 220 guest starring Batman*.

Rucka, Greg, Cliff Richards and Ray Snyder. April 2006. *Wonder Woman 226 and Superman*.

Schwartz, Julius, Mike Sekowsky and Murphy Anderson. March 1960.*The Brave and the Bold* 28.

Waldron, Cordell. 2007. "Pro-Wrestler Chris Benoit and the Bible." The Iconic Books Blog, 27 June 2007. http://iconicbooks.blogspot.com/2007/06/pro-wrestler-chris-benoit-and-bible.html (accessed 9 June 2010).

Filmography

12 Monkeys. 1995. Terry Gilliam.

28 Days Later. 2002. Danny Boyle.

28 Weeks Later. 2007. Danny Boyle.

Angel, Angel, Down We Go, aka *Cult of the Damned.* 1969. Robert Thom.

Armageddon. 1998. Michael Bay.

Children Shouldn't Play with Dead Things. 1972. Bob Clark.

The Chronicles of Narnia: The Lion, the Witch and the Wardrobe. 2005. Andrew
   Armstrong.

Core, The. 2003. Jon Amiel.

Dawn of the Dead. 2004. USA. Strike Entertainment. Zack Snyder.

Day after Tomorrow, The. 2004. Roland Emmerich.

Day the Earth Caught Fire, The. 1961. Val Guest.

Day the Earth Stood Still, The. 1951. Robert Wise.

Day the World Ended, The. 1956. Roger Corman.

Deathmaster. 1973. Ray Danton.

Deep Impact. 1998. Mimi Leder.

Donnie Darko. 2001. Richard Kelly.

Dr. Strangelove (Or, How I Learned to Stop Worrying and Love the Bomb). 1964.
   Stanley Kubrick.

Dracula A.D. 1972. 1972. Alan Gibson.

Dunwich Horror, The. 1970. Daniel Haller.

End of Days. 1999. Peter Hyams.

Esther and the King. 1960. Raoul Walsh.

Godzilla. 1954. Irhiro Honda.

Gospel According to St Matthew, The. 1964. Pier Paulo Pasolini.

Heaven's Gate. 1980. Michael Cimino.

Helter Skelter. 1976. Tom Gries.

Helter Skelter. 2004. John Grey.

I Drink Your Blood. 1970. David Durston.

Independence Day. 1996. Roland Emmerich.

Invasion of the Body Snatchers. 1956. Don Siegel.

La Jetée. 1962. Chris Marker.

King of Kings, The . 1961. Nicholas Ray, MGM/Samuel Bronston.

Last House on Dead End Street, The, aka *The Fun House.* 1977. Victor Janos [Roger
   Watkins].

Last Temptation of Christ, The. 1988. Martin Scorsese, Universal/Cineplex Odeon.

Left Behind: The Movie. 2000. Vic Sarin.

Love Commune, aka *Ghetto Freaks, Sign of Aquarius,* and *Wages of Sin.* 1970. Robert
   J. Emery.

Manson. 1973. Lawrence Merrick and Robert Hendrickson.

Manson Family, The. 2004. Jim VanBebber.

Matrix, The. 1999. Wachowski Brothers.

Multiple Maniacs. 1970. John Waters.
Omega Man, The. 1971. Boris Sagal.
On the Beach. 1959. Stanley Kramer.
Passion of the Christ, The. 2004. Mel Gibson, Icon/Newmarket.
Passion of the Christ (Director's Edition), The. 2004. USA. Twentieth Century Fox
    Home. Mel Gibson.
The Passion – Recut. 2005. USA. ICON Productions. Mel Gibson.
Postman, The. 1997. Kevin Costner.
Right at the Door. 2006. Chris Gorak.
Rosemary's Baby. 1968. Roman Polanski.
Satan's Sadists, aka *Nightmare Bloodbath*. 1969. Al Adamson.
Snuff. 1976. Michael Findlay, Roberta Findlay and Horacio Fredriksson.
Starsky & Hutch. 2004. USA. Dimension Films. Todd Philips.
Sunshine. 2007. Danny Boyle.
Superman. 1978. Richard Donner.
Sweet Savior, aka *The Love Thrill Murders*. 1971. Robert L. Roberts.
Ten Commandments, The. 1956. Cecil B. DeMille.
Them! 1954. Gordon Douglas.
Threads. 1985. Mick Jackson.
Tribulation Force. 2002. Bill Corcoran.
War of the Worlds, The. 1953. Bryon Haskin.
WarGames. 1983. John Badham.
Waterworld. 1995. Kevin Reynolds.
When the Wind Blows. 1987. Jimmy T. Murakami.
Witness. Charles Manson – The Man who Killed the Sixties. 1994. Channel 4 Television,
    produced by Peter Bate.
World at War. 2005. Craig R. Baxley.
Wrong Way. 1972. Ray Williams.

Audio Recordings

Beach Boys, The. *20/20*. 1969.
Beatles, The. *Revolver*. 1966.
— *The Beatles*. 1968.
Manson, Charles. *Lie*. ESP-Disk. 1970.
— *Unplugged*. Zylo Records. n.d.

Video Recordings

Backlash 2006. Lexington: London: Silver Vision, 30 April 2006.
Best of ITV Wrestling, The. London: ITV Sport, 2005.
Judgment Day 2004. Los Angeles; London: Silver Vision, 16 May 2004.
New Year's Revolution 2005. Puerto Rico; London: Silver Vision, 9 January 2005.
Rise and Fall of ECW, The. London: Silver Vision, 2005.

Index

Breinigsville, PA USA
26 November 2010

250025BV00003B/5/P

9 781845 533601